THE LAST YEARS
OF THE
MONROE DOCTRINE
1945–1993

Britain's Clandestine Submarines, 1914–1915

American Diplomacy during the Second World War

Morality, Reason, and Power:
American Diplomacy in the Carter Years

Dean Acheson

The Aims of American Foreign Policy

THE LAST YEARS

OF THE

MONROE DOCTRINE
1945–1993

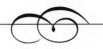

GADDIS SMITH

HILL AND WANG

A DIVISION OF FARRAR, STRAUS AND GIROUX

NEW YORK

Published simultaneously by HarperCollins*CanadaLtd*
First edition, 1994
Designed by Fritz Metsch

LIBRARY OF CONGRESS CATALOGING-IN-PUBLICATION DATA
Smith, Gaddis.
The last years of the Monroe doctrine, 1945–1993 / by Gaddis
Smith.—1st ed.
p.   cm.
Includes bibliographical references (p.) and index.
1. Latin America—Foreign relations—United States. 2. United
States—Foreign relations—Latin America. 3. Latin America—
History—1948–1980. 4. Latin America—History—1980–   . 5. Monroe
doctrine.   I. Title.
F1418.S635   1994   327.7308—dc20   94–14728 CIP

THANKS

Some years ago Virginia Wilkinson asked me to talk with her high school history class on the question "Whatever happened to the Monroe Doctrine?" My thanks go first to her for setting me on an investigation I would not otherwise have begun. Scores of archivists and librarians, the indispensable facilitators of the historical profession, helped me find answers. My Yale colleague, Diane Kunz, was a perceptive critic of an early draft. But, amid the distractions of too much academic administration, I might never have finished except for the good-tempered and endless patience and encouragement of a marvelous editor, Arthur Wang. My greatest thanks go to him.

GADDIS SMITH

CONTENTS

THE LAST YEARS
OF THE
MONROE DOCTRINE
1945–1993

CHAPTER 1

WHATEVER HAPPENED
TO THE MONROE DOCTRINE?

In December 1923, on the one hundredth anniversary of President James Monroe's message to Congress containing the doctrine bearing his name, millions of American schoolchildren sat through a reading of the famous text. New Yorkers heard it declaimed over the pioneer radio station WEAF. A full-page advertisement in *The New York Times* quoted Mary Baker Eddy, founding mother of the Christian Science Church: "I believe strictly in the Monroe Doctrine, in our Constitution and in the laws of God."[1] The original doctrine in which Mrs. Eddy so strictly believed announced three imperatives for American foreign relations: the American continents were closed to further colonization by European powers, the United States must not involve itself in the wars of Europe, and—the heart of the doctrine—the United States would view any attempt by a European power to extend its political system to "any portion of this hemisphere as dangerous to our peace and safety."

The Monroe Doctrine's warning against foreign intrusion in the Americas remained alive and vigorous after its centennial. President Franklin D. Roosevelt before and during the Second World War staunchly invoked the doctrine as the first principle of hemispheric defense against totalitarian threat, although he obviously buried the old prohibition against American entanglement in the political affairs of Europe and Asia. Victory over Nazi Germany and Japan in the Second World War was in part a victory for the Monroe Doctrine.

The Cold War followed the Second World War almost without pause. Historians, understandably drawn to the great collisions of Soviet and American power in Europe and Asia, ceased to inquire about the Monroe Doctrine. In so doing, as this book argues, they missed a significant chapter in the history of how Americans thought about the place of the United States in the world and the nature of national security. Especially for the men—and they were all men—whose adult involvement in the conduct of foreign affairs began before the Second World War, the Monroe Doctrine remained a powerful cluster of ideas. The United States succeeded in writing the Charter of the United Nations in a manner which seemed to assure an American capacity to exclude the UN from political involvement in the Western Hemisphere, thus protecting the Monroe Doctrine. Americans justifed support for brutal but anti-Communist regimes in Latin America as required under the Monroe Doctrine and then used the doctrine as cover for the overthrow of the elected President of Guatemala in 1954.

During the crisis over Soviet missiles in Cuba in 1962, the halls of Congress echoed with sentiments that would have warmed the heart of Mary Baker Eddy. Listen, for example, to Congressman John J. Rhodes of Arizona: "The Monroe Doctrine, which every Member of this body was taught as a child in school is as sacred to the American tradition as the Constitution and the Declaration of Independence . . . is not dead. And it will not die unless we ourselves kill it."[2] But Congressman Rhodes and the scores of congressmen and senators who on that occasion invoked the old text were to be disappointed. President John F. Kennedy refused to use the doctrine as explicit justification for action during the Cuban crisis. Although the Soviet Union removed its nuclear weapons from Cuba and promised not to return them, Cuba became a Soviet protectorate and Communist state within the legendary "ninety miles" of American shores.

The year 1962 thus would appear to mark the death of the

Monroe Doctrine as an absolute mandate for the conduct of American foreign policy. But the ideas and emotions evoked by the words "Monroe Doctrine" continued for another generation to influence the thinking and behavior of American leaders, especially in the administrations of Presidents Lyndon B. Johnson, Richard M. Nixon, and Ronald Reagan. American leaders simultaneously accepted the Soviet presence in Cuba and reaffirmed the principles of the Monroe Doctrine. They resolved the contradiction by defining the Cuba of Fidel Castro as an alien body no longer belonging to the American continents. They sought, in effect, to expel Cuba from the Western Hemisphere. For those Presidents the Monroe Doctrine meant preventing another Cuba. To that end they intervened in Brazil, the Dominican Republic, El Salvador, Nicaragua, and Grenada.

No post-1945 President was more enamored of the idea of the Monroe Doctrine than Ronald Reagan. He presided over a prolonged covert and often violent effort to assert American will in Latin America: the proxy war to drive the Sandinista government of Nicaragua from power and sustain the repressive government of El Salvador. In the absence of broad congressional and public support for these objectives, the Reagan Administration turned to secrecy, lying, defiance of domestic law, and contempt for international opinion and legal norms. This behavior, however, provoked ever greater opposition within the United States. The frustration of Reagan's advisers is well captured in the sarcastic comment of Robert M. Gates, deputy director of the CIA, in December 1984: "The fact is that the Western Hemisphere is the sphere of influence of the United States. If we have decided totally to abandon the Monroe Doctrine, if in the 1980's taking strong actions to protect our interests . . . is too difficult, then we ought to save political capital in Washington, acknowledge our helplessness and stop wasting everybody's time."[3]

Within less than a decade the United States did, in fact, abandon the Monroe Doctrine. The reasons touch the themes of this book. First and most obviously, the last years of the Monroe Doctrine are inseparable from the Cold War. The more serious the perceived threat to American security from the Soviet Union, the more emphatically the concept of the Monroe Doctrine was applied to policy and the selling of policy to the public. For almost half a century after 1945 the makers of American foreign policy subordinated relations of the United States with Latin America to the overarching purpose of "frustrating the Kremlin design," perceived as a coherent, implacable effort to undermine the security of the "free world" everywhere and in every way. The Soviet threat to American security in the hemisphere was sometimes real, as during the Cuban missile crisis. More often it existed largely in the American imagination and in the propensity to attribute every instance of instability in Latin America, every criticism of the United States as something ordered in Moscow.

A second theme is the pervasive lack of knowledge about or concern by high American officials for Latin America on its own terms. Because the attention of those officials during the Cold War years was dominated by events in Europe, Asia, and the Middle East, they knew almost nothing about Latin American conditions. For example, Secretary of State Dean Acheson, notwithstanding high service in the Department of State since 1941, told his staff in 1950 that he was "rather vague" about Latin America. "He wanted to know whether they were richer or poorer, going Communist, Fascist or what?"[4] Presidents, other Secretaries of State, and their immediate advisers were no better informed than Acheson. The result was a sporadic, crisis-ridden approach: long periods of ignoring Latin America alternating with moments of frantic obsession—for example, over Communists in Guatemala in 1954, over the Soviet presence in Cuba in the 1960s and after, over the Sandinistas in Nicaragua in the 1980s. Latin American governments and people were seen as pawns, not as autonomous actors with self-generated hopes, fears, and policies. If a Latin American government did not endorse and act on the world view of Washington, then it was perceived as an actual or potential puppet of the Soviet Union and thereby a threat to the Monroe Doctrine.

A third theme flows from the first two: the modification of the principles of the Monroe Doctrine to the Cold War philosophy of secrecy, covert action, and the defiance of legal and constitutional restrictions on the conduct of foreign policy. Any means was acceptable, therefore, to maintain compliant, anti-Soviet regimes and undermine those who were uncooperative. James Monroe in 1823 had contrasted American principles of candor, self-government, and respect for national independence with the devious, autocractic, imperial ways of Europe. The doctrine was proclaimed as protection of the first against the second. The abandonment after 1945 of its original ideals made the last years of the Monroe Doctrine a history of moral degradation. Sometimes the words and principles of the Monroe Doctrine were embraced openly, enthusiastically, and with complete candor. More often they were muffled in secrecy, tainted by lies, and in conflict with the public creed of democracy and human rights.

Moral degradation interacted with the fourth theme: the increasing political partisanship of the doctrine. Before 1945 the doctrine had been involved on occasion in domestic politics, but in its final years it was invoked to damage political opponents at home more than to clarify the needs of foreign policy. Previously it had been embraced equally by Republicans and Democrats. After 1945 it became the favored instrument of Republicans and Cold War conservatives of both parties. The Monroeites saw themselves standing for patriotism, strength, and a prideful unwillingness to tie American interests to the constraints of international cooperation, especially in the United Nations. They castigated domestic critics as naïve, liberal exponents of weakness. Critics in turn were unpersuaded that the principles of the Monroe Doctrine justified the covert war in Nicaragua or support for the notoriously brutal government of El Salvador.

The end of the Cold War marked the end of the Monroe Doctrine. Even perfervid wavers of the doctrine had difficulty finding a threat from beyond the hemisphere to the nation's security in Latin America when the Soviet Union unilaterally withdrew from confrontation with the West, accepted the independence of Eastern Europe under non-Communist governments, allowed the unification of Germany on Western terms, abandoned all pretense of influence in the Third World including Latin America, and then ceased to exist itself. Thus, in the early 1990s the doctrine passed into history.

The Monroe Doctrine was fundamentally the assertion of an American sphere of influence. That concept, however, has taken many shapes through history and in different parts of the world. To adopt the terminology of John P. Vloyantes, there are hard spheres of influence and soft ones.[5] A hard sphere edges toward annexation and usually involves the direct use of military force and direct control of the political and economic life of the people within the sphere. Whatever self-government exists within a hard sphere is entirely at the sufferance of the controlling power. There may or may not be local collaborators. The population within a hard sphere exercises no self-determination on the question of whether they wish to belong or withdraw. That is why in the idealist rhetoric of American thought about international relations the evil of spheres of influence and the glory of self-determination are always linked. The rights of outside countries within a dominant power's hard sphere of influence are slight to nonexistent. Other governments may be prohibited from having diplomatic relations with the sphere and their citizens may be barred from trade and travel. Examples of hard spheres are those exercised by Britain over Egypt from the 1880s to the 1950s, by Japan over "independent" Manchukuo, i.e., Manchuria, between 1932 and 1945, and by the Soviet Union over Eastern Europe during the Cold War. Soviet action in Hungary in 1956 and Czechoslovakia in 1968 is the essence of using force to maintain a hard sphere of influence.

A soft sphere, in contrast, involves no overt coercion. Its political rhetoric speaks of community of interest, shared visions of the world, and mutual benefit through voluntary association. The large power in a soft sphere does not dictate with whom the smaller powers can trade or maintain diplomatic relations—although it applies nonviolent pressure, offers positive inducements, and makes clear its preferences. It never interferes overtly in the smaller countries' internal affairs, and it is tolerant when those within the sphere pretend there is no sphere at all.

The sphere of influence which the United States sought but only partially achieved over Latin America in the years after 1945 was both hard and soft. Publicly American policymakers pretended that the sphere was a gathering of like-minded equals to advance democratic values and exclude alien totalitarianism from the American continents. That line fooled few. In practice the policymakers preferred soft methods to hard. When hard methods were employed, they preferred the covert and deniable to the open and blatant application of force. But when soft methods failed to create the conditions they desired, they moved with little hesitation to various forms of coercion.

The blend of hard and soft, open and covert, is easier to illustrate by noting the specific tools and methods applied by the American government toward Latin America than by abstract generalization. Beneath the statements of high policy and the episodic involvement of Presidents, Secretaries of State, and other luminaries were thousands of diplomats, intelligence agents, and military personnel trying every day to make reality conform with the principles of the Monroe Doctrine. Let us take brief note of the nature of this daily activity, the continuing background to the moments of crisis around which this book is organized.

With the exception of the Soviet missiles in Cuba, the perceived immediate threat to the Monroe Doctrine after 1945 was not military, but distant worst-case scenarios ultimately involving traditional military security concerns. Thus, the Rio pact of 1947 was a collective response to the threat of attack on the American continents from beyond the hemisphere. But there was almost no mechanism for coordinating the effort. The Inter-American Defense Board was a sleepy committee, meeting occasionally, an assignment on the American side for officers on the slow track.

The United States shared no useful information with the board in the belief that "information passed on to twenty countries in a body of this kind would, in many cases, find its way into the wrong hands."[6]

During the Cuban missile crisis the United States relied on its own nuclear and conventional power to persuade the Soviet Union to withdraw its missiles. On all other occasions American perceptions of a military threat were based on imaginative projection, a set of "what if" questions leading to a fearful outcome at some very distant unspecified time. The first question was what if Latin American governments equipped their armed forces with weapons from a country other than the United States? Beginning during the Second World War and for two decades thereafter, the American military sought to make the United States the sole supplier of arms and professional training for Latin America, thereby replacing a half century of European influence.[7] Weapons, training, organization, and doctrine were all to be standardized to the American model. The goal was publicly justified as necessary for effective hemispheric cooperation and defense. But there were obvious other reasons. Governments completely dependent on the United States for weapons and parts could easily be influenced and constrained from using military equipment in ways disapproved by the United States. By withdrawing or threatening to withdraw the supply of arms, the United States had a useful sanction. Conversely, regimes would gain considerable freedom of action if they had alternative suppliers. The British, French, or Swedes as arms suppliers would be bad enough—but arms from the Soviet bloc would be a serious threat to the principles of the Monroe Doctrine and the security of the United States.

Thus, a 1947 report by a State, War, and Navy interdepartmental committee urged generous supplying of American weapons lest Latin American nations turn to the Soviet Union and its satellites, thereby according the Soviet Union "a political leverage potentially dangerous to U.S. security interests." The report also said that the American defense industry would benefit by having more orders than the U.S. armed forces alone could provide.[8] The U.S. Army also stressed the "benefits of permanent United States military missions and the continued flow of Latin American officers through our service schools. Thus will our ideals and ways of life be nurtured in Latin America to the eventual exclusion of totalitarianism and other foreign ideologies."[9] The United States never came close to achieving this goal. For the first decade after 1945 there was either no legislative framework for transferring U.S. armaments to Latin America or, during the emergency of the Korean War and European rearmament, the United States had few arms to spare. Until the Korean War both the State Department and many members of Congress thought there were more liabilities than advantages in supplying arms: Latin American countries might use them for unwarranted repression or to threaten each other; since direct defense of the hemisphere was an American responsibility, the acquisition of heavy armaments by Latin American governments was a foolish waste of resources; the United States would have to take on a commitment of unpredictable dimensions or be constantly causing ill feeling by saying no.[10]

After the outbreak of the Korean War, American weapons were in short supply, costly, and not available on favorable credit terms. The U.S. military was annoyed at the increasing volume of British sales, especially of jet aircraft, but the National Security Council decided British sales should not be actively opposed.[11] The British, however, believed Americans were blocking them on the principle that the Monroe Doctrine gave the United States "the exclusive right on advising and equipping South American countries with aircraft."[12] The gap between the American aspiration of exclusive supplier and reality was enormous. Europeans provided almost all jet aircraft and new naval vessels from the beginning. By 1960 the United States was still supplying 75 percent of all arms, but the figure dropped to 20 percent in 1970, and was only 7 percent in 1980.[13]

Although the United States reluctantly accepted the growing reliance of the Latin American military on weapons from Western

Europe and later Israel, the acquisition of arms from the Communist bloc was ritualistically denounced as a violation of the principles of the Monroe Doctrine and conclusive evidence that a regime was itself Communist or soon would be. It made no difference that the United States might have closed off non-Communist sources, as with Guatemala in the early 1950s. As late as December 1984, Secretary of Defense Caspar Weinberger, while explaining the threat of Soviet weapons in Nicaragua, said that a principle of the Monroe Doctrine "was that there should be no interference, no sponsorship of any kind of military activity in this hemisphere by countries in other hemispheres."[14]

The Korean War, and especially the perilous phase following the intervention of the People's Republic of China, induced the United States to dream of using Latin American military manpower around the world. The U.S. military services thought small, miscellaneous Latin American contingents would be more trouble than they were worth—but the State Department pressed on because of large imagined political advantages. If Latin American troops participate, said a State Department memorandum, "the nationalism and patriotism of the Latin American people will be aroused in support of the entire UN action against Communist aggression"; and that, in turn, would stimulate governments to deal more effectively with Communism within their own borders.[15] A later memorandum said, "There is no better way to effectively incorporate Latin America into the free world than by permitting Latin America to share in the sacrifices."[16] Ivan White, a State Department official, let his imagination dwell on a large inter-American military force "with a portion available to combat current aggression and the balance available for overseas operations in case of a widening of hostilities, this force would constitute a new factor in the world balance of power."[17] Only Colombia welcomed this opportunity to "share in the sacrifices," sending a battalion and a frigate to Korea. All the other Latin American governments, despite heavy arm twisting from Washington, declined not only the short-term requests to help in Korea but a long-term proposal to commit trained manpower to possible global war. Americans, using language drawn from the Monroe Doctrine, could argue that in order to defend the hemisphere it was necessary to meet the enemy along the 38th parallel in Korea, or in Germany, or later in Vietnam. Latin Americans were not persuaded.

The dream of mobilizing Latin American manpower for a global struggle faded after the armistice in Korea. By the 1960s Washington's thinking focused almost entirely on the role of the military in maintaining internal security in Latin America. With U.S. military missions in almost every Latin American country and thousands of officers and enlisted men receiving training every year in the United States or the Panama Canal Zone, American policymakers convinced themselves that a new type of officer had emerged in Latin America. The old political type had been overweight, overdressed, self-decorated, corrupt, cruel, unprincipled, and without a vision of society's larger purposes. The new was envisioned as lean, mentally alert, well educated, professionally competent, honest, and above all dedicated to the welfare of the people—in short, an officer similar to the flattering image American counterparts had of themselves. The contrast was overdrawn and based on two stereotypes, but it was fervently believed and led during the 1960s and 1970s to an uncritical American faith in the capacity of military leadership to transform Latin American society by combating terrorism, stamping out corruption, building schools and roads, improving health.

Enthusiasm for the military did not apply equally to all countries. It was the greatest toward Brazil. Lincoln Gordon, U.S. ambassador to Brazil under Kennedy and Johnson, was the most articulate of civilian advocates for supporting the military. The Brazilian military, he said, "are not an aristocratic caste separate from the general public"; they are "moderately nationalist but not anti-U.S., anti-Communist but not Fascist, pro-democratic constitutionalist. The military not only have the capability of suppressing possible internal disorders but also serve as moderators on Brazilian political affairs [and an] . . . important source of trained administrators for government civil enterprises."[18] Four weeks after that fulsome appraisal, Gordon's military paragons overthrew the leftist elected government of João Goulart. Gordon was delighted.

The difficulty in the Lincoln Gordon approach came, as we shall see, when various military governing groups failed to meet the idealized stereotype—by invading the colony of America's closest ally, as Argentina did in the Falklands; by murderous treatment of political opposition—death squads, disappearances, torture, etc.—as did the Argentine junta, the Pinochet regime in Chile, and the American-supported military in El Salvador. American hardliners argued that such behavior was distasteful but inevitable in the different political culture of Latin America. But the cries of the victims of military brutality reached the United States. The outrage in Congress and among the American public was then so great that no administration could persist in giving unqualified support to repression—Monroe Doctrine or no.

U.S. military forces were employed openly in Latin America in several ways. They backed up invasions by exile groups against Guatemala and Cuba. They mounted large-scale military maneuvers to demonstrate power and supposedly intimidate leftist regimes in Cuba, Nicaragua, and Grenada. Their planes and ships collected intelligence. On occasion they went openly into combat: the Dominican Republic in 1965, Grenada in 1983, Panama in 1989. Special Forces (Green Beret) units worked to train and accompany counterparts in counterinsurgency campaigns. Covert paramilitary activity under the direction of the Central Intelligence Agency figured prominently and repeatedly during the last years of the Monroe Doctrine: the successful overthrow of the Arbenz government of Guatemala, the failure at the Bay of Pigs, the long war by U.S.–maintained "contra" forces against the government of Nicaragua, and considerable sabotage with explosives, fire, and marine mines.

If public rhetoric reflected reality, the principal instrument for defending the American continents against alien forces would have been the Organization of American States. But the OAS was barely more than a paper organization as far as the larger political objectives of the United States were concerned. It could be useful in dealing with relatively minor issues, or as a fig leaf for American unilateralism. The United States frequently, but with decreasing success, sought OAS validation for American action after the fact. But never was the U.S. government willing to let its own course be determined by an OAS vote. Presidents paid little attention. Secretaries of State had to attend meetings from time to time—but found it a burden.[19]

Political action in defense of the principles of the Monroe Doctrine included ordinary diplomatic efforts to win support from Latin American governments for U.S. policies and constant lecturing on the need for every country to be more concerned about the internal threat. Although the United States had maintained diplomatic relations with the Soviet Union continuously since 1934, Washington opposed relations between Latin American countries and Moscow. When those relations were established, the act was seen as potentially unfriendly. When a new regime broke relations, as did Brazil in 1964 or Chile in 1973, the State Department applauded. Similarly the United States favored the outlawing of the Communist Party in Latin American countries, although it was legal in the United States. The American government also urged limitations on the right of travel for suspected Communists and their sympathizers, which went beyond what courts in the United States would tolerate.

The United States devoted considerable attention to the threat from the left within Latin American labor unions. This involved quasi-covert funneling of CIA funds to local anti-Communist labor activities through the American Institute of Free Labor Development (AIFLD), an affiliate of the American Federation of Labor, and the Inter-American Regional Organization of Workers (ORIT). On the more covert side, the CIA subsidized pro-American newspapers, supported some candidates for office, and worked to discredit others. The CIA did its best to uncover Soviet agents. It gathered information on the views and activities of thousands of people and paid government officials for inside information. All of this involved hundreds of people in the field and back in Washington.[20]

Before the 1960s the United States government offered precious little in the way of economic incentives to influence the behavior of the Latin American republics. Washington repeated with liturgical monotony that Latin America's path to economic well-being lay exclusively through private investment in free-market enterprise. Government-to-government aid, said Secretary of the Treasury George Humphrey in 1956, did nothing but build up "little imitations of the Soviet Union."[21] Thus the United States barred aid to state-owned activities such as the petroleum companies of Mexico or Brazil, Pemex and Petrobras, and complained endlessly of restrictions on American business. The nationalization of American property without prompt and adequate compensation produced growls and snarls—including a congressional restriction, the Hickenlooper Amendment, barring U.S. aid to any government taking American private property without adequate compensation.

But even where aid was minuscule, Washington often used the withdrawal of that aid as a stick—for example, in suspending support for the Rama road, an extension of the Inter-American Highway, in Guatemala during the Arbenz regime. The Eisenhower Administration, much given to spelling out its policies in elaborate memoranda, put it this way: "If a Latin American state should establish with the Soviet bloc close ties of such a nature as seriously to prejudice our vital interests, be prepared to diminish governmental economic and financial cooperation with that country and to take any other political, economic or military actions deemed appropriate."[22] A much more powerful stick to use toward countries producing sugar, such as Cuba, was to reduce or end the quota on sugar imported into the United States.

In the extreme situations where the United States was waging quasi-war against a regime, the stick of an embargo on trade was employed—as with Cuba under Castro, Nicaragua under the Sandinistas, and Panama at the end of the Noriega regime. Trade embargoes were usually accompanied by efforts to induce other countries to stop or limit their trade with the target of American ire. Because these third countries were often allies—e.g., Britain, Canada, Italy—it was difficult for the United States to go beyond persuasion to the use of sanctions against them.

The Eisenhower Administration in its last two years began to extend economic aid for Latin American development, but this reached significant levels only with the Alliance for Progress announced by President John F. Kennedy in a famous speech on March 13, 1961. He said: "For the first time we have the capacity to strike off the remaining bonds of poverty and ignorance—to free our people for the spiritual and intellectual fulfillment which has always been the goal of our civilization." The rhetoric of Monroeism was almost totally absent as he outlined "a plan to transform the 1960s into a historic decade of democratic progress." To call the Alliance for Progress an instrument for fulfilling the principles of the Monroe Doctrine is too great a stretch. Only one sentence sounded the old alarm: "Yet at this very moment of maximum opportunity, we confront the same forces which have imperiled America throughout its history—the alien forces which once again seek to impose the despotisms of the Old World on the people of the New."[23]

The Alliance's grand objective was nothing less than the reordering of Latin America's political, economic, and social structure through land reform, rapid economic growth, the distribution of political power on a democratic basis, and the elimination of poverty, illiteracy, and disease. All this was to be achieved through $20 billion in public aid and private investment over ten years. At last the United States would be responding to human needs in Latin America on a scale comparable to the Marshall Plan for Europe in the 1940s.

The Alliance fell far short of its goals. Economic growth was largely offset by soaring population. Politically Latin America in the 1960s moved away from democracy to military regimes supported by oligarchies with no taste for fundamental socioeconomic reform. Those regimes, encouraged by the United States, focused on the issue of internal security. U.S. aid went increasingly to support police forces and train the military in counterinsurgency. The dominant cliché by the mid-1960s was that there could be no social progress until the threat of rural and urban guerrillas was contained. But neither the Latin American regimes nor their American paymasters made much effort to distinguish between political dissent and hardcore subversion. In theory the Alliance for Progress was a repudiation of Washington's propensity to support repressive regimes; in practice the two were too often complementary. The 1970 conclusion of Jerome Levinson and Juan de Onis remains sound: "Between the overambitious idealism of its development goals and the pointless obsessiveness of its concern for security, the United States really undermined the Alliance before it could get started."[24]

Had all the military, political, and economic tools employed by the United States in Latin America worked to perfection, the region would have been as tied to the international political policies of the United States as a state of the American union. In some respects Latin American governments would have had even less freedom than one of the fifty states, since the U.S. Constitution puts some limit on federal authority over the states. All Latin American military and police forces would have been trained by Americans and equipped with American arms. Individuals and organizations on the "far left" (as defined by the United States) would be outlawed. Governments would be strong, above all. If they could be strong and democratic, well enough, but first they must be strong and not shrink from using whatever methods were required to maintain a stable society. Latin American economies would be prosperous, open to U.S. private investment, and based on free-market principles. Latin American governments would speak with one voice, that of the United States, in the OAS. In

the UN they would support American world policies while excluding the UN from any involvement in hemispheric disputes.
The only thing missing in this fantasy was a national holiday in
every American republic on December 2, the anniversary of James
Monroe's message.

The story of the last years of the Monroe Doctrine concerns the
widening gap between this fantasy and reality. At times high
American officials believed they could close the gap by acts of will
and a dose of force. They were wrong, and often self-defeating
in their delusions. By the 1980s public and congressional support
for the fantasy had rapidly evaporated. At that moment the end
of the Cold War and the dissolution of the Soviet Union removed
the indispensable enemy.

CHAPTER 2

THE HISTORICAL LEGACY

efore turning to an account of what happened to the Monroe Doctrine in its final years, we now look briefly at the pre-1945 history of the doctrine, with an eye to how legacies of the past provided the ideas and methods which would be absorbed, modified, or abandoned after 1945.

The Monroe Doctrine, like the word of God, meant many things to different people at different times. It was first a unilateral statement of presidential opinion and policy. As operational policy it was always whatever a President or other high official said it was. Often scholars and other critics would declare that one assigned meaning or another was wrongheaded or without historical foundation. No matter. Those who invoked the doctrine always sought popular support for the fulfillment of specific objectives. They understood or intuitively sensed the emotional appeal of the doctrine and its principles and cared not for intellectual elegance or historical precision. Presidents and their advisers added and discarded interpretations to meet the needs of the moment and never admitted they were modifying the sacred text.

There were, to begin with, the three propositions in President James Monroe's annual message to Congress, December 2, 1823. The propositions were occasioned by some evidence, two years before, that Tsar Alexander intended to extend Russian territorial claims southward from Alaska along the Pacific coast, and, more recently and ominously, indications that the French—urged on by the Holy Alliance of Russia, Austria, and Prussia—were poised to use military force to overturn the independence recently gained by Latin American countries from the collapsing Spanish Empire.[1]

The first proposition declared the "American continents, by the free and independent condition which they have assumed and maintained, are henceforth not to be considered as subjects for future colonization by any European powers . . ." In later years some enthusiasts for the doctrine overlooked the qualifying adjective "future" and interpreted the doctrine as excluding all European colonies. But the American government in 1823 told the European powers they could keep what they had within existing boundaries—but there could be no new colonies, no expansion of existing ones, and no transfer of colonial possessions from one European power to another. The "no transfer" principle antedated the doctrine itself and was implicit rather than explicit in the text of the message. It stemmed from the fear that a weak and nonthreatening European colonial power, such as Spain, might transfer territory to a powerful and aggressive one, such as France. Its first appearance came in 1801–3, when the administration of Thomas Jefferson saw a threat to national security should powerful Napoleonic France secure the transfer of New Orleans and control of the Mississippi River from the weak hands of Spain. The principle was restated as late as the 1940s in opposition to possible German control of colonies belonging to countries under German occupation in Europe.

By 1945 the noncolonization proposition seemed almost, but not entirely, unnecessary. One American official, as we shall see, worried in 1947 about the consequences for British, French, and Dutch colonies in the Caribbean should Communists gain control of the governments of the mother countries. Since that feared possibility never happened, the issue was entirely theoretical. The dispute between Great Britain and Argentina over the sovereignty of the Falklands Islands, or Malvinas, as they were known to Argentina, was not theoretical. The United States maintained that the Monroe Doctrine had no bearing on the dispute and had no desire to irritate its closest European ally by giving the slightest support to Argentina. Argentina claimed that Britain had taken the islands by force 149 years before. War erupted in 1982 between Argentina and Britain and produced an embarrassing challenge to the Monroe Doctrine.

The second proposition of Monroe's original message said: "In the wars of the European powers in matters relating to themselves we have never taken any part, nor does it comport with our policy so to do." This declaration of nonentanglement, descending from Tom Paine's *Common Sense* of 1776 and Washington's Farewell Address of 1796, expressed the credo of isolationism.[2] For almost a century the absolute wisdom of nonentanglement was never seriously questioned. It was momentarily and spectacularly abandoned in 1917–18, when President Woodrow Wilson led the United States into war against Germany in order to make the world safe for democracy. Specifically Wilson advocated the creation of a universal League of Nations under moral leadership to safeguard the independence and integrity of all nations—just as the Monroe Doctrine had protected the independence of nations on the American continents. But Wilson's vision, so violative of the principle of nonentanglement in the original doctrine, was repudiated by the United States Senate.

For the next two decades the full doctrine was reasserted by unreconstructed isolationists. The Japanese attack on Pearl Harbor, December 7, 1941, finally put an apparently permanent end to the dream of isolation. After the Second World War no American leader or influential writer embraced this principle, thus burying a significant original part of the doctrine. Indeed, during the Cold War this principle was neatly reversed by what we will call the Reagan Corollary: the intrusion of a foreign threat would require the United States to divert material resources to the direct defense of its southern frontier and thus diminish its capacity to project power to Europe, Asia, Africa, the Middle East—wherever American national interest dictated.

The third proposition in the original message, the heart of the doctrine, announced that the political system of Europe—in 1823 resurgent monarchy triumphant over the lost cause of democratic revolution—was "essentially different" from the free, democratic system of America. "We owe it, therefore, to candor . . . to declare that we should consider any attempt on their part to extend their system to any portion of this hemisphere as dangerous to our peace and safety." In the second half of the twentieth century "peace and safety" would be replaced in general usage by the phrase "national security."

The perceived threats of 1823, greatly exaggerated by Americans at the time, never materialized. For the next generation Americans paid little heed to Monroe's words—until 1845, when President James K. Polk explicitly invoked them as a warning against European meddling in Texas or California. In the 1840s Monroe's statements acquired the honorific designation "Doctrine." Immediately after Union victory in the Civil War, the United States mobilized troops in Texas to back up its protest against Napoleon III's puppet Mexican empire headed by the ill-fated monarch Maximilian. The empire collapsed and Maximilian died before a firing squad. The episode fueled American self-confidence and added to the prestige of the doctrine. A century later, Soviet influence in Cuba, through Fidel Castro, alleged agent of international Communism, was routinely called the most serious threat to the Monroe Doctrine since the days of Napoleon III and Maximilian. Those who drew the comparison advocated that the United States arrange that Fidel Castro suffer a fate similar to that of Maximilian.

The next significant development in the history of the Monroe Doctrine came in 1895, when the American government intervened in a dispute between Venezuela and Great Britain over the boundary of the colony of British Guiana. Secretary of State Richard Olney, backed by President Grover Cleveland, demanded that the British submit the boundary dispute to arbitration. In one of the most oft-quoted assertions associated with the doctrine, Olney said, "The United States is practically sovereign on this continent, and its fiat is law upon the subjects to which it confines its inter-position."[3] In other words, in the Western Hemisphere what the government of the United States says, shall be. Let other powers contest this principle at their peril. The British government, confronting more serious international issues in Europe and Africa, had no wish to pick a fight with the United States. It accepted arbitration. The affair further enhanced the prestige which the doctrine enjoyed in American eyes.

To this point the doctrine was exclusively a statement of American power and purpose vis-à-vis European activity in the hemisphere. In 1904 President Theodore Roosevelt, in his famous corollary, added a justification for American intervention in the internal affairs of Latin American countries. The context was the habit of European powers in that era of rambunctious imperialism to use a weak government's inability to pay debts or maintain law and order as a pretext for seizing political and territorial control. Thus, Great Britain had taken control of Egypt in 1882 and Germany had grabbed a sphere of influence in China's Shantung peninsula in 1898.

President Roosevelt's fear was that incompetent governments in the Caribbean region, especially those failing to meet their debt obligations, might provoke European governments to impose controls in violation of the Monroe Doctrine. A European presence along the sea lanes leading to the Panama Canal, then under construction, would be a serious threat to American national security. Roosevelt used the insolvency of the Dominican Republic as the occasion for asserting what was immediately dubbed the "Roosevelt Corollary" to the Monroe Doctrine, wrapping a strategic interest in the rhetoric of international, humanitarian responsibility: "Chronic wrongdoing, or an impotence which results in a general loosening of the ties of civilized society, may in America, as elsewhere, ultimately require intervention by some civilized nation, and in the Western Hemisphere the adherence of the United States to the Monroe Doctrine may force the United States, however reluctantly, in flagrant cases of such wrongdoing or impotence, to the exercise of an international police power."[4] The United States soon took over the collection of the Dominican Republic's customs revenues and before long put the country under military occupation. The argument of the Roosevelt Corollary was subsequently applied to Haiti and Nicaragua, and its threat hovered over the entire region.

Latin American governments and writers had never shown any enthusiasm for the Monroe Doctrine. They saw it correctly as a unilateral statement designed to serve U.S. interests alone. Any benefit accruing to a Latin American nation from action under the Monroe Doctrine would be purely coincidental. With the proclamation and application of the Roosevelt Corollary, Latin American indifference became intense hostility. The very words were inflammatory south of the Rio Grande. The doctrine was now a threat to their independence and not a fraternal promise of defense against European expansion.

The doctrine was more popular than ever in the United States, but after 1904 it was a toxin poisoning inter-American relations. Some Americans understood what was happening and spoke out. For example, in 1913 Hiram Bingham, a professor at Yale and an experienced Latin Americanist, declared the Monroe Doctrine "an obsolete shibboleth . . . a display of insolence and conceit on our part." Bingham's apostasy stirred a brief, but soon forgotten flurry of controversy.[5]

Until the end of the nineteenth century the Monroe Doctrine focused on Europe as the only potential source of intrusion into the Western Hemisphere. Two simultaneous developments gave the doctrine a second, westward-looking face. On the one hand was Japan's demonstration of modern military power and imperial ambition in defeating China in 1894–95 and Russia in 1904–5—with consequent territorial gain. And on the other hand was the appearance of the United States as a trans-Pacific power in the same decade with the annexation of the Hawaiian and Philippine Islands, Guam and Wake; and the adoption of the "Open Door" for American commerce in China as a national goal. These moves were independent of the Monroe Doctrine; indeed, the acquisition of Hawaii and the Philippines was condemned by American anti-imperialists as a violation of the sacred admonition to avoid entanglement outside the hemisphere. Senator George Frisbie Hoar, for example, warned that by acquiring colonies in the other hemisphere, the United States could no longer logically deny Europeans the right to do the same in this one.[6]

Soon there were fears of sinister Japanese intentions within the Western Hemisphere, fears intensified by the rising prejudice against Japanese immigrants in California. The potential purchase in 1912 by Japanese business interests of land in lower California, Mexico, brought the Monroe Doctrine into play. The Japanese government denied its involvement, but Senator Henry Cabot Lodge introduced, and the U.S. Senate passed, what soon became known as the Lodge Corollary to the Monroe Doctrine. It stated the opposition of the United States to the acquisition "by any corporation or association which has such a relation to another government, not American, as to give that Government practical power of control" of any land "in the American continents" with the potential of threatening American national security.[7] A half century later, the presence of Soviet bases in Cuba led the historically minded to recall the Lodge Corollary.

President Woodrow Wilson, taking office in 1913, preached the politics of altruism. Theodore Roosevelt had tried to convince Latin Americans that what was good for the United States under the Monroe Doctrine was also good for them, but he was explicit in putting American national security interest first. Wilson, on the other hand, sought to purge the taint of "material interest" from the Monroe Doctrine, and indeed from all American foreign policy. The effort was noble, but he failed to convince many contemporaries and historians since that his ideals were not a hypocritical cloak for traditional selfish purpose. The fact that he ordered American troops into Mexico on several occasions and placed Haiti and the Dominican Republic under U.S. military occupation created "cognitive dissonance"—to use a bit of modern jargon—between his words and deeds. Wilson, more than any other political thinker and actor in American history, heightened the tension between "realistic" foreign policy devoted to achieving and maintaining the power necessary to protect the national interest and an "idealistic" policy devoted to the fulfillment of universal moral values: democracy, peace, nonintervention and the absence of aggression, human rights.

That tension had been present in the Monroe Doctrine from the outset, but protection of the political system of freedom and independence for all nations of the "American continents" was for Monroe and his generation as much the means of assuring the national interest of the United States as an end in itself. Monroe and Secretary of State Adams were emphatic in stating that the doctrine was a unilateral set of principles whose implementation was to be decided solely by the United States in accordance with judgments concerning the national interest. Realism remained the dominant strain—in Olney's and Theodore Roosevelt's corollary and in every other significant invocation of the doctrine—until Wilson.

In 1914 Wilson tried to convert the Monroe Doctrine into a multilateral Pan-American treaty under which all member states would guarantee each other's political independence and territorial integrity, settle disputes by peaceful means, curb the trade in munitions, and prevent their territory from being used by revolutionaries to attack other states. Drawing on ideas put forward by Colonel Edward M. House, the equivalent of a national security adviser, and using House as his negotiator, Wilson began by trying to line up the ABC powers (Argentina, Brazil, and Chile). Argentina was the most enthusiastic and hailed the idea for transforming "the one-sided character of the Monroe Doctrine into a common policy of all the American countries." House even sounded out the British government, as a major American power by virtue of Canada and her island colonies, about signing—and received a favorable response in principle. But the intervening crisis of the European war and the reluctance of Chile doomed the proposal.[8] Wilson, however, applied the idea of a mutual guarantee of independence and territorial integrity to the Fourteen Points of 1918 and thereafter in the Covenant of the League of Nations.

As Wilson struggled with the challenges presented by the great European war and gradually assigned himself the transcendent task of saving mankind from the iniquity of war, he was fully aware how involvement in a European war would contravene the Monroe Doctrine's warning against entanglement. He tried to resolve the contradiction, and answer critics, by elevating the Monroe Doctrine to a universal principle for all mankind. In a major speech, January 22, 1917, he declared: "I am proposing, as it were, that the nations should with one accord adopt the doctrine of President Monroe as the doctrine of the world: that no nation should seek to extend its polity over any other nation or people, but that every people should be free to determine its own polity, its own way of development, unhindered, unthreatened, unafraid, the little along with the great and powerful."[9]

This was one of Wilson's many expressions of the principle of self-determination, replete with profound ambiguity over the meaning of "free," "nation," and "people." On the one hand, Wilson seemed to be calling for absolute nonintervention—no nation "should seek to extend its polity over any other nation." Did that mean that a people could freely determine against democracy and that all polities were acceptable if freely chosen? Wilson's answer was no—there could be no freedom for a government to establish a system that denied freedom to the people. Thus, Wilson's universal Monroe Doctrine invited intervention to protect or establish one "polity" against another. This issue would haunt American foreign policy in general, as well as the Monroe Doctrine in particular, for generations to come. Wilson also sought to purge all taint of an exclusive United States sphere of influence from the doctrine by transforming it into a universal sphere of influence for democracy and self-determination—an interesting piece of intellectual gymnastics bound to cause confusion.

In April 1917, after Germany defied the ultimatum of the United States against the resumption of submarine warfare endangering neutrals and noncombatant civilians, President Wilson asked Congress for a declaration of war, not to make the United States commercial interests safe from German submarines, but "for democracy, for the right of those to submit to authority to have a voice in their own Governments, for the rights and liberties of small nations . . ."[10]

After fifteen months of preparation, American military power tipped the balance in favor of the Western Allies. In November 1918 Germany accepted defeat and signed an armistice. The United States and the other victorious governments soon assembled in Paris to write the peace treaty containing the Covenant (charter or constitution) of the League of Nations. The principal author of the covenant was Woodrow Wilson. Article X repeated language used by him in the proposed Pan-American pact. It required all members of the League "to respect and preserve as against external aggression the territorial integrity and existing political independence" of all other members. Since the League Covenant was part of a treaty, the United States could join only after a two-thirds vote of approval by the Senate, as required by the Constitution. Many senators entertained profound reservations. One concerned the Monroe Doctrine. Would the League be free to intervene in the affairs of the American continents, and conversely, could the League force the United States against its will to go to war anywhere in the world? In order to turn aside these doubts, President Wilson agreed, and the other nations negotiating the covenant consented, to a new article (XXI): "Nothing in this Covenant shall be deemed to affect the validity of international agreements, such as treaties of arbitration or regional understandings like the Monroe doctrine, for securing the maintenance of peace."[11] Seldom has such confusion appeared in a treaty. To call the Monroe Doctrine a regional understanding was absurd. It had never been other than a unilateral statement of United States policy—in spite of Wilson's aborted effort to fashion a Pan-American pact. And did Article

XXI refer to the entire doctrine? If so, the United States would be absolved by Monroe's admonition against entanglement in political affairs beyond the American continents, from obligations under Article X, the very "heart of the Covenant," as Wilson called it. If the Monroe Doctrine included the Olney and Theodore Roosevelt Corollaries, no Latin American government could appeal to the League without the permission of the United States; nor could a non-American nation in dispute with an American one turn to the League without Washington's blessing. In short, if Article XXI meant anything, it meant that the authority of the League covered only half the world, the "Eastern" half.

But Wilson's critics in the Senate were not satisfied. Article XXI was too vague for them, especially in failing to provide any definition of the doctrine. The critics demanded the following formal reservation, to be attached to Senate approval: "The United States will not submit to arbitration or inquiry by the assembly or by the council of the league of nations . . . any questions which in the judgment of the United States depend upon or relate to its long-established policy, commonly known as the Monroe doctrine; said doctrine is to be interpreted by the United States alone and is hereby declared to be wholly outside the jurisdiction of said league of nations . . ."[12]

This reservation, along with others designed to curb presidential power and limit the responsibilities of the United States within the League, was unacceptable to Wilson. In two rounds of voting in 1919 and 1920 the Senate failed to approve the covenant either in the pristine form on which Wilson insisted or with the reservations which he opposed. The victory of Republican Warren G. Harding in the 1920 presidential election closed the debate. The United States did not join the League. The outcome, so crushing for Wilson, was in accord with public opinion.

During the 1920s the Senate continued to defend the Monroe Doctrine against all conceivable limitations. There could be no commitments to international organizations or treaty obligations if they cast the remotest shadow on the doctrine. For example, the Permanent Court of World Justice was established at The Hague in 1922 to decide international disputes, but only in cases voluntarily submitted by all parties. There was no chance that the United States could be forced against its will to appear as defendant or be required to abide by a judgment of the Court. Even President Harding, deeply suspicious of most things connected with the League, saw no problem. In 1923 he asked the Senate to approve American participation. But Senator Henry Cabot Lodge, Wilson's nemesis in the League fight, saw a danger to the Monroe Doctrine in the Court's power to give nonbinding advisory opinions at the request of the League Council or Assembly. Lodge led a bipartisan stampede to place Monroeite conditions on American participation. The interpretation presented by Senator Claude A. Swanson made the point: "Adherence to the said protocol . . . shall not be so construed as to require the United States to depart from its traditional policy of not . . . entangling itself in the political questions . . . of any foreign state, nor shall adherence . . . be construed to imply a relinquishment by the United States of its traditional attitude towards purely American questions."[13] The United States did not join the World Court, in spite of the urging of every President in the interwar period. Under the United Nations the Court was reconstituted as the International Court of Justice, and the United States did participate. But when the Sandinista government of Nicaragua brought well-founded charges against the United States in 1984, the Reagan Administration, in effect, affirmed the principles of the Monroe Doctrine and denied the Court's jurisdiction.

The Senate also protected the Monroe Doctrine in 1928 from any conceivable curtailment through the General Pact for the Renunciation of War, commonly known as the Kellogg-Briand Pact. The treaty, inspired by idealists in the American peace movement and the French government's desire to curry favor with the United States, was proposed by Secretary of State Frank B. Kellogg and French Foreign Minister Aristide Briand. It was signed by virtually all governments of the world at Paris in 1928. The pact had two substantive articles. In Article 1 governments condemned war and renounced it as "an instrument of national policy." In Article 2 they agreed to settle disputes by pacific means. They understood, however, that the pact did not impair the right of self-defense, obligations under certain existing treaties, or special circumstances involving the British Empire. Some senators said they would vote to approve the treaty, even though it was "mere gesture," "a parchment futility."[14] And yet others saw a danger to the sacred Monroe Doctrine. Accordingly, the Senate Foreign Relations Committee declared: "The committee reports the above treaty with the understanding that the right of self-defense is in no way curtailed or impaired . . . The United States regards the Monroe Doctrine as a part of its national security and defense. Under the right of self-defense allowed by the treaty must necessarily be included the right to maintain the Monroe Doctrine which is a part of our system of national defense."[15] The doctrine was safe.

While the Senate was busy guarding the doctrine from international intrusion, the State Department in the 1920s and then President Franklin D. Roosevelt in the 1930s resumed Woodrow Wilson's effort to detoxify the doctrine in the eyes of Latin American governments. The effort began with an internal analysis prepared in 1928 by State Department lawyer J. Reuben Clark at the request of Secretary Kellogg. The so-called Clark memorandum declared, after a historical review, that the doctrine did not justify the intervention of the United States in the affairs of other American states. Thus, said Clark, the Theodore Roosevelt Corollary did not belong in the canon of authoritative interpretation and was no part of the doctrine. A draft circular to all U.S. diplomatic posts in Latin America stated the essence:

The Monroe Doctrine has nothing whatever to do with the domestic concerns or policies or the form of government or the international conduct of the peoples of this hemisphere as among themselves. The principles of the Monroe Doctrine become operative only when some European power (either

by its own motion or in complicity with an American state)
undertakes to subvert or exclude the self-determined form of
government of one of these Republics or acquire from them
all or a part of their territory . . . The Monroe Doctrine is
not now and never was an instrument of aggression; it is and
always has been a cloak of protection. The Doctrine is not a
lance; it is a shield.[16]

The Secretary of State was quite self-righteous about the principles
of the Clark memorandum—but, of course, he had the luxury of
serving at a time when even the most overwrought imagination
could not find an extra-hemispheric threat.

A second, closely related, aspect of detoxification was the ac-
ceptance by the United States of formal declarations against in-
tervention put forward by Latin American governments at the
Pan-American conferences in Montevideo (1933) and Buenos
Aires (1936). The Buenos Aires protocol, often called the "Non-
Intervention Treaty," declared—in words to be repeated in the
Charter of the Organization of American States in 1948: "The
High Contracting Parties declare inadmissible the intervention of
any one of them, directly or indirectly, and for whatever reason,
in the internal or external affairs of any other of the Parties." Dexter
Perkins, the leading historian of the Monroe Doctrine, wrote
shortly afterward: "Thus, so far as the words of a treaty are effective, the United States put behind it not only the Roosevelt
corollary, but the pretension to interfere by force of arms in the
affairs of the states of the New World; and what it promised in
the verbiage of an international agreement it carried out in practice."[17] But as Perkins sensed, words embraced could be words
ignored.

In the 1930s, however, words and deeds did seem happily congruent, thanks to President Franklin D. Roosevelt's success in
winning acceptance of the phrase "Good Neighbor Policy" as
the essence of relations with Latin America, while downplay-
ing the words "Monroe Doctrine" without in any way abandoning

the doctrine as a fundamental of foreign policy. The specifics of the Good Neighbor Policy included withdrawal of the last American forces from Haiti and the Dominican Republic, relinquishing the unequal treaty right (the Platt Amendment) of the United States to intervene in Cuba and dictate Cuba's foreign policy, and accepting Mexico's nationalization of the oil industry on Mexico's terms.[18]

Meanwhile, the aggression of Japan against China and Nazi Germany in Europe created what could be called the sauce-for-the-gander problem. As early as 1905 President Theodore Roosevelt had suggested to Japan the idea of adopting its own Monroe Doctrine in order to exclude undue European intrusion in Asia. The Japanese were much taken with the idea. In 1917 the United States gave vague official endorsement in the Lansing-Ishii Agreement, recognizing Japan's special interests in China because "territorial propinquity creates special relations between countries."[19] In 1934 the Foreign Ministry in Tokyo publicly declared that Japan had "special responsibilities in East Asia" and warned other nations against assisting China or having any relationship except that approved by Tokyo. The so-called Amau Doctrine said that Japan reserved the right to act alone to preserve "peace and order in East Asia."[20] Japan made the parallel explicit by asking the United States to recognize its "Monroe Doctrine" for East Asia, corresponding to the American doctrine for the Western Hemisphere.

Secretary of State Cordell Hull sputtered with angry indignation, and for the next seven years, until the attack on Pearl Harbor, he took every opportunity to lecture the Japanese on the differences between the defensive and benevolent Monroe Doctrine and the selfish, aggressive aims of Japan. "There is no more resemblance between our Monroe Doctrine," he told the Japanese ambassador in April 1940, "and the so-called Monroe Doctrine of Japan than there is between black and white."[21] Secretary Hull brooked no rival in the realm of self-righteousness.

The Second World War in Europe broke out in September 1939 with Germany's invasion of Poland. By June 1940 Nazi Germany had conquered France and the Netherlands, and anxious minds in Washington worried about the fate of French and Dutch colonies in the Caribbean. The United States, invoking the Monroe Doctrine, informed Germany that it would not permit transfer of any territory in the Western Hemisphere "from one non-American power to another non-American power," i.e., from France or the Netherlands to Germany. Nazi Foreign Minister Joachim von Ribbentrop piously denied that Germany had any intention of acquiring American territory and then presumed to instruct Secretary of State Hull on the Monroe Doctrine: "The nonintervention in the affairs of the American Continent which is demanded by the Monroe Doctrine can in principle be legally valid only on condition that the American states do not intervene in the affairs of the European Continent."[22] Ribbentrop's comment infuriated Hull, as intended, and illuminated an issue that would plague the disciples of the Monroe Doctrine for another half century. How could the United States under the Monroe Doctrine exclude foreign influence from an entire hemisphere and deny other great powers similar rights in their regions?

The Good Neighbor Policy paved the way for a de facto security alliance between the United States and the Latin American republics in response to the German challenge. Only Argentina was strongly uncooperative. At Panama in October 1939, a month after Germany invaded Poland, the American republics affirmed their neutrality and pledged to prevent "their respective terrestrial, maritime and aerial territories from being utilized as bases for belligerent operations." Since Britain and France already had territory and bases in the hemisphere, the Panama declaration was directed against Germany. Lest there be any doubt, an additional declaration said the American republics would enforce a ban on belligerent operations in a "zone of security" hundreds of miles broad "except the territorial waters of Canada and of the undisputed colonies and possessions of European countries . . ." The Panama declaration not only made the Monroe Doctrine a multilateral commitment, as Woodrow Wilson had once attempted, but also gave it a maritime as well as a terrestrial dimension.

But nothing the United States did in 1939 or early 1940 diminished in the slightest the power and ambition of Hitler's Germany. By the end of June 1940, Hitler, omnipotent on land in Western Europe, was preparing to invade Great Britain. This ominous condition intensified fears of German control of European colonies in the Americas. This possibility was addressed by all the American republics in the Act of Havana, July 30, 1940. The act put teeth into the ancient no-transfer principle by declaring that should any transfer of sovereignty be threatened, "the American nations, taking into account the imperative need of continental security" could take "said islands or regions" under preemptive occupation.[23] There was no doubt which American nation would do the occupying. It would not be Costa Rica.

The Act of Havana provided that, once the security emergency was over, any territory so occupied would be restored to previous status or be granted the right of self-determination. Argentina, in a little-noticed reservation to its ratification of the Act of Havana, stated that the Malvinas (Falklands) and other southern regions (the reference was to part of Antarctica and certain icebound islands) belonged to Argentina. Forty-two years later that issue would lead to war between Argentina and Britain and to accusations from Latin America that the United States had betrayed the Monroe Doctrine.

The process of defining the cartographical boundaries of the region protected by the Monroe Doctrine, reflected in the Panama and Havana declarations, raised the question of just what is the Western Hemisphere. The boundaries, obviously, did not follow the longitudinal exactitude of 0 degrees passing through Greenwich, England, thence intersecting both poles and continuing in mid-Pacific along 180 degrees of west longitude, corresponding (with a few deviations) to the international date line. Were that the case, most of the British Isles, some of France, all of Spain and Portugal, and the bulge of West Africa would be in the Western Hemisphere and under the Monroe Doctrine.

President Roosevelt, proud of his "map mind," encouraged broad, even creative, geographical definition of the territory protected by the Monroe Doctrine. Immediately after the Munich conference of 1938, with war clouds growing darker, the President told advisers that "the United States must be prepared to resist attack on the Western Hemisphere from the North to the South Pole, including all of North America and South America."[24] The next spring the United States extended the doctrine to cover the Galápagos Islands on the equator in the Pacific, belonging to Ecuador and located 1,000 miles southwest of the Panama Canal. President Roosevelt knew the islands well, having visited them on board the cruiser *Houston* during an "inspection cruise and fishing expedition" in the summer of 1938.[25] In May 1939, Under Secretary of State Sumner Welles officially declared that "any endeavor on the part of a non-American power to purchase or lease the Islands or to use any part of them for a naval, military, air, or even commercial base . . . would be a matter of immediate and grave concern to this Government."[26] The target of this warning was Japan.

The importance of the North Atlantic sea lanes turned the focus of the American government, and thus the definition of the region covered under the Monroe Doctrine, farther north and east—first to Greenland and then to Iceland. The status of Canada was clarified in 1938, when President Roosevelt declared that under the Monroe Doctrine the United States would not stand idly by if Canada were attacked.[27] The case for Greenland was relatively easy. It lies to the west of the line dropped from the North Pole and passing midway between the shores of South America and Africa. Admiral Robert E. Peary, the Arctic explorer, had recommended as early as 1916 that the United States annex Greenland under the Monroe Doctrine. In 1941, Vilhjalmur Stefansson declared that "all geographers concede that Greenland is in the Western Hemisphere." President Roosevelt agreed. In April 1941, acting explicitly with reference to the Monroe Doctrine, the United States placed Greenland under its protection in order to preclude its use by Germany.[28]

Iceland was a more difficult case. It lies west of Ireland, closer to Greenland than to Europe. Obviously, said Stefansson again, it is within the Western Hemisphere. That, however, was too great a stretch for Franklin Roosevelt's Monroe Doctrine, although not a stretch for his definition of security. The United States occupied Iceland in July 1941 with the permission of the Icelandic government, but without reference to the doctrine.

In the same period Roosevelt and his advisers were worried about possible German occupation of West Africa. The President asked Sumner Welles to draft a statement that would bring at least part of Africa under the Monroe Doctrine. Other advisers persuaded Roosevelt to drop the idea. Better, said Hull, to put our security concerns "nakedly without raising a technical Monroe Doctrine issue."[29] Perhaps the Secretary of State wanted to avoid another spitting match with Ribbentrop.

By 1941 the United States was waging an undeclared naval war against Germany in the Atlantic. The Japanese attack on Pearl Harbor and the German declaration of war on the United States ended all uncertainty. By the end of 1942 all fears of a German military threat directly in the Western Hemisphere had dissipated. The focus of United States effort was on Europe and Asia. Latin America was friendly, except for the annoying refusal of Argentina to break completely with Germany. In Washington Latin America could be and was taken for granted.

In May 1945 Adolf Hitler committed suicide and soon Germany surrendered. Japan, after losing two cities to atomic bombs and receiving the Soviet Union's declaration of war, ceased fighting in August and formally surrendered in September. The Second World War was over. Had a knowledgeable American academic or government official at that moment been asked, "How stands the Monroe Doctrine?" he might have answered along the following lines:

"The Monroe Doctrine as a statement of the determination of the United States and its fellow American republics to exclude hostile Great Power influence from the Western Hemisphere has been magnificently vindicated in the present war. No American territory fell under enemy control and the only blemish was the sympathy of Argentina for the Nazi cause. As a justification for unilateral intervention by the United States in the internal affairs of other American republics, it has long been abandoned and happily replaced by the Good Neighbor Policy, long may it be maintained. With the elimination of German and Japanese aggression, it is difficult to imagine a security threat. And yet a few individuals in Washington are entertaining farfetched worries about the Soviet Union. There are no fundamental reasons for a clash between the United States and the Soviet Union. In any event, it will be years before the Soviet Union recovers from the terrible losses in life and resources inflicted by the present war. But there is one element of uncertainty: the relation of the new world security organization to the doctrine. If that organization is entrusted with exclusive and sweeping jurisdiction over all disputes threatening the peace, as the draft recently prepared at the Dumbarton Oaks conference provides, what is left of the Monroe Doctrine?"

CHAPTER 3

THE GHOST AT
SAN FRANCISCO

T he Americans who saw themselves responsible in 1945 for designing a stable world following the consuming destruction of the Second World War were haunted by the ghost of President Woodrow Wilson, the man who had attempted almost single-handedly to do the same thing after the first terrible world war and who had failed so utterly and tragically. The new generation of planners began work in 1939. They were imbued with Wilsonian idealism and believed that the United States had a second chance to lead the world into peace—provided there was no resurgence of the narrow attitudes which had destroyed Wilson's vision.[1]

The new generation recalled that the Monroe Doctrine was connected with Wilson's failure. The Senate had insisted that the United States have the unilateral right, under the Monroe Doctrine, to exclude the League of Nations from any role in the Western Hemisphere. But during the Second World War the neo-Wilsonians hoped the Senate and the American people had learned a lesson and were ready for a universal rather than a narrow national or regional approach to security. The hopeful view was expressed by Secretary of State Cordell Hull in his address to Congress after the 1943 Moscow conference, at which the Soviets agreed in principle to support the creation of a new world organization. Said Hull, "There will no longer be need for spheres of influence, for alliances, for balance of power, or any other of the special arrangements through which, in the unhappy past, the nations strove to safeguard their security or to promote their interests."[2]

But what was the Monroe Doctrine, if not a sphere of influence? American realists, heirs of Theodore Roosevelt, would say, "Damn right, it's a sphere of influence." Pan-American Wilsonian idealists, citing the declarations of wartime cooperation, would call the doctrine a special arrangement for regional security. President Franklin Roosevelt's public position was ambiguous, although inwardly he was far closer in his ideas and intuition to Theodore Roosevelt's realism than Wilson's idealism. Franklin Roosevelt, remembering Wilson's fate, was cautious about embracing a world organization unconditionally. He left Cordell Hull and his staff to dream about redeeming the Wilsonian vision and write reams of memoranda. Roosevelt instinctively preferred a world made safe by the Great Powers, "the Four Policemen" (the United States, Great Britain, the Soviet Union, and China), each with responsibility for a region.

The chief American planner, working under Hull's direction, was Leo Pasvolsky, a Russian-born expert on Europe and a dedicated Wilsonian. The outlook of Pasvolsky and his associates was global, not regional. They had minimal interest in or knowledge of Latin America. If they thought about the Monroe Doctrine at all, they saw a sphere of influence and an unhappy precedent which could be exploited by other powers in establishing their own imperial regions. In December 1943, the American planners presented the first outline for a world organization to Roosevelt. It barely mentioned the regional approach to security and made the world body ultimately responsible for dealing everywhere with threats to the peace. Roosevelt had doubts. The traditions of the Monroe Doctrine still echoed in his mind. He insisted that the United States "not be required to furnish armed forces without our consent" and commented that American troops should be used in the Western Hemisphere and perhaps the Pacific, but not Europe.

The planning group's next draft (July 1944) responded to F.D.R.'s concerns with a grudging allusion to regional arrangements as potentially useful to the central organization. In August, September, and October 1944, the United States presided over a conference of the Big Four (the United States, Great Britain, the U.S.S.R., and China) at Dumbarton Oaks, a grand estate in Washington. The Dumbarton Oaks proposals, designed to form the basis for the Charter of the United Nations, were completed and made public in October. Power of decision in the United Nations would be concentrated in the Security Council, with the Big Four and France "in due course" holding permanent seats on the council. Chapter VIII, section C, elaborated on the regional arrangements, saying that nothing in the charter should preclude their existence "provided such arrangements or agencies and their activities are consistent with the purposes and principles of the Organization."

The governments of Latin America, indeed the governments of all small countries, were excluded from these developments—and they resented it. Brazil's President Getúlio Vargas, for example, complained in October that he was deeply embarrassed at knowing nothing about Dumbarton Oaks beyond what he read in the press. Vargas also wanted a permanent seat for Brazil on the Security Council, claimed that President Roosevelt had promised it, and was angry at the American refusal to support his claim.[3] Secretary of State Hull sought to soothe hurt feelings by meeting with groups of Latin American ambassadors. Nelson A. Rockefeller, the State Department's coordinator of inter-American affairs, did the same. In another gesture of conciliation and public relations, the United States agreed to an inter-American conference in Mexico City in February 1945 to discuss wartime and postwar cooperation. The message was: Come and talk, we have not forgotten you. The conference was named for the ancient Mayan fortress in which it was held: Chapultepec.

On the eve of Chapultepec unhappiness with Dumbarton Oaks increased within Latin American governments and among American diplomats assigned to Latin America. From Mexico City

George S. Messersmith, the American ambassador, reported that Latin American leaders believed it inevitable that the Soviet Union and Great Britain were each working to establish spheres of influence, while the United States was neglecting Latin America in preference to Europe and Asia. The ambassador warned that if Latin American governments did not receive support from the United States, especially in the economic field, they would turn elsewhere and "our position in the world will be tremendously weakened."[4] The most articulate expositor of the case for regionalism was Adolf A. Berle, former New Deal braintruster and in the middle of a career that would culminate in the Kennedy Administration. Berle in 1945 was ambassador to Brazil and a member of the American group at the Chapultepec conference. Berle called for the Dumbarton Oaks proposals to be amended so that the Western Hemisphere had priority in working out its own problems. In his diary Berle wrote that "most of those world organization people regard the hemisphere as a positive enemy. It is interesting that they have no hemispheric experience and some of them very little experience with the United States." The last remark was almost certainly a crack at Leo Pasvolsky. Berle noted that Pasvolsky opposed any separate regional commitment by the United States to use force because only the council of the new organization should be able to authorize force. Berle's response was that "this would mean that the United States and others could not prevent Argentina from seizing Uruguay without the consent of Britain and Russia—who at that moment might be backing Argentina. It would also introduce European diplomacy into every inter-American dispute." In words resonant with Monroe's message of 1823, Berle said he was against sacrificing "the hard-won liberty of the hemisphere from European disputes and intrigues as down payment for the right to participate in world organization." He noted that "the Brazilians want the Monroe Doctrine lock, stock and barrel and make no secret of it. The Uruguayans think that the British would throw them to the Argentines. The rest of South America simply thinks we don't know what we are doing—and I must say I think they are right."[5]

The conference produced a public declaration known as the Act of Chapultepec. The act advanced the general proposition that an attack on any American state was an attack on all; and that in the event of aggression the states signing the act would consult as to the measures of response. The act promised that the American republics would proceed after the war to "perfect this instrument in order that it shall be in force at all times."[6] In the opinion of the majority of Americans at work on United Nations matters, the Chapultepec conference was a bone thrown to Latin American governments, so that they would stop growling while the United States got on with the important business of world organization. But for those who put the region first and thought in terms of the Monroe Doctrine, it was a heartening conclave. For example, Senator Warren R. Austin, who attended as a "congressional adviser," told the Senate how astonishing it was to find that "the Latin-Americans, who formerly regarded the Nation up north as a sort of club over their heads, now were not only willing but eager to participate in the Monroe Doctrine."[7] Pasvolsky and his fellow universalists were not happy with the apparent commitment by the United States to establish a formal regional security commitment—but at least the Act of Chapultepec said that the treaty to be negotiated would "constitute a regional arrangement . . . consistent with the purposes and principles of the general international organization, when established."

Argentina, uninvited because of its continued diplomatic relations with Germany, was very much an issue at Chapultepec. The United States had broken diplomatic relations with Argentina, imposed economic sanctions, and was engaged in a persistent war of words. Argentina in turn had requested a formal meeting of American states to discuss the situation—an idea the United States found distasteful. Other Latin American nations, however, wanted Argentina brought fully back into the inter-American community, provided it broke with Germany. Argentina did formally declare war on Germany March 27, 1945—an act without military significance but sufficient to restore the country's good graces with fellow Latin American governments, although not with the United States.

Latin American governments lobbied for Argentina to be invited to the United Nations conference at San Francisco in fulfillment of the ideal of hemispheric solidarity. The issue was entangled with that of whether Poland, Ukraine, and White Russia should —as the Soviet Union insisted—be seated at San Francisco. If Argentina was excluded, the Latin American nations would vote against seating the two Soviet republics (whose membership in the UN had been promised by Roosevelt at Yalta and was supported by the United States at San Francisco). But the Soviet Union considered Argentina a Fascist state, almost an enemy, and voted against its presence at San Francisco. Secretary of State Edward R. Stettinius, Jr., recently appointed as Hull's successor, then struck a bargain with the Latin Americans. The United States would hold its nose, as it were, and support Argentina if they would support Ukraine and White Russia. In reporting afterward in a radio address on the conference, Stettinius said: "I wish to make clear that the vote of the United States in favor of seating Argentina did not constitute a blanket endorsement of the policies of the Argentina Government. On the contrary, with many of those policies both the Government and people of the United States have no sympathy."[8]

And so it transpired that the Soviet republics were admitted by unanimous vote and Argentina over a Soviet *nyet*. American delegate Senator Arthur Vandenberg, no friend of the Soviet Union and a great believer in the Monroe Doctrine, was delighted. This affair, he said, has "done more in four days to solidify Pan America against Russia than anything that ever happened."[9] The Soviet Union was also isolated on the question of seating the Lublin government of Poland. The conference voted no.

With the Argentine question out of the way, the United States delegation at San Francisco turned to the more significant question of regional versus universal authority, the Monroe Doctrine versus a universalist vision of the United Nations. At a preliminary meeting in Washington, Pasvolsky asked that no changes be made in the Dumbarton Oaks proposals for maintaining international security, including the paragraph on regional arrangements. Commander Harold E. Stassen and John Foster Dulles were opposed. The provisions as they stand, they said, would permit an outside power "to veto American regional action in the Western Hemisphere." Nelson Rockefeller, with the new title of Assistant Secretary of State for American Republic Affairs, raised the possibility that the Soviet Union might foment trouble in the Western Hemisphere, something feared by Latin American governments, and then use its veto to block inter-American action. Pasvolsky replied that he did not want the inter-American system destroyed, but "to weaken the authority of the Security Council in regional matters would be tantamount to throwing all Europe into the hands of the Soviet Union, and would break the world up into regional units." The battle was joined. It involved early intimations of the approaching Cold War.[10]

Assistant Secretary of War John J. McCloy, having canvassed the views of generals in the War Department, saw a serious threat to the Monroe Doctrine and to the capacity of the United States to deal unilaterally with its security interests in the Western Hemisphere. On April 26 he lunched with his boss, the venerable Henry L. Stimson, Secretary of War and former Secretary of State. Stimson had little use for Pasvolsky's universalism and was still optimistic that Soviet-American relations could be handled through mutual accommodation. He said to McCloy that "some Americans are anxious to hang on to exaggerated views of the Monroe Doctrine and at the same time butt into every question that comes up in Central Europe . . . Our position in the western hemisphere and Russia's in the eastern hemisphere could be adjusted without too much friction." Three days later Stimson entered some more comment in his diary: "The young men in the State Department are trying to push Stettinius into the view that the procedure to be established in the Dumbarton Oaks project will eventually overrule and supplant the Monroe Doctrine. I have pointed out how dangerous that would be to our public opinion; how even the League of Nations accepted the Monroe Doctrine and left it untouched, and . . . if this Administration consents to an overruling of the Doctrine, they are in for trouble. But it is pretty hard to handle such international problems indirectly and at a long distance when the protagonists are young, ignorant, and inexperienced." Stimson, staying in Washington while McCloy went to San Francisco, soon worked himself into a "red hot" state, concluding that "the Good Neighbor Policy has put serious obstacles in the path of the exercise of the Monroe Doctrine."[11]

On May 4 the American delegation to the United Nations conference, now assembled in San Francisco, heard McCloy present and support the views of the Joint Chiefs of Staff and Stimson. The Joint Chiefs said that the United States should have explicit authority to deal with the security of the Western Hemisphere. The Dumbarton Oaks proposals did not provide that authority. "It is extremely important to protect our concept of preclusive rights in this hemisphere," said McCloy. Senator Vandenberg agreed. The Dumbarton Oaks proposals spell the end of the Monroe Doctrine, he said.[12]

Vandenberg was the most politically powerful member of the American delegation. He was a veteran Republican senator from Michigan and an isolationist until the day of Japan's attack on Pearl Harbor in 1941. Then he got religion and became a well-publicized advocate of world organization under American leadership. He looked forward to becoming the chairman of the Senate Foreign Relations Committee when Republicans, as was likely, won control of the Senate in the 1946 elections. He was acutely aware that he occupied the position held after the previous war by Senator Henry Cabot Lodge. Vandenberg was determined not to be a wrecker of world organization, like Lodge. And yet he shared Lodge's devotion to American freedom of action, the prerogatives of the Senate, and the Monroe Doctrine. As editor of the *Grand Rapids Herald* in 1919 he was the first to propose—or at least so he claimed—that the Senate reserve the exclusive right for the United States to interpret the Monroe Doctrine under Article XXI of the League of Nations Covenant. In 1926 he celebrated his devotion to the Monroe Doctrine and nationalism as "the indispensable bulwark of American independence" in a flag-waving book, *The Trail of a Tradition*. One sentence will suffice to give the flavor of the man and his mind: "Upon the Doctrine, as upon a rock, the institution of Pan-Americanism has been erected in the mutual co-operation of North and South American democracies for common benefits, the most useful external political movement in which the United States engages."[13] No politician in 1945 was more steeped emotionally and intellectually in the principles of the Monroe Doctrine.

President Roosevelt, aware of Wilson's political blunder in excluding the Senate from the Paris Peace Conference of 1919, had named Vandenberg to the U.S. delegation to San Francisco. Vandenberg accepted on condition that he be free to express his own opinions and not be bound by the Dumbarton Oaks proposals "as is." On May 5 he sent Secretary of State Stettinius, head of the U.S. delegation, a warning: "I am greatly disturbed lest we shall be charged with a desertion (1) of our Pan-American obligations at Chapultepec and (2) of the Monroe Doctrine. The former is a threat to the Pan-American solidarity which becomes increasingly indispensable to our security. The latter is a threat to confirmation of the entire San Francisco charter by the Senate of the United States."[14]

The debate was entangled with a proposal from the Soviet Union to permit enforcement action under mutual-defense pacts directed against renewed German aggression. These included bilateral pacts between the Soviet Union and Great Britain, Czechoslovakia, France, Yugoslavia, and the Lublin Polish government. The French advanced a similar, more inclusive, proposal to exempt from Security Council jurisdiction all "measures provided for in regional arrangements directed against the renewal of aggressive policy on the part of the aggressor states in this war."[15] For the American universalists any exception for an inter-American system would encourage the French and Soviet tendency toward European exclusivity. For the American defenders of the Monroe Doctrine the answer was to emphasize that the European exception was temporary while the Monroe Doctrine was eternal. Meanwhile, Latin American representatives at San Francisco kept the pressure on the United States to secure regional autonomy. Several declared that their governments could never accept the possibility of a veto by a permanent member of the Security Council over an action taken under the Act of Chapultepec.[16] The Latin American viewpoint was sincere, but it was also happily encouraged by Rockefeller and other Americans in battle with the universalists.

No issue at San Francisco was argued within the American delegation at such length or so strenuously. At one extreme stood Lieutenant General Stanley D. Embick, an aging officer long involved with hemispheric defense. Embick declared, "It was important to have recognized that the normal method of action would be by regional organizations as against action normally through the Security Council. It would be essential to maintain our isolation and our preclusive control over this hemisphere."[17] Those with an ear for history could detect the sentiments of Richard Olney pontificating during the Venezuela boundary dispute of 1895: "The United States is practically sovereign on this continent, and its fiat is law upon the subjects to which it confines its interposition." The other extreme was occupied by Pasvolsky and several allies, including Hamilton Fish Armstrong, editor of the journal *Foreign Affairs* and leading light in the Council on Foreign Relations. "The general organization would be ruined if we made general exceptions for regional arrangements," said Armstrong. "The Soviet Union would demand freedom in Europe."[18] Harley Notter of the State Department, a Pasvolsky ally, was another vociferous universalist. He argued that any regional exception would give "legal sanction to our Allies to build up a system that could in time be used against us." We must fight all exceptions "in the name of American security."[19] James C. Dunn, another Pasvolsky ally and a senior State Department Europeanist, said that if enforcement action was distributed to regional organizations, the power of the United Nations would be blunted and "we would have to face the fact that any combination of powers might start up war in an area and we would have nothing whatever to say about it." "Of course," he said sarcastically, "the decision might be made that the Inter-American System was so unique and so important that one had to sacrifice everything for it."[20]

The strongest statement came from Pasvolsky himself, and he spoke with Wilsonian eloquence: "If we open up the Dumbarton Oaks Proposals to allow for regional enforcement action on a collective basis, the world organization is finished . . . We then move into a system in which we rely for our security on regional groups, large states with their spheres of influence surrounded by groups of smaller states. We will convert the world into armed camps and end up with a world war unlike any we have yet seen."[21] Except for the grim prediction of world war, Pasvolsky accurately described the condition of international relations that would develop during the Cold War.

John Foster Dulles occupied a middle ground. He believed in the continuing validity of the Monroe Doctrine, but he saw the danger in placing regional authority before that of the Security Council. The United States, he said, was faced with "the highest decision of national policy—whether or not to build on hemisphere solidarity alone and throw away all of Europe or whether to save our voice in Western Europe."[22] Speaking on the telephone from Washington, Secretary of War Stimson added his weight to the regionalist argument. We should, he said, insist on a "hemisphere free of the veto of the Security Council" even if that risked Soviet opposition. Resurrecting a Wilsonian metaphor, Stimson denied that a single exception for the hemisphere would "cut the heart out of the document . . . I think it's not asking too much to have our little region over here" if Russia "is going to take these steps . . . of building up friendly protectorates around her."[23]

There were three, rather than two, positions in the debate, but all shared suspicion of the Soviet Union. The Pasvolsky purists opposed a reassertion of the Monroe Doctrine because the Soviets, and perhaps others, would use it as precedent for their own exclusive spheres—with possibly dire consequences for the well-being of people within such spheres and for world peace. A smaller group in the middle could be called the unpanicked realists. They considered a Soviet sphere of influence in Eastern Europe inevitable, something with which the United States would have to live, and not something leading to another world war. At the same time they believed in protecting the special position of the United States in the Western Hemisphere. People holding this position could be conservative like Stimson, or on the left like Secretary of Commerce Henry A. Wallace.

The third position prevailed at San Francisco. Its advocates were more suspicious than Pasvolsky of the Soviet Union and in traditional fashion turned to the Monroe Doctrine and the inter-American system as necessary protection against a hostile threat from beyond the hemisphere. In the years ahead there would be a high correlation between fear and denunciation of the Soviet Union and international Communism and spread-eagle praise of the Monroe Doctrine. Vandenberg, leader of this group, dismissed the Pasvolsky argument that American embrace of the Monroe Doctrine might be used by the Russians and others to justify their spheres. Vandenberg's diary is illuminating:

It speedily developed that not only are the South Americans hot about protecting Chapultepec, but the Australians are equally anxious not to be left unprotected in their far corner of the earth. They want liberty of regional action if some of the Big Powers veto action in the Council. Other potential regional groups are forming and they could be highly dangerous—particularly the Arabian bloc in its impact on Palestine. Our great problem is to find a rule which protects legitimate existing regional groups (like Pan-Am) without opening up the opportunity for regional balance of power groups.[24]

Here again was the sauce-for-the-gander problem. Just as Secretary of State Hull on the eve of the Second World War had said that the morally pure Monroe Doctrine could never be justification for Japanese or German spheres of influence, now Senator Vandenberg denied that anything the Soviets, or the Arabs, might seek to establish in their alleged sphere had any legitimacy. Only the inter-American system under the Monroe Doctrine was legitimate.

The commodious concept of "self-defense" helped the American delegation break its internal stalemate and find a solution to the "great problem." Harold Stassen moved the thinking in this direction by suggesting three additions to the charter under the heading "Self-Defense":

1. Nothing in this Charter shall be construed as abrogating the inherent right of self-defense against a violator of the Charter.
2. In the application of this provision the principles of the Act of Chapultepec and of the Monroe Doctrine are specifically recognized.
3. It is also clear that all regions are fully entitled to use all peaceful means of settling disputes without the permission of the Security Council.[25]

During several days of discussion, the self-defense argument won broad agreement within the delegation—except on the desirability of including specific reference to the Act of Chapultepec and the Monroe Doctrine. Rockefeller said that mention of the act would have a "sales value for the Latin American group," that it had a "symbolic value similar to the Monroe Doctrine." Stassen agreed: "The Act is the modern Monroe Doctrine."[26] But when the issue was raised in a five-power meeting (the United States,

Great Britain, the Soviet Union, China, and France), British Foreign Secretary Anthony Eden—after listening to a patriotic speech on the history of the Monroe Doctrine from Senator Tom Connally—was very opposed, even nasty. "I did not come here for the purpose of signing a regional agreement," he said. "If what was wanted was a Latin American regional arrangement that was all right with him but he would have nothing to do with it."[27] In 1954, when Guatemala sought to bring a complaint before the Security Council and was opposed by the United States, Eden's suspicions of American purpose were confirmed, as we shall see, and his anger was even greater.

After extended debate, with innumerable tributes by Americans to the Monroe Doctrine, the U.S. delegation decided it was not essential to mention Chapultepec or the Monroe Doctrine by name. The United States accepted as adequate the language that became Articles 51, 52, 53, 54. The British, French, and Chinese approved. So did the Soviets, after some balking. The Latin American representatives told Rockefeller that they accepted the texts. The "great problem" had been solved in words. The future would tell whether words could meet all circumstances to everyone's satisfaction.

Article 51 affirmed the "inherent right of individual and collective self-defense against armed attack" without in any way affecting the authority and responsibility of the Security Council. Measures taken under the right of self-defense were to be reported immediately to the Security Council.

Article 52 authorized "regional arrangements or agencies" (an oblique reference to Chapultepec) consistent with the purposes of the United Nations. United Nations members belonging to such regional entities were enjoined to try to settle disputes by peaceful means before turning to the Security Council. On the other hand: "This Article in no way impairs the application of Articles 34 and 35," which affirmed the unlimited right of the Security Council to investigate any actual or potential threat to international peace and security, and the absolute right of any member to bring such matters to the attention of the General Assembly or the Security Council.

Article 53 directed the council in appropriate circumstances to employ regional agencies, but stated that no enforcement action could be taken by a regional agency without authorization of the Security Council. Article 54 directed regional agencies to keep the Security Council informed of their activities relating to peace and security.

Senator Vandenberg was ecstatic. "We have preserved the Monroe Doctrine and the Inter-American system," he wrote a constituent after the conference was over. "We have retained a complete veto—exclusive in our own hands—over any decisions involving external activities."[28]

During the remainder of 1945 and through 1946 the United States, Great Britain, and the Soviet Union negotiated unsuccessfully over the shape of the postwar world. President Truman and one segment of his advisers believed that the United States had an obligation to insist that the Soviet Union live up to the amorphous wartime agreements for the establishment of democratic governments in Eastern Europe. Others in the United States and Great Britain questioned whether it was appropriate to challenge the Soviet Union in its sphere. For example, British Foreign Minister Ernest Bevin, not yet a hard-line cold warrior, put forward an idea he called "the three Monroes." The United States would be responsible for maintaining "international order" in the Pacific (and presumably Latin America), Great Britain in the Mediterranean broadly defined, and the Soviet Union in southeastern Europe. Each power, however, would agree not to interfere in the purely internal affairs of the countries in its sphere and would permit all outside countries to have freedom of access and trade within the sphere.[29] The trouble with Bevin's idea from the universalist point of view was that the line between maintaining "international order" and intervening in internal affairs was impossible to draw. But at least Bevin wanted to insist on certain minimal standards of behavior for each Great Power.

American Secretary of Commerce Henry Wallace, on the other hand, was less concerned about what the Soviets might do in their sphere. He saw American warmongers pushing for a showdown with the Soviet Union and believed that the best course was for both sides to stay out of each other's affairs. For example, in November 1945, after listening to Assistant Secretary of State Spruille Braden, Rockefeller's successor, expound on the Communist danger in Latin America, Wallace suggested that it should be possible to strike a deal with the Russians who "might feel about the Balkan states in somewhat the same way as we feel about Latin America." Wallace put the idea even more expansively in the September 1946 Madison Square Garden speech that led to his dismissal from Truman's cabinet: "On our part, we should recognize that we have no more business in the political affairs of eastern Europe than Russia has in the political affairs of Latin America . . ."[30]

The views of Bevin and Wallace raised the old sauce-for-the-gander issue yet again. How could the United States simultaneously maintain that peace was indivisible and assert that only American nations, with the United States in the dominant position, could be heard on issues of the Western Hemisphere? In March 1947, in the most famous speech of his presidency, Harry Truman resolved the problem by extending to the entire world the definition of American interest in protecting small nations from external coercion. His speech, immediately named the Truman Doctrine, was called the most important statement of foreign policy since Monroe's message of 1823. "Like the Monroe Doctrine, it warned that the United States would resist efforts to impose a political system or foreign domination on areas vital to our security," wrote James Reston in *The New York Times*.[31] After describing a world faced with the choice between two "ways of life"—one free, the other based on "terror and oppression"—Truman said it must be the policy of the United States to support everywhere "free peoples who are resisting attempted subjugation by armed minorities or by outside pressures." Truman thus divided the world by ideology, not geography, and declared long-term war on the ideology of "subjugation." The Monroe Doctrine remained intact for the Western Hemisphere because that hemisphere was—in Truman's geography—the heart of democracy. But unlike Stimson in 1945 or Wallace in 1946 Truman did not believe in giving the Soviet Union a free hand in Eastern Europe; nor would he accept the idea of any "Monroes" other than the American brand. The fact that Truman's speech was instantly named the Truman Doctrine, and has been known as such ever since, was an implicit acknowledgment of the continuing emotional appeal of the original doctrine.

The success of Senator Vandenberg and company at San Francisco in protecting the autonomy of the hemisphere from foreign intrusion under the Monroe Doctrine required the creation of a new treaty structure for inter-American collective security. Latin American governments were impatient over the delay, and in August 1945 Brazil issued an invitation for the American republics to meet in Rio de Janeiro to perfect the formal treaty of inter-American security promised at Chapultepec. The United States said no—not yet. The reason was American unwillingness to be associated in signing such a treaty with the Argentine government of President Juan Perón. In 1945 the outspoken American ambassador in Buenos Aires, Spruille Braden (the only bull to carry around his own china shop, said Dean Acheson), had waged a personal war against Perón as if the popular Argentine dictator were Adolf Hitler incarnate. By any definition of diplomatic protocol Braden was guilty of egregious intervention in Argentine internal affairs—not only egregious but counterproductive in that his attacks increased Perón's popularity. But Braden's campaign was redolent of Monroeism and Wilsonian intervention. The United States would champion American democratic values, the exclusion of alien ideology, even against a country's popular leader.

The anti-Argentina policy remained in effect through 1946, when Braden was back in Washington as Assistant Secretary of

State for American Republic Affairs. Arguing against Braden was his successor as ambassador, George S. Messersmith, formerly ambassador to Mexico. Messersmith, flattered by Perón's attention, believed it was time to welcome Argentina back into the community of American states. As memories of Argentina's affinity with Nazi Germany faded and the Cold War began, Perón spoke of his determination to stand with the United States in war with the Soviet Union. Messersmith's approach soon prevailed over Bradenism. The United States would no longer refuse to sit at the same communal diplomatic table with Argentina. Braden resigned from the Department of State in July 1947, and the next month delegations from the United States and the other American republics convened, after a two-year delay, in Rio, to conclude the treaty promised at Chapultepec.

Senator Arthur Vandenberg, champion of the Monroe Doctrine at San Francisco and now chairman of the Senate Foreign Relations Committee, was one of the American delegates, and in many ways overshadowed Secretary of State George Marshall. He certainly took the conference with great seriousness and attended carefully to detail. In the Inter-American Treaty of Reciprocal Assistance (to use the official name) the parties agreed to undertake the peaceful settlement of disputes among themselves before turning to the United Nations. They agreed that an attack on the territory of any one was an attack on all. Collective decisions on how the victim of aggression should be assisted and the aggressor punished required a two-thirds vote of approval—thus, said Vandenberg, taking the veto out of the inter-American system; however, no state could be required to use force without its consent. Aggressions on the high seas or in the air fell within the meaning of the treaty if they occurred within precisely described boundaries. This provision, largely the work of Vandenberg, carried through the process of geographical boundary-drawing begun less formally during the Second World War. The area was a gigantic ellipse beginning at the North Pole, sweeping southward in two lines encompassing Greenland on the east and Alaska on the west, passing an average of three hundred miles off the continental coasts, to meet again at the South Pole.

But what of disputes over sovereignty between an American and a European state within the ellipse? When Argentina again sought the removal of British occupation over the Falklands, the response from the United States, delivered by Arthur Vandenberg, was curt: "The Argentine delegation is entitled to enter on the record any unilateral statement it desires. But the basic fact will remain that this treaty does not touch or involve or change any sovereignty in the regional zone here defined. These are questions of fact and this treaty does not directly or indirectly affect these questions of fact."[32] Thirty-five years later this "question of fact" would be contested in war between Argentina and Great Britain with, as we shall see, some curious ramifications for the Monroe Doctrine.

For the ceremonial conclusion of the Rio conference, President Truman arrived on the battleship *Missouri*, on the deck of which, precisely two years before, the surrender of Japan had marked the end of the Second World War. Returning to Washington, Senator Vandenberg presented the treaty to the Senate with these words: "We have sealed a New World pact of peace which possesses teeth. We have translated Pan-American solidarity from an ideal into a reality . . . This is sunlight in a dark world." The Senate approved by a vote of 72–1.[33] For Vandenberg the Monroe Doctrine had never been so alive and well.

Before continuing we should note that inclusion of a wedge of the Antarctic continent in the area of the Rio treaty raised a complicated problem. Although American mariners and explorers had been prominent in expeditions to the great frozen and uninhabitable continent, the United States government had long ignored Antarctica. The first official American action toward Antarctica was the expedition of 1939 under the command of Admiral Richard Byrd, prompted partly out of scientific curiosity and partly out of the possible strategic importance of the continent. Both the Japanese and the Germans were then active in the region.

The military involvement of Antarctica in the Second World War was minimal, but with the onset of the Cold War, Admiral Byrd and some others warned that the Soviets might be coming to the Antarctic and the United States should take preemptive action. In a secret policy review the Department of State suggested that the statement of the Monroe Doctrine—that the United States would "consider any attempt on their part [Europe] to extend their system to any portion of this hemisphere as dangerous to our peace and safety"—provided a basis for dealing with Antarctica.[34] If, as Senator Vandenberg and others affirmed, the Rio pact was a multilateral expression of the Monroe Doctrine, then Antarctica was covered. But the United States had a long-standing position that it neither claimed territory on Antarctica nor recognized the claims of others. The others, however, included Chile, Argentina, and Great Britain—with overlapping claims within the sector covered by the Rio treaty.

Here was an invitation for trouble. At the very time the United States was working closely with Great Britain in the containment of the Soviet Union, Chile and Argentina were challenging the British presence in their sectors of Antarctica as a violation of the Monroe Doctrine and a ground for invoking the Rio pact. On several occasions blood was nearly shed as Argentine and Chilean vessels challenged the British, who sent reinforcements. Shots were fired, but without casualties.

The matter was serious enough to be put to George Kennan's Policy Planning Staff (PPS). In June 1948, PPS noted that the conflict between Britain and the two Latin American claimants "is a source of embarrassment . . . because of our close relations to Great Britain and our commitments in the Western Hemisphere," embarrassment "susceptible to exploitation by the U.S.S.R. to the further disadvantage of the United States." The solution was to make a serious effort to reach a broad international settlement, excluding the Soviets.[35] During the next decade the United States rejected any idea that the Monroe Doctrine applied to the issue and by vigorous diplomacy succeeded in preventing armed conflict—in contrast to the failure through passivity on the Falklands issue. The Antarctic treaty of 1959 neither recognized nor denied territorial claims, prohibited military activity, and kept the continent open for the peaceful uses of all nations including the Soviet Union. The coldest region on earth became the first region to be excluded from the Cold War.

After Rio, the next step was to transform the old Pan-American Union, a politically bland organization dating from 1889, into the Organization of American States. For this purpose the American republics met in Bogotá, Colombia, in the spring of 1948. The American delegation, led by Secretary of State George C. Marshall, had modest objectives. On the negative side, it sought to disabuse the Latin Americans of any hope of massive economic aid from the United States and to discourage them from pressing for the abolition of existing European colonies in the hemisphere. On the positive side, the United States sought to tidy up the text of the OAS Charter and, more important, to engage the conference in serious discussion of the threat of Communist subversion. What might have been a boring occasion became exciting, even dangerous, at the outset when the leader of the Colombian Liberal Party, Jorge Gaitán, was assassinated in downtown Bogotá. A mob killed the assassin and hanged the body in front of the presidential palace. Days of rioting, looting, destruction of property, and armed violence followed. The building in which the conference was being held was gutted and records destroyed. Marshall told the other chiefs of delegation that it was imperative to keep on—as a signal of courage in the face of revolutionary movements with worldwide implications. But Acting Secretary of State Robert Lovett in Washington cabled Marshall that there was strong congressional and public sentiment for ending the conference as soon as possible without giving the impression of running away. Marshall replied that his continued presence in Bogotá would do more to combat Communism and reported revolutionary activities throughout Latin America than his return home.[36] The conference ran its course.

When Marshall did return in May, he put Latin America aside in order to concentrate on the implementation of the European recovery program, the early negotiations for what became NATO, and soon the response to the Berlin blockade which the Soviets imposed in June. Except for the two conferences just discussed, the late 1940s were a quiet time in United States relations with Latin America—or a period of reprehensible neglect, depending on one's point of view. The great events of American foreign policy were elsewhere. Senator Arthur Vandenberg, now chairman of the Senate Foreign Relations Committee, retained his devotion to the Monroe Doctrine but became an effective advocate of new American commitments under the Truman Doctrine, the Marshall Plan for the economic revival of Europe, and the North Atlantic Treaty, which he called "the most important step in American foreign policy since the promulgation of the Monroe Doctrine."[37]

The Marshall Plan for the economic reconstruction of Western Europe, subject of almost limitless self-congratulation by Americans then and since, was resented in Latin America as sorry proof of American priorities. Latin America at the time received virtually no American foreign aid. President Truman did nothing to allay concerns when he was asked at a press conference whether the United States would consider a Marshall Plan for Latin America. "Well, I think there has always been a Marshall plan in effect for the Western Hemisphere. The foreign policy of the United States in that direction has been set for one hundred years, known as the Monroe Doctrine."[38] It is difficult to say whether that comment demonstrated more confusion about the Marshall Plan or about the Monroe Doctrine.

A more intriguing hypothetical connection between the Marshall Plan and the Monroe Doctrine came from the pen of John Moors Cabot, an experienced Foreign Service officer and Latin

American hand. Cabot noted in November 1947 that four European countries had colonies within the security zone of the Rio treaty (Britain, France, the Netherlands, and Denmark). Should a Communist government gain power in one or more of these countries—as seemed all too possible that year—then the colonies might become "a potential or actual menace to our security." The Monroe Doctrine, he said, certainly justified American action, but the prohibition on the use of force in the UN Charter would be an obstacle. Cabot's solution was that the European governments should be required, as a condition of receiving Marshall Plan assistance, to agree that the American republics had the right under the Act of Havana of 1940 and the Rio treaty to occupy their colonies and establish a provisional administration should Communist control be threatened. By such a course, said Cabot, the United States would assure its continental security and show the Latin American republics that there was something in the Marshall Plan for them.[39] Cabot's idea was never pursued, because none of the European colonial governments ever became Communist, and yet his memorandum stands as a fascinating intellectual link between the Monroe Doctrine of the Nazi and the Cold War eras.

One can find scattered throughout the archives of the late 1940s individual expressions of deep concern mingled with boilerplate prose about Communist and Soviet intentions in Latin America. For example, the Army's secret intelligence weekly summary cited the Monroe Doctrine as a fundamental policy and warned of Communist involvement in the Venezuelan oil industry and Communist intentions in Cuba and Brazil to "undermine United States influence in Latin America and to aid the U.S.S.R." In a report of the strategic significance of Central America, Army intelligence observed: "Where dictatorships have been abolished, the resulting governments have been weak and unstable."[40] The FBI, which had responsibility for Latin America prior to the establishment of the CIA in 1947, supplied similar material. Director J. Edgar Hoover reported in January 1946 that Communism was making considerable headway in Latin America by playing on the theme of

U.S. imperialism. In July Hoover saw a "noticeable accentuation of the anti–United States and pro-Soviet line" and the "redoubled efforts on the part of Soviet Russia to entrench herself diplomatically and commercially in Latin America."[41] This was all pretty dreary, predictable stuff and no one at a high level, except Hoover, paid it much heed. But by the end of 1949 the period of high-level complacency was about to end and the Monroe Doctrine was about to be rediscovered.

CHAPTER 4

THE KENNAN COROLLARY
AND GUATEMALA

The American approach to Latin America has always been affected by the larger context of foreign policy. Indeed, had there never been real or imagined threats to national security from beyond the hemisphere there would never have been a Monroe Doctrine. In late 1949 and early 1950 a dramatic shift in the larger context caused American officials to perceive greater dangers in Latin America than at any time since the high tide of Nazi expansion in 1940–41. The new perceptions led to unprecedented use of the Monroe Doctrine to justify covert intervention against a Latin American government and a general willingness to temper support for democracy in order to stand against Communism.

The shift occurred quickly. During the first part of 1949 the United States seemed to have won the Cold War. The North Atlantic Treaty was signed in April; in May the Soviets lifted the Berlin blockade, a significant retreat, perhaps even recognition that a comprehensive settlement on Western terms might be in the offing. But in August 1949 the Soviet Union detonated its first nuclear explosion, ending the American atomic monopoly. In October the People's Republic of China was formally established in Beijing, signifying the triumph of Communism in the Chinese civil war. The end of the atomic monopoly and the "loss" of China replaced the optimism of mid-1949 in Washington with a growing assumption that the world was now on the eve of war. In the winter and spring of 1950 a group of State and Defense Department officials, headed by Paul Nitze of State, prepared the foundation policy statement for the United States in this seemingly perilous on-the-eve-of-war situation. It was in the form of a 30,000-word report to the National Security Council. Known ever since simply as NSC–68, and widely cited after being declassified and published in 1975, the report used language alarmist in the extreme. A few excerpts will suffice to make the point: "The Soviet Union . . . is animated by a new fanatic faith, antithetical to our own, and seeks to impose its absolute authority over the rest of the world. Conflict has, therefore, become endemic and is waged, on the part of the Soviet Union, by violent or non-violent methods in accordance with the dictates of expediency . . . The issues that face us are momentous, involving the fulfillment or destruction not only of this Republic but of civilization itself." The Kremlin "design, therefore, calls for the complete subversion or forcible destruction of the machinery of government and structure of society in the countries of the non-Soviet world and their replacement by an apparatus and structure subservient to and controlled from the Kremlin."[1]

The pervading sense of worldwide danger made the highest officials in the American government think about Latin America in terms of global strategy, not in terms of the problems within individual countries or the region or even in terms of the perennial issues between the other American republics and the United States. These men—Secretaries of State, national security advisers, Presidents, directors of the Central Intelligence Agency, and their top advisers throughout the entire period from 1945 to the end of the Cold War—all lacked deep knowledge or experience of Latin America. The foreign policy and national security professionals in the group were experts on Europe, Asia, and relations among the Great Powers. They knew the leaders of Britain, France, Germany, Italy, Japan, Israel, the Soviet Union, and the many other countries of Europe, Asia, and the Middle East—but not the leaders of the

American republics. None of the members of the high foreign policy establishment in the United States had ever lived in Latin America. None had more than the most rudimentary knowledge of Spanish or Portuguese—if that. And most were condescending and prejudiced toward the people and culture of Latin America. For Harry Truman, Latin Americans were, like Jews and the Irish, "very emotional" and difficult to handle.[2] Secretary of State John Foster Dulles thought he knew how Latin Americans should be handled. "You have to pat them a little bit and make them think you are fond of them."[3] President Eisenhower's attitude was revealed in a remark to President Arturo Frondizi of Argentina, a nation whose population was almost entirely white and European in origin: "Argentines are the same kind of people we are."[4] High officials in their franker moments admitted to feelings of unease, distrust, and racial prejudice toward Latin American politicians. The result was that much of American policy toward Latin America as developed by the highest American officials had little to do with Latin America as such—but everything to do with how those officials saw the United States projecting power around the world and being threatened by the projected power of the Soviet Union. The fear of that projected power led them to the protean principles of the Monroe Doctrine as the foundation of policy toward Latin America.

The above generalizations are nowhere better illustrated than in the case of what we call the Kennan Corollary to the Monroe Doctrine. George F. Kennan was in 1950 the best known and acclaimed senior American diplomat and foreign policy intellectual. His views on the "sources of Soviet conduct" and the nature of the conflict between Russia and the West had earned him the reputation of father of "containment." He was the founder and head of the State Department's Policy Planning Staff, 1947–50. He and his associates had influenced the shape of the Marshall Plan, the response to the Berlin blockade of 1948, the North Atlantic Treaty of 1949, and the effort to find some stability in relations with China. But neither Kennan nor his staff knew anything about

Latin America.[5] He noted on a global review of foreign policy in 1948, "This document should properly have included a chapter on Latin America. I have not included such a chapter because I am not familiar with the problems of the area, and the Staff has not yet studied them."[6]

In early 1950 Kennan determined to repair the gap in his knowledge by touring Latin America. The result was a 10,000-word memorandum for the Secretary of State on "Latin America as a problem in United States foreign policy."[7] Because of his brutal frankness and extremely negative evaluation of Latin American character, the report was classified SECRET and very closely held within the Department of State until its publication more than thirty years later. The report, per se, did not influence policy. But as an unvarnished statement of widely held attitudes and for its claim that the Monroe Doctrine justified, indeed demanded, support by the United States for repressive political regimes in Latin America, it is a seminal document—ranking with Monroe's original message, Richard Olney's and Theodore Roosevelt's elaborations, and the Clark memorandum of 1928.

Kennan left Washington by train for Mexico City on February 18, 1950, and thence by plane to Caracas, Rio, São Paulo, Montevideo, Buenos Aires, and back via Lima and Panama City. "I found the journey anything but pleasant," he noted in his memoirs. The luxury of the very rich and the dismal life of the poor dismayed him. He was unnerved when Communist-inspired propaganda attacked him personally, when he was several times burned in effigy, and when huge security forces were mobilized to protect him. The self-centered pomposity of political leaders disgusted him. Reflecting prejudices more common to North Americans of the eighteenth and nineteenth centuries, he concluded that Latin America was cursed beyond redemption by geography, history, and race. "The handicaps to progress are written in human blood and in the tracings of geography; and in neither case are they readily susceptible of obliteration . . . and the answers people have suggested to them thus far have been feeble and unpromising."[8]

But Kennan believed that the failure of the United States to keep Latin America within its own sphere could be catastrophic in the confrontation with the Soviet Union. Especially in a war, if "a considerable portion of Latin American society were to throw its weight morally into the opposite camp, this, together with the initial military successes which the Russians would presumably have in Europe, might well turn the market of international confidence against us and leave us fighting not only communist military power, but a wave of defeatism among our friends and spiteful elation among our detractors elsewhere in the world." After talking to American ambassadors and presumably CIA station chiefs, Kennan reported that Communists were a clear and present danger throughout Latin America. "Here, as elsewhere, the inner core of the communist leadership is fanatical, disciplined, industrious, and armed with a series of organizational techniques which are absolutely first rate."

Kennan's prescription for how the society of the United States should meet the challenge of Communism was a rededication to fundamental moral values. The last paragraph of his famous "long telegram" of February 1946 declared: "Finally, we must have courage and self-confidence to cling to our own methods and conceptions of human society. After all, the greatest danger that can befall us in coping with this problem of Soviet communism is that we shall allow ourselves to become like those with whom we are coping."[9] But he had no such confidence in or prescription for Latin America, nor did he believe it was necessary for the United States to cling to its ideals when dealing with Latin America.

The overriding objective for Kennan was to apply the Monroe Doctrine in the changed circumstances of the mid-twentieth century. After a long historical review of the meaning of the doctrine, drawing heavily on the work of historian Samuel Flagg Bemis (whose efforts to reaffirm the Monroe Doctrine as justification for removing Fidel Castro will be described in Chapter 6), Kennan argued that Communist infiltration, "designed to make the Latin American countries pawns in the power aspirations of regimes beyond the limits of this continent," was precisely the kind of threat the doctrine was meant to combat.

What to do? Kennan said that Americans could not defeat the threat alone. That had to be done by Latin American governments, impelled or coerced by the United States. We should provide incentives for effective anti-Communist action, and also, where necessary, "coercive measures which can impress other governments with the danger of antagonizing us through excessive toleration of anti-American activities and would yet not be susceptible to exploitation by our enemies as constituting intervention or imperialism or illicit means of pressure."

The public rhetoric of American foreign policy, enshrined in the Truman Doctrine and innumerable other declarations, proclaimed that democracy, freedom, the rights of the individual were the answer to Communism. But in Latin America Kennan saw a political culture too weak and selfish to support a democracy strong enough to resist the superior determination and skill of the Communist enemy. Kennan's answer, his corollary to the Monroe Doctrine, was clear, direct, and bleak:

> We cannot be too dogmatic about the methods by which local communists can be dealt with. These vary greatly, depending upon the vigor and efficacy of local concepts and traditions of self-government. Where such vigor and efficacy are relatively high, as in our own country, the body politic may be capable of bearing the virus of communism without permitting it to expand to dangerous proportions. This is undoubtedly the best solution of the communist problem, wherever the prerequisites exist. But where they do not exist, and where the concepts and traditions of popular government are too weak to absorb successfully the intensity of the communist attack, then we must concede that harsh governmental measures of repression may be the only answer; that these measures may have to proceed from regimes whose origins and methods would not stand the test of American concepts of

democratic procedures; and that such regimes and such methods may be preferable alternatives, and indeed the only alternatives, to further communist success.

Those who know and admire George Kennan's entire career realize that this memorandum, setting forth a Kennan Corollary to the Monroe Doctrine, is inconsistent with much of his subsequent thought. It was the product of the culture shock of a Europeanist who had never visited Latin America before, an uncharacteristic susceptibility to the views of the American ambassadors with whom he talked, the near-hysterical sense of a worldwide Communist menace in that year 1950, and Kennan's preference for "realism" over moralistic rhetoric. It would be an overstatement to claim that the Kennan Corollary permeated all of American policy toward Latin America through the 1980s. On many occasions the United States condemned right-wing governments engaging in harsh repression and supported regimes and individuals committed to democracy and respect for human rights. But through the 1980s the approach recommended by Kennan in 1950 had staunch advocates who applied it to particular situations—most notably, Guatemala in 1954, Brazil in 1964, Chile in 1973, El Salvador in the 1980s. In so doing they unwittingly hastened the death of the Monroe Doctrine by associating it with torture, death squads, and the very denial of democratic ideals that the original doctrine honored and vowed to protect. Less than a month after Kennan delivered his report, Assistant Secretary of State Edward G. Miller, Jr., spoke publicly about the Monroe Doctrine. His words were polite and designed to avoid offense, but the message was close to Kennan's. In the tradition of the Monroe Doctrine, said Miller, we today "consider any attempt to extend the Communist system to any portions of this hemisphere as 'dangerous to our peace and safety.' " The problem is never purely military. "Extreme weakness in the political and social structures of small states has always made them vulnerable to diplomatic pressures and to penetration by political and economic means." Miller then praised Theodore Roosevelt's corollary for authorizing "certain protective interventions" appropriate to time and circumstances. Miller said that today, 1950, no such intervention was necessary, but if it were, there should be action by "the organized community of American states."[10] The reference to collective action was a necessary ritual. Kennan, the realist, never once mentioned the "American community," the Organization of American States, or the Rio treaty. For him they were myths, mere paper nullities. Although he could on occasion be eloquent on the necessity of grounding foreign policy on moral principle, here Kennan was echoing the amoral instrumentalism of NSC–68, an almost exactly contemporaneous document:

> The integrity of our system will not be jeopardized by any measures, covert or overt, violent or non-violent, which serve the purposes of frustrating the Kremlin design, nor does the necessity of conducting ourselves so as to affirm our values in actions as well as words forbid such measures, provided only they are appropriately calculated to that end and are not so excessive or misdirected as to make us enemies of the people instead of the evil men who have enslaved them.[11]

George Kennan never again expressed himself at length on Latin America. At the end of 1950 he took an extended leave from the Foreign Service and for the remainder of his long career would return only briefly to government service. As scholar and commentator he would focus on Soviet-Western relations and the dangers of nuclear war, and on writing diplomatic history. But his 1950 report on Latin America remains the single most illuminating document in the last years of the Monroe Doctrine. No other better expresses the hard assumptions behind the interventions and threats of intervention undertaken in the subsequent decades and justified by the Monroe Doctrine and amoral realism—even though those ordering the interventions were unaware of Kennan's 1950 report.[12]

The first application of the Kennan Corollary was the American covert intervention in Guatemala in 1954. Here was the post-1945 high-water mark for the Monroe Doctrine as public declarative policy and also the first extensive use of secrecy and lying in supposed defense of democracy against an alien creed, the first use of the deniable covert coercion Kennan had discussed, the first deliberate overthrow of a democratic regime because it refused to act against the left, and its replacement by a regime meeting the test of harsh repression at the heart of the Kennan Corollary. The ramifications of what happened in 1954 would unroll for decades.

From 1931 to 1944 Guatemala had been ruled by an archetypal Central American dictator, Jorge Ubico—friendly to the United Fruit Company and large landowners generally, unfriendly to organized labor, repressive of dissent, and little concerned for the economic and social welfare of the mass of the Indian population.[13] Ubico had no trouble maintaining a good image in the United States. For example, in November 1939 he entertained Senator Harry S. Truman, visiting in connection with a survey of national defense issues. Truman, writing to his wife, noted Ubico's reputation "for eliminating graft in this country—the only one south of the Rio Grande where it has been done."[14] But even dictators can lose their grip, and in July 1944 Ubico, faced with broad opposition in Guatemala City, resigned. After a violent interval under a self-proclaimed provisional President, General Federico Ponce, Guatemala held presidential elections in December 1944. The winner was a charismatic professor of literature and philosophy, Juan José Arévalo.

Arévalo inaugurated a broad movement of political, social, and economic reform, and incurred the enmity of the right. His enemies spoke darkly of Communist influence and one tried to enlist U.S. support for a coup. General Ponce, accompanied by an American adventurer named John Rendon, in March 1948 asked the State Department for assistance in overthrowing Arévalo and ending the "influence of Moscow," which threatened Guatemala and the entire Western Hemisphere. The department told Ponce that such assistance would violate the American commitment not to interfere in the internal affairs of another state and also warned him that the United States government would "do everything within its power to discourage revolutionary activities."[15] But at the same time the State Department accused the Arévalo government of "lack of concern" for traditional good relations with the United States because it was giving "cooperation and assistance to pro-Communist elements in Guatemalan national life."[16]

Arévalo's term as President ran through 1950. In 1951 Jacobo Arbenz, a reform-minded officer, won the presidential election. He proceeded to extend the agrarian and other reforms begun by Arévalo: higher taxes on the wealthy, social welfare programs, more rights and better wages for labor. The United Fruit Company, largest landowner and employer in Guatemala, was not happy. The company portrayed the Guatemalan government as sliding toward Communism and as a threat to American security throughout the hemisphere. Conservative journalists, members of Congress, and some officials in the State Department agreed with the company's analysis.

In 1949 the State Department began an undeclared and low-key diplomatic and economic war against Guatemala. The war was directed by Edward G. Miller, Jr., a New York lawyer/businessman, and Secretary of State Dean Acheson's choice as Assistant Secretary for Inter-American Affairs. Miller was forceful, blunt, and totally unsympathetic to the Guatemalan government's efforts to wrest control of its economy from the United Fruit Company and its subsidiary, the International Railway of Central America (IRCA). We have already noted his views on the Monroe Doctrine. During his first month at State, Miller met with officers of IRCA and agreed that unless actions of the Guatemalan government were checked, it would "mean eventual elimination of American control of this important railroad." Miller then warned the Guatemalan ambassador that his government better behave in a more accommodating manner if it expected any favors from the United States.[17]

Richard Patterson, the new American ambassador in Guatemala City, was an hysterical, paranoiac anti-Communist. Before taking up his post in 1949, he conferred at length with officers of United Fruit and with American business and political conservatives, including former President Herbert Hoover. Hoover asked him to convey the following message to President Truman:

> We now have an Atlantic Pact to combat Communism. Let's have a Western Hemisphere Pact. There are 240 Communist papers in South America that have little or no advertising. Where does this money come from? South American countries are in constant Communist jeopardy. In a Western Hemisphere Pact—(1) ask the Governments to systemize their laws of title, (2) do away with Communist control, and (3) give security to American capital in that contracts made by American interests with South American Governments, if not lived up to by those Governments, then the United States could impose economic sanctions, (4) do away with continuous taxation.[18]

Even with due allowance for Hoover's advanced age and reactionary politics, it is difficult to imagine a program more antithetical to the Good Neighbor Policy, still the supposed foundation of U.S. relations with Latin America, and more likely to encounter outraged opposition in Latin America.

Ambassador Patterson sought to perform his duties in the spirit of Herbert Hoover. He wrote to Samuel Zemurray, chairman of United Fruit, that the contest in Guatemala was between "labor leaders and all others opposed to their cancerous doctrine . . . I want you to know that I am giving my undivided attention to trying to protect and promote American interests." In another message Patterson advised the company to encourage "an all-out

barrage in the United States Senate . . . This takes the onus off
the United Fruit Company and puts it on the basis of a demand
by our Senators that all American interests be given a fair deal."[19]
The company, having reached the same conclusion, followed Patterson's recommended course with great success.

There was one dissenting voice in Patterson's embassy. Labor
attaché James F. Fishburn said it was folly for the United States
government to involve itself in a labor dispute between the fruit
company and the Guatemalan government, because such action
allowed "the Communists to pose as the champions of labor and
national sovereignty in the same breath. Any such situation is also
a death trap for us, a trap which . . . could threaten our entire
Good Neighbor Policy . . . We will not send in troops if all goes
wrong and can only retreat miserably. On the other hand, if we
cause a friendly government to decide in our favor, we weaken
the internal labor support of that group. And, today, strong labor
support is essential for any democratic government in Latin America."[20] Fishburn's views were treated with contempt in the embassy and back in Washington. "If we flounder around looking
for non-existent policies that the Communists cannot twist and
exploit, we will have gone miserably and ridiculously on the defensive," wrote one Foreign Service officer in rebuttal.[21]

In the spring of 1950, Ambassador Patterson fled back to the
United States, a target of justified complaints from the Guatemalan
government that he had been intervening in the country's internal
affairs and believing that his life was in danger from Communists.
The next U.S. ambassador, Rudolph Schoenfeld, was quieter and
more balanced, a rather colorless professional but no apologist for
the Guatemala government. But two developments soon led to
further deterioration of U.S. relations with Guatemala. The first
was the outbreak of the Korean War and a consequent increase of
American fear of international Communism. The second was the
inauguration in Guatemala of President Arbenz in March 1951.
Everything Arévalo had done, Arbenz intensified. He refused to
make any soothing gestures toward Washington and he ostenta-

tiously welcomed advice from the far left. Throughout 1951 the United States increased the pressure, cutting promised foreign aid, blocking a Guatemalan effort to purchase airplanes in Italy, trying to enlist the American Roman Catholic hierarchy in an anti-Communist crusade in Guatemala. Assistant Secretary Miller's temper was growing shorter. "I think that the Guatemalans, like so many other people, will be more cooperative if it sinks through their skulls that they need us more than we need them."[22]

But the United Fruit Company believed it needed direct U.S. government action, not merely a change in Guatemalan thinking produced by economic slaps on the wrist. In a February 1952 meeting with Miller at the State Department, the chairman of the board of IRCA said that "communist infiltration in Guatemala is a modern day violation of the Monroe Doctrine, just as serious as physical intervention of a foreign government in Latin America was in the 19th century." He said the United States should invoke the Monroe Doctrine, taking whatever measures were necessary, including military force. Miller gave a circumspect and legally correct response. He said the Monroe Doctrine is now a multilateral concept within the inter-American system, and the United States could not intervene directly in the affairs of another state. If Communist action became more overt or if there was evidence of direct Soviet military infiltration, that would be another story, requiring that our position be reconsidered.[23]

Thus matters stood as the Truman Administration in 1952 entered its last months in office. The economic squeeze continued with the further blocking of Guatemala's efforts to purchase military material in Europe, the denial of equipment for constructing the Guatemalan section of the Inter-American Highway, the maintenance of export controls to Guatemala (with an exception for goods needed by the United Fruit Company), and various calculated diplomatic indignities. Ambassador Schoenfeld believed that Arbenz was beginning to get the message.[24] But Guillermo Toriello, the articulate Guatemalan Foreign Minister, said to Acheson that his country was pained and bewildered. What had they done to deserve so many acts of hostility from the United States? Guatemala, he said, was only "attempting to remove the evils which gave communism a base."[25]

The possibility of covert military action against Arbenz had been raised by the Central Intelligence Agency and others, but was rejected by Secretary of State Acheson and President Truman.[26] The United States also firmly rejected and discouraged a proposal from Presidents Anastasio Somoza of Nicaragua and Rafael Trujillo of the Dominican Republic that a group of Caribbean region countries invade Guatemala, with U.S. backing. As the State Department told the Nicaraguan ambassador, repeating the 1948 admonition to General Ponce, "the principle of non-intervention was one of the very keystones of the Inter-American system." Intervention was barred by major treaties. The war in Korea was being fought precisely on this issue.[27]

In January 1953 the administration of President Dwight D. Eisenhower began. John Foster Dulles was Secretary of State and his brother, Allen Dulles, was director of the Central Intelligence Agency. Walter Bedell Smith, previous CIA head, moved to the State Department as Under Secretary. President Eisenhower and the Dulles brothers had no inhibitions about covert intervention. Their interpretation of the Monroe Doctrine followed the Kennan Corollary rather than the Acheson State Department's insistence on nonintervention. They believed that the Democrats had been too passive in the face of world Communism, relying on the negative policy of containment, shrinking from an active policy of liberation. And they were impatient. John Foster Dulles, who saw peril everywhere in the world, sounded the alarm over Latin America in an early meeting of the National Security Council. "Anti-American forces [are] on the march . . . and we might well wake up ten years from now to find that our friends in Latin America had become our enemies."[28]

New policymakers with new attitudes produced the overthrow of the Arbenz regime and its replacement by precisely the kind of government envisioned by Kennan—harsh, repressive, with origins and methods violating "American concepts of democratic procedures." The episode is one of the most minutely studied in the history of U.S.–Latin American relations and its details need not be repeated here. The objective of ousting Arbenz was pursued along three tracks: covert support through the Central Intelligence Agency of a rebel force organized in Honduras, open denunciation of the perceived Communist threat in an effort to secure collective action through the Organization of American States, and continued economic pressure. Some historians argue that the United States acted to make Guatemala safe for the United Fruit Company, and more broadly to advance American corporate interests in Latin America. As evidence they point to the company's access to the highest reaches of the U.S. government, always extraordinary, but quite phenomenal in 1953–54, and to its intensified lobbying in Congress and its campaign with the press. One major, more persuasive, account places the affair in the broader context of the Dulles-Eisenhower view of a worldwide struggle with international Communism, with the plight and outcries of United Fruit providing background music, not fundamental motivation. The best study focuses on the Guatemalan revolution itself and the handicaps, some self-imposed, under which Arbenz struggled.[29] Here we will only summarize the main flow of events while concentrating on the episode as a chapter in the history of the Monroe Doctrine.

John Moors Cabot, a senior American diplomat with extensive Latin American experience, was Dulles's choice as Assistant Secretary of State for Latin America. In April Cabot called on Arbenz in Guatemala City. He had, Cabot concluded, "the pale, cold-lipped look of the ideologue and showed no interest in my suggestions for a change of course in the government's direction. He had obviously sold out to the Communists and that was that." Cabot believed Arbenz had to go, but at first believed that covert action, such as that employed against Prime Minister Mohammad Mossadegh in Iran in 1953, was inappropriate. Far better, he thought, to work collectively through the OAS. "By September [1953]," Cabot wrote, "I realized that no such action was remotely possible. After much soul-searching I went to Bedell Smith and said I thought a CIA-organized coup was the only solution. He nodded and smiled, and I got the impression that the plan was already under way . . . My principal concern was to keep secret any United States involvement in the projected coup."[30]

Plans for covert action were indeed under way, but so was an approach by Secretary of State Dulles to the Organization of American States at the Foreign Ministers' meeting in Caracas in March. Dulles, born in 1888, belonged to a generation taught to revere the Monroe Doctrine as the first and most fundamental of American foreign policies. As a young man he watched Woodrow Wilson's efforts to make the doctrine the policy for the world under the League. In 1945 at the United Nations founding conference in San Francisco he had joined forces, as we have seen, with Senator Vandenberg in securing revisions in the charter designed to preserve the doctrine. As private citizen and Republican Party authority on foreign policy he had warned in 1947 that "Soviet policy in South America subjects the Monroe Doctrine to its greatest test," and in 1949 he said that the "unilateral Monroe Doctrine has been merged into the multilateral Pact of Rio.[31] When he was Secretary of State the doctrine remained firm in his mind. For example, he remarked in 1953 to the Dominican ambassador that the doctrine's opposition to "alien political systems" in the Americas, originally directed against the Holy Alliance, "applied equally today to international communism."[32]

Now Dulles saw an opportunity to meet the problem of Guatemala by persuading his fellow Foreign Ministers within the OAS to extend the Monroe Doctrine to outlaw foreign ideologies, declaring their presence tantamount to aggression. Armed with such a resolution the United States could then take action against Communism while avoiding the charge of intervention. On the eve of the conference the State Department issued a threat to the other OAS governments. By agreeing to the principle of nonintervention and limiting its freedom of action, said a circular sent to all capitals, the United States was relying on the OAS to take collective action. "The issue of Communism in the hemisphere provides a test case," and if the OAS fails to take a strong stand, then "some question must be raised regarding the soundness of the OAS relationship."[33] In other words, the United States was prepared to abandon nonintervention and go it alone. There was the authentic voice of the original, unilateral Monroe Doctrine.

At Caracas, Dulles presented his resolution declaring that the domination or control of the political institutions of an American state was a threat to the sovereignty, independence, and peace of the American states, "and would call for appropriate action in accordance with existing treaties." Immediately the thrust was weakened when the conference accepted an amendment, offered by Colombia, which inserted "consultation to consider adoption of" before the word "appropriate"—thus transforming an authorization of individual action into a call for another meeting. The resolution passed 17–1, with Guatemala opposed, and Mexico and Argentina abstaining. A Uruguayan diplomat captured the mood of the conference when he told *The New York Times*: "We contributed our approval without enthusiasm, without optimism, without joy, and without feeling that we were contributing to the adoption of constructive measures."[34] Roy Rubottom of the State Department called the resolution a Pyrrhic victory. Because the conference was hosted by the brutal Pérez Jiménez regime in Venezuela, the resolution was "untouchable and almost unmentionable."[35] Publicly Dulles hailed the Caracas declaration as a great victory, comparable in its importance to the original proclamation of the Monroe Doctrine. Privately he said he was disappointed, admitting that the resolution was "not adopted with genuine enthusiasm," and noting that it could have been worse had Mexican Foreign Minister Padilla Nerva "really thrown himself into the fight against."[36]

After Caracas, movement along the covert track increased at a moderate rate until the arrival May 15 in Guatemala of a Swedish ship, the *Alfhelm*, with a cargo of arms from Czechoslovakia. This event was politically useful to the United States as "proof" that the Arbenz regime was under foreign control.[37] Militarily it was a threat to the planned invasion from Honduras. The United States took two actions. On the one hand it accelerated the preparations and on the other it set up a naval patrol to stop and examine "suspicious foreign-flag vessels on the high seas off Guatemala." If the vessels did not cooperate they were to be taken forcibly to Panama.[38]

For appearances' sake, but without much hope of a positive outcome, Dulles directed the State Department to prepare an elaborate indictment of "Communist penetration" into the hemisphere for presentation to the OAS. With characteristic rhetoric Dulles publicly invoked the Monroe Doctrine again and declared in a speech in Seattle: "I hope that the Organization of American States will be able to help the people of Guatemala rid themselves of the malignant force which has seized them . . . If they do not succeed, the whole body of the Organization of American States may be corrupted and we shall see in the American continents the same forces which have brought war and captivity and misery to so many hundreds and millions in Europe and Asia."[39] In Seattle Dulles kept informed of the progress of the planned CIA operation via coded phone conversation.[40]

The invasion, led by Colonel Carlos Castillo Armas, began on June 18, 1954. The Guatemalan government appealed to the United Nations Security Council, whose president that month happened to be the American representative, Henry Cabot Lodge. Guatemala reported that attacking forces were coming from Honduras and possibly also from Nicaragua and asked the Security Council to send an observer team immediately. The United States delegation had already arranged for Colombia and Brazil, the two Latin American governments then represented on the council, to parry the Guatemalan request by introducing a resolution that the issue should be referred to the Organization of American States. Ever since the San Francisco conference of 1945, said the Colombian ambassador,his government had "sought to avoid any direct appeal to the Security Council without going first to the regional organization, because, in that case any action taken on this continent to prevent aggression would be at the mercy of the veto." France, unhelpfully from the American point of view, offered an amendment to the resolution calling for an immediate cease-fire. French Ambassador Henri Hoppenot could not resist needling the United States by quoting back a comment the previous day by Ambassador Lodge in favor of hearing a complaint from Thailand: "I hope that I will never live to see the day when a small country comes to the United Nations and asks for protection against war and is simply greeted with the question: what is the hurry?" Hoppenot added that he could not believe that the United States was "either directly or indirectly the instigator of the events." The record does not indicate whether the Frenchman was keeping a straight face.

Lodge replied that "the United States has no connexion whatever with what is taking place." But since the United States could not oppose a cease-fire without tipping its hand, Lodge voted for the combined Brazilian-Colombian-French resolution. So did every other member of the Security Council, with the exception of the Soviet Union, whose nay vote constituted a veto. Ambassador Semyon Tsarapkin explained the veto by remarking that Guatemala could hardly find justice in the OAS, an organization dominated by the United States. The issue is whether U.S. aggression could be stopped in Latin America. Lodge retorted that there had been no aggression but rather "a revolt of Guatemalans against Guatemalans." France then reintroduced the cease-fire resolution standing alone, without reference to the OAS, and it passed unanimously.[41]

There was no cease-fire, as the Guatemalan government reported in a series of insistent telegrams to the Security Council. On June 22 Guatemala asked that the council meet again. Ambassador Lodge telephoned Secretary of State Dulles and said the move was a "carefully planned Communist plot." Yes, said

Dulles, we face the end of "our entire American system if we let it get involved in the Security Council and the communist plotting that goes on up there." Lodge and Dulles said they both were angry and betrayed by the French.[42] Lodge delayed two days, but on June 24 called the council into session, not to hear what Guatemala had to say, but to vote on whether to put the issue on the agenda at all.

There followed an extraordinary clash between the United States and its NATO allies, France and Britain. The problem was that the French and British governments believed Guatemala had a right to be heard. Dulles spoke with President Eisenhower and said that the issue of the priority of regional organizations, for which he and Senator Vandenberg fought successfully at San Francisco, was at stake. Ambassador Lodge at the UN was instructed to get tough with the allies. The telephone conversation between Lodge and Dulles tells the story:

DULLES: The President said he thinks you should let the British and French know that if they take independent line backing the Guatemalan move in this matter, it would mean we would feel entirely free without regard to their position in relation to any such matters as any of their colonial problems in Egypt, Cyprus, etc. . . .

LODGE: I will do that.

DULLES: He [the President] wanted to avoid making it in the form of a threat. But make it a clear understanding that if they don't take into account our needs and considerations in this matter, it will be a two-way street, and they must accept it.

LODGE: Yes, I see. It's a terrible thing. I will get this to them. Will determine just when and how to do it.

DULLES: Use your own judgment as to time.

LODGE: If there is open split between British and French, Russians will be very much pleased. But we cannot put off meeting much longer.[43]

Lodge followed instructions. British Foreign Secretary Anthony Eden happened to be in Washington to discuss the situation in Indochina, and Dulles spoke sharply to him on Guatemala, saying that Russia was "trying to wreck the Latin American system, [and] destroy the Monroe Doctrine which was the first assumption of international responsibility by the United States." If the Soviets gained a foothold in the hemisphere, he warned, the United States would have to divert forces from elsewhere around the world.[44] Dulles concluded that "Eden did not understand the problem," but was satisfied that he would at least instruct Sir Pierson Dixon, British ambassador to the UN, to abstain.[45] Meanwhile, Dulles telephoned French Foreign Minister Henri Bonnet. Under such intense pressure the British and French had little choice. They buckled, and both abstained on the motion to put the Guatemalan complaint on the agenda. Dulles also tried but failed to persuade New Zealand, but could not change its vote in favor.

The resolution failed with 4 in favor (Denmark, Lebanon, New Zealand, and the Soviet Union), 5 against (Brazil, Colombia, China, Turkey, and the United States), with Britain and France abstaining. In the debate the Colombian ambassador helpfully repeated Washington's message, calling Guatemala's attempt to engage the Security Council a "most inacceptable intervention in American affairs by totalitarian communism." Lodge then said that the issue had been faced at San Francisco in 1945; had not the primacy of the regional organizations been protected, the U.S. Senate would not have voted for the UN Charter. And now the first practical test was before the council. Would the UN destroy itself in 1954 as it almost did in 1945? Semyon Tsarapkin, the Soviet ambassador, said the issue was whether the United Nations had any authority to deal with aggression in the Western Hemisphere. The conclusion of British Ambassador Dixon was to the point in his report to London: "Lodge's enunciation of what came very near a new kind of Monroe Doctrine amounted to a warning not only to international Communism but also to the

United Nations itself to keep their hands off the American continent."[46] Precisely. Not since Richard Olney in 1895 had proclaimed that the will of the United States was beyond challenge in the hemisphere had such broad pretensions been advanced.

Eden, who at San Francisco in 1945 had deplored the American move to establish a separate hemispheric system, and many of the permanent officials of the Foreign Office, were incensed. But not Prime Minister Churchill. At dinner the next night at the White House his comments on the "Communist government in Guatemala" and his support for peace maintained regionally indicated his sympathy for the United States. Back in London two days later Churchill told John Colville, his private secretary: "Anthony Eden was sometimes very foolish: he would quarrel with the Americans over some petty Central American issue which did not affect Great Britain and could forget about the downtrodden millions in Poland."[47]

The endgame for the Guatemalan affair came quickly. In order to establish that the issue was before the OAS, the United States (joined by Brazil, Costa Rica, Cuba, the Dominican Republic, Haiti, Honduras, Nicaragua, and Peru) called for a July 7 meeting of OAS Foreign Ministers—not to hear a Guatemalan complaint but to charge Guatemala with aggression against Honduras and more broadly against the Americas by abetting the penetration of Communism. The United States also arranged for a visit to Guatemala of an OAS peace commission. Arbenz said he would welcome the commission's visit, but the United States managed to have it delayed in Mexico City in order to give the military operations, especially the noisy and heavily publicized bombing by supposedly Guatemalan fighters for freedom, a chance to succeed.

Success was achieved by June 30. Arbenz fled. The peace commission never left Mexico. Soon the U.S. ambassador to Guatemala, John Peurifoy, was busy arranging for Castillo Armas, rather than one of several rivals, to take over the government. The new regime in Guatemala withdrew the complaint before the Security Council. And on July 2 the United States asked that the

planned OAS Foreign Ministers meeting be canceled because the
new Guatemalan government "had affirmed its opposition to communist penetration and had given evidence of its determination to
see that the penetration was terminated."[48]

In London the British government put up an unconvincing defense of its role in the face of criticism from UN enthusiasts and
critics of the United States in the House of Commons.[49] At the
Foreign Office, an official commented that "the ghost of Guatemala
will be with us a long time . . . The differences of view between
ourselves and the Americans as regards the U.N.'s scope and
functions have been shown up to be more serious than we
feared."[50]

Secretary of State Dulles used the moment of triumph for a
major address on the Monroe Doctrine and some elaborating em-
broidery of the facts. We have prevailed, he said, over

the evil purpose of the Kremlin to destroy an inter-American
system . . . This intrusion of Soviet despotism was, of course,
a direct challenge to our Monroe Doctrine, the first and most
fundamental of our foreign policies.

It is interesting to recall that the menace which brought
that doctrine into being was itself a menace born in Russia.
It was the Russian Czar Alexander and his despotic allies in
Europe who, early in the last century, sought control of South
America and the western part of North America . . .

Guatemala is a small country. But its power, standing
alone, is not a measure of the threat. The master plan of
international communism is to gain a solid political base in
this hemisphere, a base that can be used to extend Communist
penetration to the other peoples of the other American Governments. It is not the power of the Arbenz government that
concerned us but the power behind it.[51]

Later Ambassador Peurifoy in a speech in Miami declared, presumably without smiling, that "in proving that communism can

be defeated, we relied on the traditional American principle of honesty in the conduct of foreign affairs and the American doctrine of continental liberty from despotic intervention, first enunciated by President Monroe 131 years ago."[52] Of course, the United States had relied on the very opposite of honesty. When the truth became known in years ahead, the whole affair would do great damage to any lingering pretension that truth and the Monroe Doctrine as applied in the Cold War years were sisters.

The Castillo Armas regime in Guatemala and its successors into the 1990s mocked democracy and maintained a reign of terror against the poor, following closely the model recommended in the Kennan Corollary.[53] No other Latin American government for four years after 1954 imitated the Arbenz regime's toleration of the left, and official Washington could find no cause for alarm.

The dominating issues in those years were the Suez and Hungarian crises of 1956, American support for the Diem regime in Vietnam, the recurrent war scares with Communist China over the offshore islands of Quemoy and Matsu, the Soviet triumph in being the first to launch an earth satellite in 1957. President Eisenhower and Secretary of State Dulles paid no attention to Latin America. If the British and French hoped that the United States would be supportive during the Suez crisis of 1956, as Dulles seemed to promise in 1954 in return for the abstentions on the Guatemalan affair, they were sorely disappointed.

The one episode in that period to attract headlines began in April 1958 as a routine courtesy tour of Latin America by Vice President Richard M. Nixon. The Vice President believed he had more important things to do than go on a trip to Latin America—but at the persistent urging of Assistant Secretary of State Rubottom, Secretary of State Dulles, and President Eisenhower he consented. The result was more dramatic than he or anyone else could have imagined. He encountered some minor heckling from "Communists" in several capitals. But in Caracas, Venezuela, on May 13, his and Mrs. Nixon's cars were surrounded by a hostile rock-

throwing mob. They barely escaped with their lives to the sanctuary of the U.S. embassy. U.S. troops were started on the way
to effect a rescue—although that proved unnecessary.[54]

The dramatic close call caused the administration, prodded by
the President's brother, Milton Eisenhower, and Nixon to think
more deeply about Latin America than in the past. They believed
that the mob violence against the Vice President was of Communist origin and coordinated on a hemispheric scale. But they
also recognized that many people in Latin America had legitimate
reasons to hate the United States.

In Venezuela especially, the principle of the Kennan Corollary
had been followed with a vengeance—which explains in large
measure the violent reception inflicted on Nixon. From 1945 to
1948 Venezuela had been governed by the democratic and moderately left Acción Democrática (AD) Party and its leader, Rómulo
Betancourt. The U.S. government was lukewarm in its support
and often complaining about alleged poor treatment of American
oil interests. In November 1948 the AD government was overthrown by Lieutenant Colonel Marcos Pérez Jiménez. Pérez Jiménez proceeded to imprison, torture, and kill political opponents
and suspend civil rights. Few regimes could exceed his in terms
of harsh repression. The United States decided it would be better
to recognize the new military junta rather than risk chaos by assisting the AD to regain power. Secretary of the Army Kenneth
C. Royal, for example, noted that the deposed Gallegos government had depended on support from labor unions sympathetic to
Communist aims. By recognizing the new government, the U.S.
Army mission could continue and would be able to work with
the generally pro-American military.[55] Recognition followed
without further delay.

Pérez Jiménez lasted for a decade, outlawing the AD, filling the
jails with political prisoners, employing torture. The Korean War
led the United States to look on Venezuela's petroleum as vital to
national security. By 1952 Venezuela was the world's largest oil
exporter, and a State Department paper hailed the country as an

"outstanding example to the rest of the world of cooperation between foreign investors and the government for their mutual benefit."[56] In 1954 Dulles had no compunctions about the Caracas conference being hosted by Pérez Jiménez. Only Costa Rica refused to attend, with a statement that "at least one country, by its absence, should emphasize the agony of people being sacrificed in the fight against our own totalitarianism in America."[57] In 1956 President Eisenhower welcomed Pérez Jiménez to Washington and gave him a medal. But finally, in January 1958, Pérez Jiménez was overthrown by a broad-based popular movement. He and his hated chief of the secret police, Pedro Estrada, received sanctuary from the U.S. government and fled to Florida.

Four months later Richard Nixon arrived in Caracas. He and the State Department believed he would have an opportunity to express support for democracy. It was not to be. Nixon's near-disaster precipitated the first wide-ranging, extensive top-level policy discussion of Latin America in the Eisenhower years. The Guatemala issue had been narrowly and secretly discussed. Nixon's views were, comparatively, liberal.

For years a dictum of Secretary of the Treasury George Humphrey had enjoyed broad support within the administration: "Wherever a dictator was replaced, Communists gained . . . The United States should back strong men."[58] Humphrey was also totally opposed to foreign aid or lending to governments. "The way to bring indigenous capital out in Latin America," he believed, "is to create in Latin America a satisfactory climate for investment."[59] He believed the best of all climates had been created by Pérez Jiménez. But Nixon argued that the United States should show its moral disapproval of dictators—whether of the right or the left; and should participate in a "new program for economic progress in the hemisphere."[60] Secretary Dulles thought Nixon was exaggerating the problem with dictators[61]—but within a year Dulles would be dead of cancer. The President, however, was ready for change. Fidel Castro, soon to appear on the scene, would add further impetus.

CHAPTER 5

AGROUND AND SHATTERED
ON CUBA

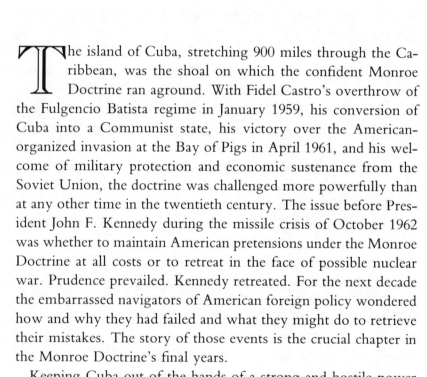

The island of Cuba, stretching 900 miles through the Caribbean, was the shoal on which the confident Monroe Doctrine ran aground. With Fidel Castro's overthrow of the Fulgencio Batista regime in January 1959, his conversion of Cuba into a Communist state, his victory over the American-organized invasion at the Bay of Pigs in April 1961, and his welcome of military protection and economic sustenance from the Soviet Union, the doctrine was challenged more powerfully than at any other time in the twentieth century. The issue before President John F. Kennedy during the missile crisis of October 1962 was whether to maintain American pretensions under the Monroe Doctrine at all costs or to retreat in the face of possible nuclear war. Prudence prevailed. Kennedy retreated. For the next decade the embarrassed navigators of American foreign policy wondered how and why they had failed and what they might do to retrieve their mistakes. The story of those events is the crucial chapter in the Monroe Doctrine's final years.

Keeping Cuba out of the hands of a strong and hostile power was one of the oldest objectives of American foreign policy. The island's size and location—the proverbial "ninety miles from our shores"—gave it undeniable strategic significance. In hostile hands the island could obstruct American trade and influence in the Caribbean. At worst it could become a base for an attack on the

United States. The retention of Cuba in Spanish hands during most of the nineteenth century was tolerable. Feeble Spain alone could never threaten the United States. But Spain's weakness opened the possibility of another power seizing or buying the island. From time to time some American leaders advocated the acquisition of Cuba by the United States, but a combination of international and American domestic politics blocked this possibility. Instead, the United States warned against the transfer of Cuba to another power, invoking a principle closely linked to the Monroe Doctrine.[1]

In the 1890s American political leaders decided that Spain's continued possession of Cuba had become intolerable. The island's economy and social stability were being disrupted for the second time in a generation by a war for independence, a war which the insurgents could not win and the Spanish could not squelch. The United States now had a growing economic stake in Cuba and new imperial ambitions of its own throughout the Caribbean. The view from Washington was that the peace and safety of the United States demanded an end of the internal war in Cuba, and that could be achieved only by the departure of Spain. Madrid in 1898 preferred to lose Cuba in an honorable war rather than abject surrender. And war it was. Spain, defeated on land and sea, sued for peace.[2]

The Cuban insurgents welcomed help from the United States in their fight for independence. But authentic Cuban independence was a potential obstacle to the achievement of American strategic control of Cuba and the Caribbean, the real reason for intervention. The idea of annexing the island, politically unpopular in the United States, was formally disclaimed by a Senate resolution. Puerto Rico, however, was pocketed as a nearby and available spoil of victory. Instead, the United States required the new Cuban government to assign control of its foreign relations to the United States and accept an American right of intervention in Cuban internal affairs "for the protection of life, property, and individual liberty." The United States guaranteed Cuban independence from all other powers except itself. The instrument of this subservience was the Platt Amendment, whose provisions were incorporated into Cuba's constitution.

The specific terms of the Platt Amendment carried echoes of the Monroe Doctrine and its corollaries. Cuba could not "in any manner authorize or permit any foreign power or powers to obtain by colonization or for military or naval purposes or otherwise, lodgment in or control over any portion of said island." Cuba also could not incur debts in excess of her capacity to service through ordinary revenues—an anticipation of the Roosevelt Corollary. The United States would be the judge of Cuban compliance and stood ready to intervene if necessary. Finally, Cuba agreed to provide the United States with land for one or more naval bases; thereby the United States acquired the base at Guantánamo Bay at the southeast corner of the island.[3]

President Franklin D. Roosevelt, confidently implementing his Good Neighbor Policy, relinquished the Platt Amendment's right of intervention in a new treaty with Cuba in 1934. But control by Washington over Cuba's foreign relations remained undiminished. It was inconceivable until 1959 that any Cuban government would conclude a significant agreement with a foreign power without the permission of the United States. Complacency was the pervading characteristic in the American posture toward Cuba in the first decade after 1945. In 1947 almost 90 percent of Cuba's trade was with the United States—92 percent of exports, 84 percent of imports. The State Department's 1948 assessment was that developing nationalism and a growing spirit of independence would make dealing with Cuba slightly more difficult, but there was no cause for deep concern. The election of Carlos Prío as President in 1948 was a routine event. His regime, predicted the CIA, "can be expected fully to support the United States in its anti-Soviet policies."[4] Even the March 1952 coup in which former President Fulgencio Batista seized power was welcomed in Washington. Prío had been corrupt and prone to irritate the United States on minor economic issues. And so, said Assistant Secretary

Edward G. Miller, Jr., "from the cold-blooded standpoint of U.S. interests, we have nothing to worry about Batista who is a proven friend of ours and who might possibly be tougher on the commies than Prio was."[5] The Batista government obliged, promising "to eliminate the freedom and privileges which the Communists were now enjoying in Cuba," and breaking diplomatic relations with the Soviet Union. Secretary of State Acheson praised the new government and recommended to President Truman that the United States extend recognition. That was done.[6]

In the mid-1950s Batista wallowed in the corrupt opportunities of office, was brutal toward critics, and formed a cozy relationship with American organized crime. Havana, never a puritanical place, developed its eminence as a center of gambling, pornography, and prostitution, attracting American tourists eager to get drunk, get laid, and look for Ernest Hemingway. All this was of no concern to the American government. Nor did Washington pay much attention at first to the anti-Batista revolutionary band organized by the young Fidel Castro.

The State Department began to take Castro seriously at the turn of the year 1957–58. But the department's assessments focused on the uprising as a symptom of Cuba's internal problems and not as an indication of Moscow at work. The department was unimpressed by Batista's habit of crying red. The problem was Batista's corruption and lack of popular support—not international Communism or a threat to the Monroe Doctrine. The solution was to induce Batista to show some respect for democracy and human rights. Ambassador Earl Smith, a political appointee of conservative bent, was less inclined to bring pressure on Batista than the professionals on the Cuban desk in the department. He believed Batista might be assassinated or alternatively would welcome "honorable retirement," but Smith considered Castro's movement appallingly disorganized. After Batista, he said in February 1958, "there is no responsible group able to take over the government. Vandalism, chaos, and bloodshed would surely ensue."[7] Concluding that Batista was hopeless, State Department officials wished for "the emergence of a military civilian junta which would oust Batista but not permit Castro a dominant position"—but could find no way to convert a dream to reality.[8]

The brutal character of Batista's effort to crush Castro's challenge placed the Eisenhower Administration in a dilemma. To encourage Batista's political demise might bring chaos. To stand by him until the inevitable end would leave the United States tainted with Batista's sins and faced with an understandably hostile successor regime, not to mention tarnishing the American reputation throughout Latin America. Understanding a dilemma and dealing effectively with it are different things. A few American diplomats and politicians believed Batista should be supported at all costs, but the dominant view was that of Assistant Secretary Roy Rubottom, supported by Milton Eisenhower: Batista was the problem.

In March 1958 the United States imposed an embargo on arms shipments to Cuba, but retained the military training mission and continued to hand out medals to Batista's officers—a mixed signal at best. Not until December, days before Castro seized power, did the United States tell Batista unequivocally that he would have to go. Later Rubottom and other anti-Batista officials would be attacked for their views in a way reminiscent of the McCarthyite charges that stupid or disloyal State Department officials had "lost China." As Ellis Briggs, a conservative American ambassador of the old school, recalled, Rubottom and Milton Eisenhower "sold down the river a man whose primary plank in foreign policy was close collaboration with the United States, in favor of a known lunatic and anti-American."[9] Batista flew out of Cuba to the Dominican Republic before dawn on New Year's Day, 1959. Fidel Castro immediately entered Havana and soon established a government. The United States recognized the new government and appointed a career ambassador known for his liberal views, Philip W. Bonsal, to replace Smith, a man disqualified by his association with Batista. Bonsal did his best to be patient and conciliatory with Castro, although Castro's strident anti-

Americanism and the wholesale execution of people associated with Batista made the task difficult. Amid reports that Castro hoped to unseat other Latin American governments and might even stir up trouble in Puerto Rico, Bonsal argued that the United States should not adopt a hostile stance until there was clearer evidence of Castro's character, clearer to both the Cuban people and the American people.[10] Robert C. Hill, ambassador to Mexico and a man well to the political right, vehemently disagreed at a conference of American diplomats in San Salvador in April 1959. Hill said that Castro "has long been a tool of Moscow and Peking."[11] Hill's accusation, widely echoed throughout the Republican Party in the United States, soon led to the proposition that Castro's presence was a challenge to the Monroe Doctrine. Had John Foster Dulles been alive, he might well have agreed with Hill that Castro was another Arbenz, only far more dangerous.

In April 1959 Castro visited the United States. President Eisenhower arranged to be unavailable, but Vice President Richard Nixon did receive him for a long conversation. Nixon's first estimate was that Castro was "incredibly naïve about Communism" rather than "under Communist discipline." But in the weeks ahead the Vice President reached another conclusion: "Castro's actions when he returned to Cuba convinced me he was indeed a Communist, and I sided strongly with Allen Dulles in presenting this view in the NSC and other meetings."[12] And President Eisenhower wrote: "We will check in a year!!" on the margin of a report that Castro said during his visit that Cuba would remain "in the western camp" in the Cold War.[13]

The succeeding months saw a flurry of small Castro-sponsored guerrilla attacks against the Dominican Republic. None was successful, but they undermined what little sympathy Castro retained within the U.S. government. More irritating were Castro's internal "confiscatory" actions against American investments in Cuba. For example, Robert Kleberg, head of the vast King Ranch in Texas and owner of extensive property in Cuba, had an hour interview with Eisenhower on June 25. Kleberg said that "Cuba

is being dominated and run by agents of Soviet Communism
. . . Russia is challenging the United States in our own hemisphere
and we must take the necessary steps to keep the hemisphere
free."[14] Eisenhower was impressed with Kleberg, but Secretary
of State Christian Herter warned that the kind of hostile action
against Cuba which Kleberg desired would alienate most of Latin
America and delight Communist propagandists.[15] But on the same
day Representative Daniel Flood, a colorful jingoistic Democratic
congressman from Pennsylvania, warned of the "red tide" sweeping across the Caribbean and threatening the Panama Canal. He
described "an extension of alien imperialism into the strategic
center of the Americas. It constitutes the gravest challenge to the
Monroe Doctrine since threats of European occupation of Latin
American States early in this century forced upon President Theodore Roosevelt an enlargement of that doctrine to include what is
known as the Roosevelt Corollary."[16]

The shuttlecock of accusations and insults accelerated throughout the rest of the year. Anti-Castro exiles flying light airplanes
from Florida dropped incendiary bombs on cane fields. In Havana
several people died during a raid by an exile flying a B–25 bomber.
It is impossible either to affirm or to deny that the U.S. government was responsible for these harassing raids.

On November 5, 1959, the Senate Judiciary Committee held
well publicized hearings on the "Communist Threat to the United
States Through the Caribbean," and on the same day Secretary
of State Christian Herter told President Eisenhower that Castro's
continuation in power was incompatible with American security.
Herter recommended that the United States inaugurate a secret
policy of building up a coherent Cuban opposition, people capable
of replacing Castro and establishing economic and political policies
consistent with good U.S.–Cuban relations.[17] Here was the first
high-level endorsement of the path that would lead to the Bay of
Pigs.

By the end of 1959 the Monroe Doctrine was being increasingly
invoked in the press and Congress as the answer to Castro and

his connections to the Soviet Union. An influential and widely quoted statement was the long article entitled "A Way to Stop the Reds in Latin America," in *U.S. News & World Report* by the dean of American diplomatic historians, Samuel Flagg Bemis of Yale University. Bemis painted a frightening picture of the nation threatened on four fronts—east, west, north, and now south— with the balance of power about to "tip fatally against the United States in the present deadly crisis of power and politics which we call the cold war." Bemis said that the Organization of American States had shown itself too weak to turn back the threat; therefore, unilateral action should be taken under the Monroe Doctrine. He called on Congress to make clear by resolution "to our friends and enemies, all over the globe, that this Government is determined . . . within the purview of the pristine Monroe Doctrine . . . not to permit the intervention of international communism to endanger the peace and security of the United States, and of all the republics of this hemisphere—indeed, the balance of power for freedom against slavery in the entire globe."[18] Bemis's call was cited with approval by scores of editorial writers and heeded by Congressman Craig Hosmer in the House and Senator Prescott Bush, father of a future President, in the Senate.[19] Hosmer wrote President Eisenhower asking the administration's support for a resolution drafted by Bemis. House Joint Resolution 540 quoted the Monroe Doctrine and called for the United States to be ready to take unilateral action "to forestall intervention, domination, control and colonization by international communism in the New World."[20] The Bemis-Bush-Hosmer campaign caught the administration's attention, and at a National Security Council meeting on January 14, the role of the doctrine was discussed. Assistant Secretary of State Rubottom opposed taking action against Cuba under the doctrine. It would be better, he said, to get the OAS Foreign Ministers to recommend action under the Caracas resolution of 1954.[21] But Eisenhower had doubts similar to those of Professor Bemis on the utility of the Organization of American States. "If the OAS is not going to support us, they show themselves as fair weather friends and we may have to take action . . . We could quarantine Cuba," the President said to a meeting of top advisers on January 26.[22] Admiral Arleigh Burke, chief of naval operations, also believed in unilateral action. He wrote that Cuba was becoming a very serious threat; action was imperative. "The U.S. has never renounced the Monroe Doctrine."[23]

In February 1960, Soviet Deputy Premier Anastas Mikoyan visited Cuba and signed an agreement for the purchase of sugar by the Soviet Union and the extension of economic aid.[24] Meanwhile, the number of incendiary attacks against Cuban cane fields by "unidentified aircraft" increased, and on March 4 a French vessel, La Coubre, unloading general cargo and ammunition, blew up in Havana with heavy loss of life. Castro said the United States was responsible. Ambassador Bonsal denied American complicity and denounced the accusation as shameless venom. Bonsal afterward concluded that "Castro's reaction to the . . . explosion was perhaps what tipped the scales in favor of Washington's abandonment of the policy of non-intervention."[25] Someday, but not yet, it may be possible to determine who, or what, was responsible for the destruction of La Coubre.

Bonsal was wrong. The scales had long since tipped. For several months the CIA had been planning the creation of a paramilitary force of Cuban exiles for an invasion to overthrow Castro, and on March 17 President Eisenhower gave his full approval. American purpose, said the secret policy statement, "is to bring about the replacement of the Castro regime with one more devoted to the true interests of the Cuban people and more acceptable to the U.S. in such a manner as to avoid any appearance of U.S. intervention." Eisenhower said he knew of no better way to handle Castro. "The great problem is leakage and breach of security," he said. "Everyone must be prepared to swear that he has not heard of it."[26]

Month by month the United States increased its pressure on Cuba and Castro turned more and more to the Soviet Union for support, establishing diplomatic relations with Moscow in May

1960, becoming almost entirely dependent on Soviet petroleum, and receiving large amounts of Communist-bloc arms, mostly from Czechoslovakia. In July the United States reduced Cuba's sugar quota in the American market to zero. "Castro retaliated by nationalizing all U.S.–owned industrial and agrarian enterprises" and banks.[27] The economic war was now total.

The deteriorating state of U.S.–Soviet relations after the U–2 affair of May and the shooting down of another American plane, a RB–47, over Russia on July 1 interacted explosively with the Cuban question. On July 9 Soviet Premier Nikita S. Khrushchev said the Soviet Union would support Cuba in its struggle. "Now the United States is not so unreachable as it once was . . . In case of necessity, Soviet artillerymen can support with rocket fire the Cuban people if aggressive forces in the Pentagon dare to start intervention against Cuba."[28]

Then on July 12 Khrushchev made a spectacular attack on the Monroe Doctrine, using the pungent overheated prose that was his trademark. At a press conference in the Kremlin, with Foreign Minister Andrei Gromyko at his side and a bust of Lenin in the background, he said: "We consider that the Monroe Doctrine has outlived its time, has outlived itself, has died, so to say, a natural death. Now the remains of this doctrine should best be buried as every dead body is so that it should not poison the air by its decay." He said the original doctrine of 1823 expressed noble democratic ideals and resistance to European colonialism. But today it belonged to "the imperialists of the United States of America, the colonialists, who, like vultures, snatch the last crumb out of the mouths of the dying children and old folk just to wax fat and rich. And it is through the Monroe Doctrine that they want to assure themselves the right to go on with this robbery forever."[29] Nothing Khrushchev might have said would have been more infuriating to American sensibilities. The State Department instantly replied that "the principles of the Monroe Doctrine are as valid today as they were in 1823 when the Doctrine was proclaimed," i.e., the prevention of despotic systems of government being extended to the independent states of the hemisphere. The Rio treaty of 1947, said the department, is the modern, multilateral embodiment of the doctrine.[30]

This was the context in which Cuba and the United States each sought to discredit the other in the Organization of American States and the United Nations Security Council. The United States on June 27, 1960, accused Cuba before the OAS of threatening the peace and stability of the hemisphere, and supported the charge with a long list of provocations and false allegations of American aggression.[31] Cuba took its case to the Security Council in July, while Khrushchev's contemptuous comments on the Monroe Doctrine were still echoing in the air. Cuban Foreign Minister Raúl Roa spoke for over an hour, mixing allegations of U.S.–supported attacks on Cuba with hostile quotations from the American press and various politicians. For example, he cited an editorial from William F. Buckley, Jr.'s National Review advocating military operations against the regime by "Free Cuba" forces and urging Congress to invoke the Monroe Doctrine and declare that a European power is committing indirect aggression against the United States and other American nations by its creation of a satellite state. Roa charged that "the United States is trying to conceal its true aims and justify its policy of harassment, retaliation and aggression by deliberately distorting the character . . . of the Cuban Revolution, representing it now as a Soviet appendage, now as a pawn of 'international communism' on the American continent."[32]

The United States response, delivered by Ambassador Henry Cabot Lodge, was to praise the moral purpose of the Monroe Doctrine, deny all Cuban charges, and argue that Cuba's complaints should be heard in the OAS, not the Security Council. This was the same argument used in 1954, also by Henry Cabot Lodge, to keep the allegations of the Arbenz regime from being investigated by the Security Council. Lodge succeeded again. The council resolved 9–0, with the Soviet Union and Poland abstaining, that Cuba should go first to the OAS.

Eisenhower, in the final months of his presidency, may have

had doubts about the planned invasion by exile forces after Castro caught and summarily executed twenty men involved in a mini-raid. This, said an intelligence report, was "a serious blow to the chances of a genuine revolt."[33] The President also wondered if the drastic economic warfare, now including an embargo on all exports except food and medicine, made it appear that the United States was acting against the Cuban people rather than Castro. He worried especially about Mexican condemnation. "If Mexico were to become disgruntled and if we were to see the Communists come into power there, in all likelihood we would have to go to war about this." And then there was the Soviet Union. What if Cuba announced a defensive alliance with Russia?[34]

In November Democrat John F. Kennedy defeated Richard M. Nixon for the presidency by the narrowest of margins. During the televised debates between the two candidates, Kennedy accused the Eisenhower Administration of failing to remove Castro and suggested that he as President would support the armed overthrow of Castro by Cuban forces in exile—precisely what the Eisenhower Administration was secretly planning. Vice President Nixon believed his first obligation was to protect the secrecy of what would become the Bay of Pigs invasion; therefore, he replied with a statement he did not at all believe: "If we were to follow [Senator Kennedy's] recommendation . . . we would lose all of our friends in Latin America . . . and we would not accomplish our objective . . . It would be an open invitation for Mr. Khrushchev . . . to come into Latin America and to engage us in what would be a civil war and possibly even worse." Nixon's dissembling made Kennedy appear tough and himself weak. Kennedy's position was popular among voters and may have won him the election. Nixon never forgot.[35]

As 1960 ended and Castro turned increasingly to the Soviet Union for assistance, the champions of the Monroe Doctrine were in deep distress. Professor Bemis wrote Senator Bush about "this ominous hour" and predicted that the Soviets would soon have submarine bases and missile launching pads in Cuba: "We have suffered nothing less than a staggering defeat of the Monroe Doctrine."[36] In January the outgoing Eisenhower Administration broke diplomatic relations with Cuba. Kennedy, inaugurated on January 21, inherited and kept on track the CIA program for invading Cuba with a small army of exiles—although not without some dissent from close advisers.

In April 1961 the attack was launched at the Bay of Pigs. It failed completely. President Kennedy decided against committing U.S. forces and soon all the invaders had been killed or captured by Castro's army. The story, in all its details, is well known and need not be repeated here.[37]

The failure at the Bay of Pigs had broad consequences for the history of the Monroe Doctrine. Castro's ties to the Soviet Union were immensely strengthened, leaving no doubt in the minds of American officials and politicians that Cuba was now a Soviet satellite "ninety miles from our shores." President Kennedy was politically vulnerable. The charge that he had failed to defend the Monroe Doctrine was too tempting for Republicans to ignore. In the next two years they made the best of it. President Kennedy could no more tolerate Castro than could the most outspoken American jingo, but after the Bay of Pigs he was caught in a dilemma. The main thrust of his Latin American policy was the Alliance for Progress, with its plenitude of liberal rhetoric about the need to improve the lives of the people of Latin America through social reform, economic growth, and democracy. Communism would be stopped by eliminating the poverty and inequality which were its breeding ground. More heavy-handed intervention against Castro was bound to be condemned throughout much of Latin America, thus jeopardizing the alliance.

Kennedy's solution was to try to remove Castro through secret, deniable attempts at assassination while harassing his regime in a variety of small ways through "Operation Mongoose" headed by General Edward Lansdale, famed for clandestine operations in Vietnam. The United States also imposed a tight embargo on trade with Cuba and did everything possible to prevent non-Soviet nations from trading with Cuba.[38] The Kennedy Administration also followed the Eisenhower practice of using the OAS as a forum for expatiating on Cuba's ties to international Communism in violation of the principles of hemispheric freedom from alien political creeds. In January 1962, at an OAS Foreign Ministers meeting in Punta del Este, Uruguay, the United States won approval, by a one-vote margin, of a resolution declaring that the adherence of any American nation to "Marxism-Leninism is incompatible with the inter-American system," that Cuba is a Marxist-Leninist regime, and therefore, that Cuba is excluded from the OAS. Mexico opposed the resolution; Argentina, Brazil, Chile, Bolivia, and Ecuador abstained. The "aye" votes thus represented less than a third of the population of Latin America.[39] Some victory.

Thus matters stood when Khrushchev in May 1962 decided to place intermediate-range nuclear missiles in Cuba. The resulting crisis was the most dangerous in the four decades of the Cold War. Nuclear war was narrowly averted. The crisis has been endlessly analyzed from almost every angle except as the climactic chapter in the post-1945 history of the Monroe Doctrine. At no other time was the doctrine so often mentioned, invoked, and used as a weapon in domestic politics. And when the crisis was over, with a seemingly permanent Soviet military protectorate established over Cuba, Khrushchev's boast that the doctrine was dead seemed to have come true.

For President Kennedy the crisis began as a political challenge from Republicans eager to depict him as weak and ineffectual on the eve of the 1962 congressional elections, and not as a serious issue of national security. The CIA in the summer of 1962 held to a position first presented in 1960 that the Soviet Union would not run the risk of military confrontation with the United States over Cuba. The mounting volume of Soviet-bloc arms shipments to Cuba, including surface-to-air missiles, excited little alarm in the American intelligence community and was repeatedly described as defensive. Within the cabinet only John McCone, director of Central Intelligence, challenged the prevailing assumption and said there might be some truth behind the rumors of intermediate nuclear missiles soon to be installed.[40] The Soviets early on emphatically denied that they were sending offensive weapons.

With the end of the summer, as politicians and editorial writers returned from vacation, the Monroe Doctrine was rediscovered by scores of commentators—and overwhelmingly in a way critical of President Kennedy. At the President's August 29 press conference a reporter asked, "What the Monroe Doctrine means to you today in the light of world conditions and in Cuba?" Kennedy's answer: "The Monroe Doctrine means what it has meant since President Monroe and John Quincy Adams enunciated it, and that is that we would oppose a foreign power extending its power to the Western Hemisphere . . . That's why we worked in the OAS and in other ways to isolate the Communist menace in Cuba."[41] The answer did not address the issue of what the United States might do should the Soviet Union place nuclear missiles in Cuba.

In preparation for that possibility Attorney General Robert F. Kennedy, the President's brother, in mid-August asked Norbert A. Schlei, recently appointed assistant attorney general, to prepare a memorandum on the legal basis for direct action. Schlei's memorandum stressed the inherent right of self-defense under Article 51 of the UN Charter, urged action through the OAS if possible, but gave heavy emphasis to the Monroe Doctrine as a "regional variation in the international law of self-defense." Schlei included a long annex on the historical evolution and application of the doctrine.

On September 4 President Kennedy met with McGeorge Bundy, Robert Kennedy, Schlei, and officials from the State Department and the CIA to prepare another statement on the Cuban crisis. The President had read Schlei's memorandum and did not like it. "The Monroe Doctrine—what the hell is that?" he "snapped" at Schlei.[42] The outburst stemmed not from ignorance—John Kennedy did not need instruction on something learned by every schoolchild of his generation—but from sensitivity to the way the doctrine was being used against him by domestic political enemies. Furthermore, he was never comfortable with rigid myths and doctrines, seeing them as obstacles more than aids to constructive thinking. He preferred to approach problems pragmatically with an eye on solutions and not to be tied to preconceptions. The public statement, he indicated, must not mention the doctrine—and it did not.

President Kennedy's assurance that the shipment of Soviet arms and military personnel did not yet constitute a threat intensified rather than quieted the mounting debate over the Monroe Doctrine. *The Wall Street Journal* on September 5, for example, noted that both Eisenhower and Kennedy affirmed that the doctrine was alive, but neither "had chosen to implement it; both have relied instead on the so-called machinery of the inter-American security system . . . Where a once-weak nation was bold enough to put its shield over the nations of the hemisphere, a strong nation has hoped that its weak neighbors will somehow shield it from a danger on its own doorstep."[43] In the Senate the opening salvos were fired by Senator Bush, who recalled the resolution drafted by Professor Bemis, and introduced in 1960 by Senator Kenneth Keating, the most vociferous of those warning that missiles might be in Cuba. Keating accused President Kennedy of rendering the Monroe Doctrine meaningless and, worse, a "pair of handcuffs" restricting U.S. action through the imposition of what amounts to an OAS veto. The sharpest barb was inserted by Senator Strom Thurmond. He attacked Kennedy for not using the doctrine as justification for expelling the Castro regime. "It is to admit that the clear historical meaning of the Monroe Doctrine has been abandoned as a cornerstone of United States foreign policy and that there has been substituted therefore, in desecration of the name of Monroe Doctrine, a policy of expediency, hesitation, and indecision."[44]

Over the next three weeks senators and congressmen by the score outdid each other in patriotic embrace of the Monroe Doctrine. James Monroe, 139 years after delivering his famous message, made the cover of *Time* magazine. *Time*'s cover story, "The Monroe Doctrine and Communist Cuba," reported the chorus of demands in Congress that President Kennedy vindicate the Monroe Doctrine by removing the Soviet presence from Cuba. These demands, said *Time*, reflected the "intense American conviction that the Monroe Doctrine—almost like the Declaration of Independence and the Constitution—is an enduring cornerstone of national policy."[45] *Life* magazine, second giant in the publishing empire of Henry R. Luce, urged that a blockade be mounted around Cuba in the name of the Monroe Doctrine to prevent the importation of arms and declared that the "Soviet buildup near Florida is the most direct challenge to the Monroe Doctrine since Maximilian invaded Mexico. The reassertion of the doctrine against this threat will reassure our uneasy allies and put spine in the inter-American system."[46] An occasional voice suggested that the furor over the doctrine was silly. Eleanor Roosevelt said the doctrine was "out of date."[47] Walter Lippmann, magisterial columnist, wrote that the doctrine "did not give the United States any right to perpetual dominance over Latin America." Furthermore, since it "had been based on the notion of the separation of the two hemispheres and United States abstention from the political affairs of Europe" and since the United States now had "a score of military bases in Europe and Asia, the United States could no longer logically invoke the Monroe Doctrine."[48] History and logic were on Lippmann's side, but not the political emotion of the moment.

In the Senate and House, a fierce partisan struggle took place. Democrats and Republicans, Kennedy friends and foes, all agreed that the Monroe Doctrine was alive, noble, and worthy of being reaffirmed by joint resolution. The issue was whether the resolution should support President Kennedy in the course he was following or condemn him for weakness and demand direct action against Communism in Cuba. The Democratic majority in both Houses arranged a text acceptable to President Kennedy. It opened with a "whereas" tribute to Monroe and resolved that the United

States was determined to prevent, by all necessary means including the use of military force, aggressive or subversive activities from Cuba to any part of the hemisphere; and "to prevent in Cuba the creation or use of an externally supported military capability endangering the security of the United States."

Kennedy's critics derided the text for accepting the continuation of Castro's regime and failing to declare that an existing violation of the Monroe Doctrine had to be met. If only Theodore Roosevelt were alive, said one romantic, "the beard would have been shaved off Castro in the first week after he came to power . . . because Teddy Roosevelt was an American through and through." Another deplored the fact that "watchful waiting" had replaced the Monroe Doctrine and declared we must prove ourselves "lineal descendants of those rugged old pioneers whose flag bore the motto, 'Don't Tread on Me.' We either take the leadership or surrender it." A third warned that the doctrine was "on its deathbed, suffering from the fatal disease of lack of exercise and complicated by the faulty diagnosis of a physician who does not understand it." The President's strongest defender was Congressman Emanuel Celler: "Despite the waving of arms and frenetic speech of these Pinafore admirals and papier-mâché generals, the President moves with courage, caution and conscience, and guards our interests."[49]

On September 26 the Republican opposition proposed to amend the joint resolution to declare the Monroe Doctrine already violated by the Communist presence in Cuba and to urge the President to take all necessary steps, including military force, to remove the violation. The vote on the amendment was a clear indication of the partisan nature of the debate. The amendment failed by a vote of 140 (all Republicans) to 251. The original resolution then passed and was signed into law by President Kennedy on October 3.

Meanwhile, persistent cloud cover impeded U.S. photographic surveillance of Cuba. Only on October 15 did photographs confirm that construction of Soviet missile sites was under way. President Kennedy and his advisers had no time to think about doctrines, debating points, or criticism from the political right. The task, said the President on October 16, was to remove the missiles "one way or the other."[50] How that was accomplished without going to war is one of the most intensely studied episodes in American history, comparable to the coming of war with Japan in 1941 and Kennedy's assassination in 1963.

The first phase, until October 22, involved the secret discussions within the special "Executive Committee" over alternatives—an air strike, invasion, or quarantine (euphemism for blockade). Dean Acheson, invited by the President to participate, argued for a surprise bombing attack. Robert Kennedy disagreed passionately and said such action would be comparable to Pearl Harbor in reverse. He did not want his brother to be remembered in history as the American Tojo. Acheson was contemptuous of the analogy. The Japanese, he said, attacked without warning thousands of miles from their shores. But in the present situation the Soviets had installed weapons "capable of lethal injury to the United States" within ninety miles of our shores, all in defiance of the warning given by James Monroe a hundred and forty years before. Robert Kennedy "could not accept the idea that the United States would rain bombs on Cuba, killing thousands and thousands of civilians in a surprise attack"—Monroe Doctrine or no Monroe Doctrine.[51]

President Kennedy decided to impose a quarantine in the hope that more violent measures would not be necessary. The crisis now had moved far beyond the issue of the Monroe Doctrine. In the minds of President Kennedy and his advisers, the future standing of the United States in the world, perhaps survival itself, was at stake. Secretary of State Dean Rusk's opinion on October 18 was that American inaction "would free the Soviets to act any place they wished and at their own will [and] . . . would make our situation unmanageable elsewhere in the world."[52] This anticipated an argument much favored by President Ronald Reagan two decades later—that a Soviet presence in the hemisphere would tie down American resources and limit the capacity to act globally.

McGeorge Bundy, the President's national security adviser, feared that the Soviet nuclear presence in Cuba could tempt them into a first strike and would, in any event, produce a catastrophic shift in the balance of power.[53] Vice President Lyndon B. Johnson was not part of the decision-making group, but when consulted as a matter of courtesy, he said he favored a surprise air strike and was opposed to a blockade because it would merely be "locking the barn door after the horse was gone."[54]

The second phase opened with Kennedy's October 22 address to the nation and the world announcing the missile sites and describing the American response. Here was the central message: "This urgent transformation of Cuba into an important strategic base—by the presence of these large, long-range, and clearly offensive weapons of sudden mass destruction—constitutes an explicit threat to the peace and security of all the Americas, in flagrant and deliberate defiance of the Rio Pact of 1947, the traditions of this nation and hemisphere, the Joint Resolution of the 87th Congress, the Charter of the United Nations, and my own public warnings of September 4 and 13." The president did not mention the Monroe Doctrine by name, but the reference to "traditions of this nation" and the congressional Joint Resolution—which did explicitly invoke the Monroe Doctrine—demonstrated Kennedy's effort to satisfy the Monroe Doctrine choir without becoming entangled in debate over mere words.[55]

During the last week of October the Soviet Union and the United States were "eyeball to eyeball"—in Secretary of State Dean Rusk's famous phrase. The U.S. Navy established the quarantine line, and the Soviets accelerated the construction work on the missile sites. That the United States might invade Cuba seemed by October 25 more probable than not, with October 29 or 30 as the target date. President Kennedy ordered the State Department to make plans to install a civil government in Cuba following an invasion and occupation.[56] The danger may well have been even greater than the Americans realized. According to recollections of a former Soviet general involved in the crisis, Soviet forces in

Cuba were also equipped with nine short-range tactical nuclear weapons and the local commander had authority to use them in the event of an American invasion.[57]

The critical days were October 26, 27, and 28, during which Kennedy and Khrushchev nervously exchanged letters, secretly agreed that in due course the United States would remove its nuclear missiles from Turkey (a public *quid pro quo* was politically unthinkable for Kennedy), and then reached a preliminary understanding that the Soviets would remove offensive missiles from Cuba and introduce no new ones "under appropriate United Nations observation and supervision." In turn, the United States would lift the quarantine and agree not to invade Cuba "upon the establishment of adequate arrangements through the United Nations."[58]

The paladins of the Monroe Doctrine believed Kennedy had betrayed the sacred text and they never forgave him. Robert Murphy, old diplomat among warriors, deplored Kennedy's "docile submission to a dangerous violation of the Monroe Doctrine."[59] Spruille Braden, old Latin American hand and uncompromising anti-Communist, called Kennedy's promise not to invade an "all-out defeat for the Monroe Doctrine" and a violation of America's pledged word.[60] Professor Bemis, who never believed the Soviets had withdrawn all the missiles, remained convinced that the United States had betrayed the doctrine and suffered a grievous defeat. Bemis told friends that he had violated a personal lifelong principle by voting for Kennedy, a Democrat, in 1960. In 1964 he voted for Barry Goldwater.[61] And in October 1963 Dean Acheson, who never forgave Robert Kennedy's Pearl Harbor analogy, said the Monroe Doctrine should be kept alive and thrown directly at the Soviets. "If they should be in doubt as to the meaning . . . there would be a way, though a dangerous way, to find out."[62]

President Kennedy still resented the way critics had used the Monroe Doctrine. He chose Dallas, Texas—heartland of jingo criticism—as the place to speak his mind. Dissent, he said, is inevitable. "But today other voices are heard in the land—voices preaching doctrines wholly unrelated to reality . . . doctrines which apparently assume that words will suffice without weapons, that vituperation is as good as victory and that peace is a sign of weakness . . . I realize that this Nation often tends to identify turning-points in world affairs with the major addresses which preceded them. But it was not the Monroe Doctrine that kept all Europe away from this hemisphere—it was the strength of the British fleet and the width of the Atlantic Ocean." The President was in a motorcade on his way to deliver that speech on November 22 when he was killed by an assassin's bullets.[63]

CHAPTER 6

NO MORE CUBAS:
THE MONROE DOCTRINE UNDER
JOHNSON AND NIXON

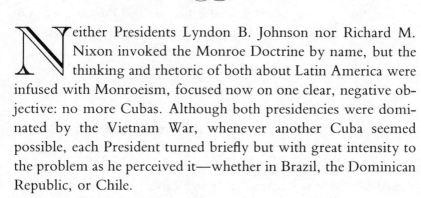

Neither Presidents Lyndon B. Johnson nor Richard M. Nixon invoked the Monroe Doctrine by name, but the thinking and rhetoric of both about Latin America were infused with Monroeism, focused now on one clear, negative objective: no more Cubas. Although both presidencies were dominated by the Vietnam War, whenever another Cuba seemed possible, each President turned briefly but with great intensity to the problem as he perceived it—whether in Brazil, the Dominican Republic, or Chile.

The intellectual problem of how to go on reaffirming the principles of the Monroe Doctrine when it had been so blatantly breached with the establishment of Cuba as a Soviet protectorate was neatly solved by expelling Cuba from the American mental image of the Western Hemisphere. The objective map continued to place the island off the tip of Florida. But on the American political map Cuba had been exiled somewhere behind the Iron Curtain, perhaps anchored off Leningrad. Every day through the 1960s, into the 1970s, even into the 1990s, thousands of American government officials devoted their careers to keeping Cuba politically and economically out of the hemisphere. On the political front this meant trying to prevent other governments from reestablishing diplomatic relations with Cuba, tedious harping to others on the menace of Cuba as the tool of international Communism, even more tedious drafting of Monroeite resolutions for consideration at meetings of the OAS, and ritualistic condemnation of Castro before congressional committees and in public speeches. On the economic front this meant maintaining a stringent embargo against Cuba, denying Americans the right to travel to the island, and pressuring friends and allies to cooperate in keeping the noose tight: no trade, no travel, no air service. Every ship going to Cuba was monitored and the complaints addressed to European governments were endless. On the military-strategic side, it meant naval patrols, U–2 and electronic surveillance; maintenance of the U.S. base at Guantánamo in Cuba itself; and substantial forces at the ready in south Florida and Puerto Rico. On the covert side, it meant sabotage in Cuba and even the attempted assassination of Fidel Castro by CIA "assets." President Johnson, however, did order an end to assassination attempts and restraint in CIA activities.[1] "We had been running a damned Murder, Inc., in the Caribbean," Lyndon Johnson said.[2]

The CIA continued to cultivate close relations with anti-Castro groups in exile and to oversee the use of Army Special Forces against insurgents in countries whose leaders shared the American hatred for Castro—most notably in Bolivia, where in 1967 U.S. forces made possible the tracking down and killing of Castro's revolutionary colleague Ernesto "Che" Guevara.[3]

The U.S. government was never satisfied with its efforts to isolate Cuba. European nations and Canada continued to trade. Mexico never broke diplomatic relations, and gradually other Latin American governments re-established ties. Far more satisfying to Presidents Johnson and Nixon, however, was their prevention of "another Cuba." Johnson took dramatic action twice —in relation to Brazil and the Dominican Republic—and Nixon once, toward Chile. The very low probability of "another Cuba" in all three cases is beside the point. Johnson, Nixon, and their supporters believed they were acting to prevent threats of the highest order.

Were it not for Vietnam, Lyndon Johnson's foreign policy might be remembered primarily for his approach to Latin American issues: the violence-tinged resentment of Panama over the status of the canal; the encouragement for the military officers who overthrew the leftist regime of President João Goulart in Brazil in 1964; and, in a far better known episode, the military intervention in the Dominican Republic in 1965.

Brazil came first. The American perception and fear of Communist influence in Brazil had been growing for several years. It contrasted with the mutually congratulatory tone of U.S.–Brazilian relations throughout most of the period since the Second World War. Those early years must be briefly reviewed, for they did much to shape American and Brazilian assumptions in the crisis of 1964. Brazilian politicians, military officers, and diplomats never tired of telling their American counterparts that Brazil was different—a near-great power, not just another Latin American republic, a nation almost as large as the United States, with a population and potential for growth comparable to that of the United States in the nineteenth century. Recall that Brazil in 1945 had sought permanent membership in the United Nations Security Council, along with the United States, the Soviet Union, Great Britain, France, and China.

American visitors to Brazil liked what they saw. For example, Secretary of State Dean Acheson on his first trip to Brazil in July 1952 was nearly overcome with awe and admiration. He wrote his friend Supreme Court Justice Felix Frankfurter that "the amazing greatness of Brazil one has to see to apprehend. It is altogether fantastic. Like the U.S. just before the Civil War and without that threat developing. Great, undisciplined, as full of energy as a colt, rich, vulgar, cultivated, poor, technically competent, naïve, administratively hopeless—every contradiction, every possibility. I am in love with it. And it almost killed me with kindness."[4]

The military relations of the United States with Brazil were closer than with any other Latin American nation. Brazil sent an infantry division to Europe during the Second World War and collaborated closely with American air and naval forces in hemispheric defense. Close personal friendships were formed among the officers of the two countries. For example, Major Vernon "Dick" Walters was the U.S. combat liaison officer with the Brazilian division. In future years he would play a significant role in U.S.–Brazilian relations and American foreign policy in general.[5] Americans saw their Brazilian colleagues as men of integrity, high professionalism, and patriotism. A U.S. Army assessment in 1946 declared Brazil's military leaders "hard-headed, patriotic realists who are fully cognizant of world trends and potential situations. In their minds, Brazil is irrevocably committed to complete collaboration with the United States, and this includes full integration of military plans and methods."[6]

On the civilian side, however, the relationship was not idyllic. Americans complained that Brazil's economic nationalism interfered with the free flow of trade and investment, and specifically the repatriation of profits to the United States. Brazil wanted assistance in developing its government-owned petroleum industry. Never, said the United States, never until you turn petroleum over to private enterprise. Brazilians complained that the United States was giving billions to Europe under the Marshall Plan and neglecting Brazil. Brazil's point of view was not appreciated in the State Department. "It seems to me, to put it as bluntly as possible," wrote Assistant Secretary Edward G. Miller, Jr., to the American ambassador in Rio, "that the Brazilians are indulging in too much complaining and too little effort to help themselves."[7] The relationship also suffered from the turbulence of Brazilian presidential politics.[8] Getúlio Vargas, facing demands from the military that he resign, committed suicide in 1954. The next year Juscelino Kubitschek was elected President. He was an ambitious dynamo who presided over four years of very rapid economic growth, and in 1958 proposed "Operation Pan-America," a grand scheme calling for lots of money from the United States and anticipating the Alliance for Progress of the Kennedy Administration. The conservatives of the Eisenhower Administration considered Kubitschek out of touch with reality, but he was still a good friend of the United States. Not so Jânio Quadros, elected in 1960 and inaugurated January 31, 1961, ten days after the inauguration of John F. Kennedy in Washington.

The sins of Quadros, from Washington's point of view, were unforgivable. He received Che Guevara, guerrilla hero of Castro's revolution in Cuba, and awarded him a high decoration. He exchanged congratulatory messages with Soviet Premier Nikita Khrushchev and moved toward the resumption of diplomatic relations with the U.S.S.R. and the establishment of relations with the People's Republic of China. John M. Cabot, the American ambassador, noted with diplomatic understatement that "these matters are exclusively Brazil's concern but, although we may have no legitimate grounds for complaining about them, they nevertheless impinge on our interests."[9]

Quadros was, not surprisingly, anathema to military and conservative elements in Brazil. There were rumors of a coup. Suddenly, on August 25, 1961, Quadros resigned. The CIA speculated that Quadros hoped to excite a popular tidal wave of support so that he could return with his critics confounded. If that was his plan, he miscalculated. There was no organized popular support. His resignation stood. Vice President João Goulart became President.

If Quadros was bad from the American point of view, Goulart was intolerable. Significantly, at the moment of Quadros's resignation, Goulart was on shipboard returning from a goodwill trip to the People's Republic of China. American diplomats predicted correctly that the military would try to prevent Goulart's assumption of the presidency. The military tried and failed. Goulart was duly sworn in. The American embassy in Rio advised Washington to handle the military with great tact at a time when its prestige was undermined. The "armed forces, although ostensibly acting in contravention of the constitution, were beyond doubt sincerely motivated by desire to preserve ultimate democratic values."[10]

Throughout 1962 and 1963 the CIA and the embassy in Rio

chronicled Goulart's sins and predicted that there would be a coup. President Kennedy in September 1962 ordered that a special team be dispatched to Brazil, modeled on the team headed by General Maxwell Taylor and Walt Rostow that had reported in the fall of 1961 on Vietnam. The special group on counterinsurgency, headed by General Taylor, approved the Brazilian visit and agreed that it should be headed by General William H. Draper, Jr., a veteran cold warrior acclaimed for his work with the American occupation of Germany in the 1940s. Draper was accompanied by Defense, CIA, AID, and USIA senior officials.[11] Ambassador Lincoln Gordon said he welcomed the arrival of the Draper mission. Perhaps responding to the Vietnam parallel, he described the situation in Brazil as a "political war" which would determine Brazil's future "domestic and external orientation and with it most of this continent."[12] The Draper mission took place during October 1962, simultaneous with the Cuban missile crisis, and thus received relatively little attention. Draper saw Brazil through spectacles similar to those of Ambassador Gordon. The government under Goulart was lurching dangerously to the left; Communist power was increasing; the stakes were huge.

Aid to Brazil under the Alliance for Progress continued, but it was deliberately channeled to Brazilian states with governors perceived as opposing Goulart and away from states and regions, such as the impoverished northeast, where Goulart had support. In Washington this was called the "islands of sanity" approach.

The missile crisis of October 1962 intensified American alarm. Colonel Walters was dispatched to Rio to brief his friends in the Brazilian Army. He remained as military attaché. In December 1962 the National Security Council decided the United States must encourage "Brazilian moderate democratic elements in Congress, the armed forces and elsewhere who advocate democratic and foreign policies we can support." For Ambassador Gordon the armed forces were all that counted. We must tell the Brazilian military, he reported to Washington, that "we want to help them and are prepared to do so effectively so long as they remain an effective bulwark of democracy." By expediting shipments of M–14 rifles, helicopters, and C–130 cargo planes to Brazil, the United States would be assuring the military of its friendship. "This would increase the influence they have on shaping the regime and would also increase their awareness they could count on us in an emergency."[13] Since Gordon and the Department of State already assumed that Goulart's policies were the opposite of what the United States could support, the thrust of Gordon's policy was unambiguous. There are times when it is unnecessary to spell out c-o-u-p.

In February 1963 Gordon cabled almost hysterically that Brazil could be lost to Communism at any moment, thus undermining American "efforts to protect the hemisphere no matter what happened in other Latin American countries." In other words, if Brazil goes, no more Monroe Doctrine. Gordon also suggested that if the administration failed to do everything possible and Brazil did indeed fall, there would be dire political consequences in the United States. The reference to the political recrimination over "who lost China" was unmistakable.[14]

Meanwhile, Khrushchev spoke admiringly of the Goulart regime and promised a glorious future for Brazilian-Soviet trade.[15] By mid-year the U.S. government was noting with alarm the numerous charter flights shuttling between Cuba and Rio—"another example of Castro's determination . . . to break out of the hemisphere's isolation of Cuba" and thwart efforts to use travel controls against subversives.[16] Almost weekly the CIA or the Rio embassy predicted a military coup, always with the assumption that it was the only way to prevent Brazil from descending into Communism.

In November 1963 General Draper invoked the Monroe Doctrine. Eisenhower, he said in a letter to President Kennedy, could have kept Communism out of Cuba had he acted in time. A Communist Brazil would have ten times the impact "in turning Latin America toward Moscow or Peiping." The crisis could come at any moment. "Strong action to keep communism out of Brazil and out of Latin America is something our Congress and our people will understand and to which they will respond enthusiastically. I believe that you would receive almost unanimous bipartisan support for action which would demonstrate to the world, and to Latin America in particular, that the Monroe Doctrine still lives and that it will not permit outside interference in this hemisphere." On November 21 Kennedy aide Ralph Dungan asked the State Department to answer the letter over the signature of the Secretary of State. The answer, said Dungan, should provide details of what the United States was doing to protect its interests in Brazil and be so phrased as to prevent General Draper from saying "I told you so" if the situation did turn bad. In other words, the answer should provide President Kennedy with some political protection against a recurrence of the firestorm over Cuba.[17] The next day President Kennedy was assassinated in Dallas.

Now the problem of Brazil was on Lyndon Johnson's desk and he took it seriously. Ambassador Gordon in March 1964 sent urgent cables through CIA channels predicting that Goulart was about to seize dictatorial power and that Brazil would then fall under Communist control. A "democratic rebellion" by the military, possibly leading to a very bloody civil war, was in the offing.[18] This time a coup was indeed about to occur. On March 30 the U.S. consul in São Paulo was asked by those plotting the coup how quickly a U.S. fleet could reach Brazil.[19] On the same day the CIA reported the probability that the "revolution will not be resolved quickly and will be bloody" and that the Brazilian Navy might remain loyal to Goulart. The CIA in the finest tradition of spycraft reported that Brazilian Communists were getting their teeth fixed, a necessary preliminary to a prolonged guerrilla war from rural bases.[20]

On March 31 the coup was under way and an American carrier task force was steaming toward Brazil. The orders from the Joint Chiefs of Staff to the fleet were to maintain secrecy and be ready to carry out additional orders. Gordon in Rio expected U.S. armed intervention would be necessary, although he cautioned against "getting out front in a losing cause." His hope was that those conducting the coup would set up a government with "some color of legitimacy" which the United States would recognize and then assist in the interests of "upholding constitutional government." American forces were rapidly alerted. A cargo airlift with fighter escorts (code-named Brother Sam) was readied at Ramey Field in Puerto Rico to ferry vital supplies to the rebellion. Plans were developed for U.S. forces to seize and defend an airfield on the Brazilian end.[21]

Goulart, however, had no significant military support. Within forty-eight hours the coup had succeeded. The American airlift never took place and the naval task force returned north. We are dealing, therefore, with a great might-have-been. But had Brazil fallen into the predicted civil war between the forces of the coup and those loyal to Goulart, Lyndon Johnson was ready to fight. American warships were on the way and planes could have arrived in half a day. The probability was high for a large-scale American military intervention, quite likely the largest in the history of the Western Hemisphere, and certainly dwarfing the intervention in the Dominican Republic the following year.

It seems likely that the overthrow of Goulart would have taken place without American encouragement. Intervention by the military was an old Brazilian tradition and the officers who moved so decisively against Goulart needed no help from the United States or anyone else. There is no evidence that the United States promised to provide combat assistance to the coup, should it run into difficulty. The contingency planning for air and naval operations seems—at least until the most secret records are someday opened—to have been on Washington's initiative. But from the extensive contacts between the Brazilian officers and American political and intelligence officials, there was never any doubt in the Brazilian mind of the American attitude: the officers should do what they had to do and the United States would welcome the consequences.

The new government under General Humberto Castelo Branco,

whose friendly ties with the United States went back to World War II, moved quickly to imprison leftists and otherwise restrict political freedom. Brazil broke diplomatic relations with the Soviet Union and ended the contacts with Cuba. Euphoria among Americans was unrestrained. "I am convinced that if the revolution had not occurred, Brazil would have gone the way of Cuba," wrote military attaché Walters.[22] The CIA's conclusion was that the "Brazilian revolution . . . marked a serious setback for Soviet interests. Moscow's hopes . . . have been frustrated."[23] Visiting Americans found much to praise. Presidential aide Jack Valenti, after returning from a trip to Brazil with Senator J. William Fulbright, wrote: "This immense country is obviously the United States of the future in Latin America. The people, the country and the challenges are greatly similar to this nation at the time when we moved westward to settle the land, and eastward to industrialize."[24]

Within a few months of coming to power the Brazilian military had the opportunity to reciprocate the friendship and support extended by Washington—by joining the United States in the military occupation of the Dominican Republic. And that brings us to the best known of Lyndon Johnson's actions to ensure that there would be no more Cubas while he was President.

Sharing the large island of Hispaniola with Haiti, the Dominican Republic is only fifty miles from Puerto Rico across the Mona passage. For more than a century it had been second only to Cuba as an object of American strategic concern and intervention in the Caribbean. President Ulysses S. Grant wanted to annex the country, but was rebuffed by the Senate in 1872. President Theodore Roosevelt's 1904 corollary to the Monroe Doctrine, asserting an American police power, was a response to instability in the Dominican Republic. From 1915 to 1934 the country was under American military government. After the withdrawal of American forces, the country was ruled by Rafael Trujillo, a military dictator merciless toward opposition and skilled in the accumulation of personal wealth at the expense of a desperately poor population. Trujillo was a stench in American diplomatic nostrils, but he was vocally anti-Nazi during the Second World War and anti-Communist thereafter. In 1946 the American ambassador in Santo Domingo described the regime as "based on fear and the suppression of fundamental civil liberties." Trujillo, he said, "could not make any substantial concessions to our concept of democracy and still retain power."[25] The United States refused Trujillo's request to be allowed to purchase arms and Trujillo complained of being treated as if he were a Hitler or a Mussolini. But Washington did nothing to dislodge Trujillo from power.

In 1951 the United States put itself in Trujillo's debt by asking and receiving permission to set up a missile tracking station in the Dominican Republic. Trujillo was assured there was no danger of the missiles falling on the island, but yes, there was a possibility that they might carry nuclear warheads.[26] Also in 1951, the United States asked Trujillo to contribute a battalion to the Korean War. He said no.[27] The State Department's glum conclusion was that "unless we are prepared forcibly to remove Trujillo—and such a step would be contrary to our non-intervention commitments—a policy of other than normal relations would merely antagonize him . . . without removing him or advancing the cause of democracy in the Dominican Republic."[28] Trujillo's behavior grew worse year by year. When Assistant Secretary of State John M. Cabot visited during a tour of the Caribbean in April 1953, he concluded that "never, not even in Russia, have I seen such a reign of terror as existed in Santo Domingo."[29] But even the abduction from New York and subsequent murder on Trujillo's orders of Dr. Jesus de Galíndez, a critic of the regime, and the disappearance of an American who had incriminating knowledge of the affair did not change U.S. policy. Noting the claim of the U.S. Air Force that the maintenance of the missile tracking station was "vital," the State Department confined itself to mild protest. "This course of action will not, of course, satisfy all members of the Congress or the U.S. and Latin American liberal elements," admitted Assistant Secretary Roy Rubottom in February 1957.[30] Putting the best face on the situation, the secret briefing by the administration in support of the military aid program for 1958 said: "While repressive methods of dictatorial power in the Dominican Republic are unsavory to the United States, the present government has brought stability and considerable progress to the country" and Trujillo is a strong opponent of Communism and a supporter of the United States in the United Nations.[31] There spoke the voice of the Kennan Corollary.

Fidel Castro's success against Batista, a Cuban despot not half as brutal as Trujillo, was a warning to the Eisenhower Administration. If Trujillo was not replaced by a non-Communist successor responsive to the needs of the people, he could well be overthrown by a Dominican Castro, probably with the real Castro's help. Haiti would follow and the result would be a picket line of Communist islands across the vital sea lanes to the Panama Canal. In June 1959 a band of 200 exiles and a sprinkling of other nationalities invaded the Dominican Republic with Castro's support—but were virtually wiped out by Trujillo's forces. Afterward, Trujillo's violations of human rights reached new depths.

The problem in 1960 as seen from Washington was that Trujillo's sudden departure, especially if he was assassinated or violently overthrown, would create a vacuum almost certain to be filled by a Castro-backed Communist regime. The classic solution was to find a way to persuade Trujillo to leave while arranging for a moderate successor regime. Eisenhower tried working through General Edwin Norman Clark, an old friend. Clark, who had long ties with Trujillo, tried to induce the dictator to accept asylum in the United States with his fortune deposited in a foundation headed by U.S. and Latin American leaders.[32]

Secretary of State Christian Herter considered the Clark approach too weak and urged direct military action to prevent the dreaded "Castroite takeover." Herter said the United States should arrange for an "appropriate" group to overthrow Trujillo. The United States would respond to the new regime's request for assistance to prevent a Communist-inspired invasion or insurrection. "This could include putting naval vessels into port and/or the landing of U.S. forces in the Dominican Republic provided there were reasonable assurance that they would not have to fire on the local inhabitants or meet serious resistance from armed military or civilian elements."[33] The CIA fiddled with this idea—but without immediate success.

In June 1960 Trujillo went on the offensive: his agents wounded Venezuelan President Rómulo Betancourt in an assassination attempt. The OAS meeting in Costa Rica in August declared the Dominican Republic guilty of aggression, imposed an arms embargo, and agreed that all members would break diplomatic relations with Trujillo's government.[34] The United States went along, but without enthusiasm. There was some byplay in the United Nations Security Council when the Soviet Union charged that the imposition of sanctions against the Trujillo regime was properly a matter for the UN, not the OAS. The Soviet ambassador quoted Article 53, which said, "No enforcement action shall be taken under regional arrangements or by regional agencies without the authorization of the Security Council." To which the United States replied that the Soviet Union was interfering in the affairs of the American republics—thereby holding to the Monroeite principle that barred UN authority from the hemisphere.[35] Thus matters stood when John F. Kennedy was inaugurated. His administration was soon too entangled in Cuban affairs to pay much attention to the Dominican Republic. But on May 31, 1961, Trujillo was assassinated in circumstances which remain murky to this day.

Ten months later, Juan Bosch, poet and lifelong opponent of Trujillo, won the country's first free election for President. The American ambassador, John Bartlow Martin, considered Bosch "a divider, a splitter, a schemer, a destroyer," but preferable to the military plotters who wanted him out. But Martin could muster no enthusiasm for Bosch in Washington. Bosch personified the kind of ineffective Latin American democrat described by George

Kennan in his 1950 memorandum on the need, under the Monroe Doctrine, to support harsh repressive regimes. Within the Dominican Republic Bosch was unpopular with the wealthy because of a land-reform program and hated by the military. By the summer of 1963 the air was full of rumors that Bosch would soon be toppled by a military coup. Ambassador Martin flew to Washington to rally support for Bosch. Martin failed. Instead, President Kennedy said Bosch should deport thirty to fifty leftists and the United States would be glad to take them off his hands. Martin went back to Santo Domingo and advised Bosch to be strong in dealing with both the left and the military right. Bosch lacked the necessary power. He was overthrown in September 1963 and deported by the new regime. There were no tears in Washington.[36]

A triumvirate whose nominal head was Donald Reid Cabral took over. The country's democratic moment had been short. From Puerto Rico, Governor Luis Muñoz Marín cabled President Kennedy, urging strong action against the military regime, saying that here was a test of American devotion to democracy, predicting that the military might well prepare the way for Communism as Batista had done in Cuba. The response in Washington was tepid. Even Ambassador Martin, again on a visit to Washington, was no longer a supporter of Bosch.

"I take it we don't want Bosch back," said Kennedy to Martin.

"No, Mr. President."

"Why not?"

"Because he isn't a President."[37]

Officially the United States deplored the coup and delayed establishment of normal diplomatic relations. By early 1964, however, with Lyndon Johnson now President, the United States decided to accept the triumvirate in the absence of any satisfactory alternative. State Department analysts warned that Communists might take advantage of the situation by posing as the champions of freedom and democracy.[38] The trap in that argument, however, was that any champion of freedom and democracy could be suspected of being a Communist in disguise. On the other hand, the

Latin Americanist on the National Security Council staff said the greater danger was the return of a Trujillo-type dictatorship.[39]

By early 1965 the military regime was proving itself ever less effective in governing. The CIA placed the Dominican Republic high on its list of twelve hemispheric countries ripe for Communist success. President Johnson was deeply disturbed. Suddenly, on April 24, a rebel group seized the principal radio station in Santo Domingo, called for the return of Bosch, and began an attack on the military government.

The United States could have worked for a negotiated cease-fire and assisted in the transition to a democratic regime. Bosch, after all, had been fairly elected and illegally deposed. But from the beginning Lyndon Johnson, haunted by the fear of another Cuba, assumed that a rebel victory would mean another Communist regime. He had shown during the 1964 coup in Brazil a capacity for acting fast. Now he soon responded in similar fashion. The task of the American intelligence community became the collection of evidence supporting an *a priori* conclusion.

By the fourth day of the uprising, April 28, President Johnson and his advisers had concluded that the military regime lacked the determination to prevail—so much for the effectiveness of harsh, repressive regimes. The President ordered the landing of 500 Marines, ostensibly to protect American and other foreign lives. The force would ultimately number 23,000, reflecting the military's conviction that the failure at the Bay of Pigs and currently in Vietnam was the result of not committing enough forces to win. The same day Johnson received a cable from Ambassador W. Tapley Bennett, Jr., in Santo Domingo, which perfectly reinforced his instincts: "All indications point to the fact that if present efforts of forces loyal to the government fail, power will be assumed by groups clearly identified with the Communist party . . . My own recommendation and that of the Country Team is that we should intervene to prevent another Cuba from arising out of the ashes of this uncontrollable situation."[40]

Pat Holt, the experienced Latin American specialist on the staff of the Senate Foreign Relations Committee, said that Lyndon Johnson was his own Dominican desk office for the three months of the crisis.[41] The evidence bears out this assessment. For example, at the April 29 meeting of his highest advisers, Johnson said: "We have resisted Communism all over the world—Vietnam, Lebanon, Greece—why are we disregarding our doorstep?" He demanded the evidence on Communists in the rebellion, and when Secretary of State Dean Rusk said that not all the rebels were Communist, Johnson answered that not all Cubans supporting Castro were Communist either: "I am ashamed of the little we have done." Under Secretary of State George Ball said we had done considerable in putting a force ashore without an angry response. Johnson was not satisfied and said he was determined that Castro not take over.

The group then agreed with the President on the need to present irrefutable evidence of the Communist danger and to convince the public that if the United States failed to act, Castro would soon be in command of the island. They also agreed that a Castro victory in the Dominican Republic "would be the worst domestic political disaster we could possibly suffer." The political note appeared a few days later when Johnson told congressional leaders, "If I send in Marines, I cannot live in the hemisphere. If I don't I can't live at home."[42] This self-pitying description of a dilemma was vintage Johnson. He would repeat it, with variations, to describe the problem of fighting in Vietnam.

The Marines and Army units moved rapidly into the city of Santo Domingo, ostensibly to bring an end to the fighting, but in reality to make the rebel position untenable. They succeeded.[43] The United States also succeeded in winning, by a 14–5 vote, an OAS decision to form an inter-American peace force. Brazil contributed the largest number of troops, and after most U.S. troops withdrew in late 1965, a Brazilian general took over command. The Soviet Union denounced the United States for using the OAS, an imperialist tool; and the United States, as in the past, made sure that the United Nations Security Council kept its nose out of the affair. Soon Joaquin Balaguer, perennial conservative once associated with Trujillo, won an election and the United States forgot about the Dominican Republic.

Thus, Lyndon Johnson and the advisers on whom he relied were able to take great satisfaction in their Latin American policy. There were no more Cubas—not in Brazil, not in the Dominican Republic. Evidence that Communists were even close to taking over in either country was flimsy to nonexistent. It existed primarily in Lyndon Johnson's active imagination—and that was enough.

A persistent theme of latter-day Monroeism was that by keeping the hemisphere secure, and not having to erect defenses on "our own doorstep," the United States could deploy forces all over the world. Alas for Lyndon Johnson, the success in the hemisphere left him free to decide in the summer of 1965 to go for victory in Vietnam through the large-scale use of American combat forces, ultimately over 500,000. From that moment he paid no more attention to Latin America.

Latin America fell off the mental map of high Washington officials in the late 1960s, years when the Vietnam War dominated American foreign policy and domestic politics. The State Department toyed with the idea of asking Latin American countries individually or through an OAS resolution to contribute troops for Vietnam, but did not pursue what was a wildly foolish idea.[44]

President Johnson's only personal additional involvement with Latin America was to attend the OAS conference of heads of state in Punta del Este, Uruguay, in 1967. On the plane flying down, Johnson asked, "What the hell are we doing this for?"[45] Good question. The conference produced a lengthy declaration describing an "action program" for trade, development, and limits on armaments. There was no action. Johnson's mind was on the catastrophe of the Vietnam War. Within a year he would announce what was, in effect, his resignation as President. In November 1968 Richard Nixon won the election for President over Vice President Hubert Humphrey.

Only twice did an issue involving Latin America attract significant attention from President Nixon or his national security adviser, Henry Kissinger. The first was brief—an exchange with
Moscow over Cuba as a base for Soviet submarines. The submarine affair was the equivalent of a delayed and mild aftershock
from the missile crisis of 1962. Recall that Premier Nikita Khrushchev had withdrawn the Soviet missiles from Cuba and President John F. Kennedy, in turn, had promised that the United States
would not invade Cuba. The Kennedy-Khrushchev accord was
not a contract or treaty meticulously drawn by lawyers but, rather,
a loosely worded and qualified exchange of messages indicating
that neither Great Power intended to push the other beyond a
certain dangerous point over Cuba; neither wanted to cross a line
which would bring retaliation from the other. Both leaders, and
their successors, had been deeply shaken by the prospect of nuclear
war. Neither side wished to undergo again the terror of 1962, or
to encounter something worse. Either side could have claimed,
had it so wished, that it was no longer bound by the understanding
because the other had failed to fulfill or had violated the agreement.
The Soviets could have claimed that the continuation of CIA-
supported sabotage in Cuba and above all the attempted assassinations of Fidel Castro violated the no-invasion pledge. The Americans could have declared the accord invalid because the anticipated
United Nations verification that the missiles had been withdrawn
was never permitted by Castro. The Americans could also have
claimed that non-invasion was contingent on Cuba's forsaking all
attempts to spread its revolution into other Latin American countries and that Castro through the 1960s was up to his whiskers in
such activity. Neither the Soviet Union nor the United States
denounced the accord, because its preservation remained in the
interest of each. But the neuralgic borderline of the acceptable,
having never been stated with precision, could at any moment be
touched. How each resulting mini-crisis was resolved then provided some definition of what was necessary to keep the accord

alive. The process also helped American officials explain to themselves and the public how they were still upholding the principles of the Monroe Doctrine even while accepting a Soviet presence so close to American shores.

By 1970 Soviet nuclear missile–carrying submarines were cruising continuously near the shores of the United States, just as American submarines in the Arctic and North Pacific Oceans hovered close to the Soviet Union. Prolonged submarine cruises are hell on the crew, especially if there is no chance to get ashore, breathe some fresh air, and enjoy the sailors' traditional opportunities for rest and recreation. Cuba, as a Soviet ally in a tropical climate adjacent to the North American cruising grounds, was an ideal stopping place for the submarine fleet. Accordingly, in 1970 the Soviets secured Castro's permission and began to build a submarine base at Cienfuegos, on Cuba's south coast. This motivation, however, may have been incidental to a larger and, from the American point of view, more ominous purpose.

The opinion of Raymond Garthoff, diplomat and distinguished analyst of Soviet-American relations, deserves to be quoted. Garthoff notes how the forced withdrawal of missiles from Cuba in 1962 was regarded by the United States as a reassertion of the Monroe Doctrine, an "outstanding American victory in the cold war." For the Soviets it was a humiliating defeat. But by 1970 "Soviet leaders believed the U.S.S.R. was acquiring strategic parity and wanted that new status recognized. One way would be to circumscribe the limitations forced upon them in 1962 restricting their military presence in Cuba."[46] In September 1970, a U–2 flight discovered the submarine base under construction. Nixon and Kissinger interpreted the construction much as Garthoff did later. The base was unacceptable. Nixon's first impulse was to retaliate. He asked Kissinger for "a report on a crash basis on (1) What CIA can do to support any kind of action which will irritate Castro; (2) What actions we can take which have not yet been taken to boycott nations dealing with Castro; (3) Most important, what

actions we can take, covert or overt, to put missiles in Turkey—
or a sub base in the Black Sea—anything which will give us some
trading stock."[47] Kissinger thought Nixon's ideas were "time-
wasting options" and concentrated instead on a diplomatic settlement. "The Soviet Union can be under no doubt that we would
view establishment of a strategic base in the Caribbean with utmost
seriousness" and would consider it a clear violation of the Kennedy-Khrushchev understanding of 1962, he told a press conference. The statement was on "background" and could be attributed
only to a White House source. No knowledgeable reader doubted
who that source was or could fail to recognize a strong statement.

Soviet Ambassador Anatoly Dobrynin was, according to Kissinger, "ashen" when confronted with the issue.[48] The Soviets
immediately promised they would not have a naval base in Cuba.
In the process both the Americans and Soviets publicly reaffirmed
and made more explicit their commitment to the 1962 accords.
The American side wrote out and gave the Soviets their statement
of the understanding: "The U.S.S.R. will not establish, utilize, or
permit the establishment of any facility in Cuba that can be employed to support or repair Soviet naval ships capable of carrying
offensive weapons, i.e. submarines or surface ships armed with
nuclear-capable, surface-to-surface missiles." After further diplomatic interchange "support and repair" was narrowed to exclude
using Cuba as a base for submarine tenders who did their actual
tending at sea.[49]

The satisfactory outcome of the submarine base issue encouraged President Nixon to deal forcefully with what appeared to be
another Cuba in the making: the pending inauguration of Salvador
Allende as President of Chile. Salvador Allende, articulate man of
the left long prominent in Chilean politics, was no invention of
Moscow—not even Nixon could make that claim. But he was
highly critical of capitalism and the influence of the United States
in Latin America. He was on friendly terms with Fidel Castro.

Nixon, a man prone to obsessive hatreds, was grimly fascinated by Allende. He believed the comment of a visiting Italian businessman that "if Allende should win, and with Castro in Cuba, you will have in Latin America a red sandwich. And eventually, it will be all red."[50] Seldom has a metaphor, a delicatessen version of the domino theory, been so oblivious to geography and political diversity.

The importance attached to Chile was not new. Its copper, in the age before fiber optics, was a strategic mineral. Its 2,000-mile coastline on the Pacific, including Cape Horn and the entrance to the Straits of Magellan, could not be allowed to fall into hostile hands, especially if for some reason the Panama Canal was out of operation. During the Korean War, when World War III appeared all too imminent, Claude Bowers, the American ambassador in Santiago, reiterated this fear: "In the extreme south of Chile . . . there are a great number of heavily timbered unoccupied islands that are ideal hideouts for enemy submarines . . . In a new war involving Russia the danger here will be infinitely greater than during the last war."[51] American intelligence and diplomatic officials had monitored the strength of the Communist Party and Chile's relations with the Soviet Union with great care since the 1940s. They praised the democratically elected governments of Chile, but often feared the worst.

On the positive side, Ambassador Bowers in 1952 was delighted that new President Carlos Ibáñez agreed to the U.S. suggestion that he abandon plans to establish diplomatic relations with the U.S.S.R., sell minerals behind the Iron Curtain, and repeal the Law for the Defense of Democracy under which Communists were roughly handled.[52] By dutifully employing tools and methods from the armory of the Monroe Doctrine, Ibáñez retained American goodwill. In 1955 a U.S. intelligence report praised his curtailment of Communists, but regretted that "Chilean public opinion has been largely apathetic towards Communism and has looked askance upon any repression of political liberties, even the Communists may exploit these to their own advantage."[53]

Under Chilean law an individual could serve as President for one six-year term. Ibáñez, age eighty-one, retired in 1958 and the CIA provided some financial support to conservative Jorge Alessandri, who won over socialist candidate Salvador Allende. Allende's chances in 1964 appeared ominously good. "Of all the Latin American nations, Chile offers the Communists their best prospects for entering and potentially dominating a government through the electoral process," the CIA warned in April.[54] The National Security Council staffer for Latin America, Gordon Chase, saw a double reason for concern: "A Communist election victory in September 1964 ('another Communist penetration in the Western Hemisphere') is intolerable for national security and domestic political reasons."[55] In other words, another Cuba could doom Lyndon Johnson's chances for election. The CIA spent heavily to support Eduardo Frei and discredit Allende. Frei won.

In 1970 Allende was back again, and formidable. The CIA generously distributed money to assure his defeat, but Allende won 36 percent of the vote, more than any opponent, and was scheduled to be confirmed by Congress in October. The American ambassador in Santiago was Edward M. Korry, a onetime newspaper man with a flare for vivid writing and an incapacity to take a relaxed attitude. His message was that Allende in office would have dire and far-reaching consequences for the United States. "It is a sad fact that Chile has taken the path to communism with only a little more than a third (36 percent) of the nation approving this choice," Korry said in a cable which Nixon read carefully and underlined. "It will have the most profound effect on Latin America and beyond; we have suffered a grievous defeat; the consequences will be domestic and international . . ."[56] Nixon ordered Henry Kissinger to prevent Allende from being inaugurated. Kissinger, simultaneously handling the controversy with the Soviet Union over a possible submarine base in Cuba, switched on his geopolitical imagination. Cuba at least was an island, he told a press briefing "on background," and therefore easy to isolate. But Chile had a long border with Argentina and another with Peru, already heading in dangerous directions, and next to Peru was Bolivia.[57]

The traditional soft CIA methods of influencing an election having failed, President Nixon ordered the CIA "to leave no stone unturned . . . to block Allende's confirmation." CIA director Richard Helms's notes on Nixon's instructions read:

> One in 10 chance perhaps, but save Chile!
> worth spending
> not concerned risks involved
> no involvement of embassy
> $10,000,000 available, more if necessary
> full-time job—best men we have
> make the economy scream
> 48 hours for plan of action

More CIA shenanigans contributed to a bungled coup and the death of the Chilean chief of staff, General René Schneider, but failed to prevent Allende's inauguration.[58]

From the Kissinger-Nixon point of view, Allende's sins as President were manifold and grievous. He entertained members of the Puerto Rican Independence Party, erected a statue of Che Guevara, opened diplomatic relations with Cuba and received Castro as a guest, opened contact with North Korea and North Vietnam, and seized private corporate property without adequate compensation. The United States conducted an open war of economic sanctions against Allende, condemned his every action, and funneled money through the CIA to political opponents. That much was public at the time or admitted soon after. Chile's economy did indeed "scream," as Nixon had wished, but its problems were partly of Allende's own making. He alienated virtually everyone but his own radical advisers and would have been in deep trouble even if the United States had remained passive.

In September 1973 Allende died—either killed or a suicide—during the coup that installed the military dictatorship of General Augusto Pinochet. Chile became the very model of the harsh repressive regime envisioned a generation earlier by George Kennan in his corollary. The Nixon Administration extended warm support and looked the other way while the Pinochet regime imprisoned, tortured, and murdered indiscriminately. The United States applauded when Pinochet broke diplomatic relations with the Soviet Union and expelled a group of Cubans.

Did the United States give direct aid and encouragement to the generals who launched the coup of September 1973, or indirect support conveyed through the military junta in Brazil? Kissinger absolutely denies that the United States had anything to do with Allende's overthrow[59]—but the evidence is not all in. There is, of course, a difference between causing an outcome and welcoming it. The welcome to Pinochet was never in doubt. At a minimum one can say that the Chilean plotters took comfort in the knowledge that their success would be rewarded by good relations with the United States—exactly the same sort of comfort available to their Brazilian colleagues during the overthrow of Goulart in 1964.

Kissinger and Nixon had the satisfaction of knowing that another Cuba, continental and 2,000 miles long, was not established on their watch. But their complicity in events which inflicted political repression and brutality on Chile was soon uncovered by the press and congressional investigations. The ill-conceived, mendacious covert operations in Chile inflicted deep and lasting wounds on the principles of the Monroe Doctrine. Kissinger's claim that the United States had done no more than provide modest subsidies to democratic institutions so that they could resist Allende's oppression was not true and not believed by congressional and public opinion. And even if true, the outcome in Chile was the establishment of a murderous military regime welcomed by the Nixon Administration. In 1976 the murderous arm of the

Pinochet regime reached Washington, D.C., with the car-bomb assassination of Orlando Letelier, once Foreign Minister under Allende, and an American associate who happened to be in the car.[60] That was something to disconcert even the most dedicated believer in the Kennan Corollary. Toleration for harsh repressive regimes had its limits.

Nothing of great significance involving Latin America or the Monroe Doctrine occurred in the short presidency of Gerald Ford.

CHAPTER 7

PREMATURE OBITUARY: THE DOCTRINE AND JIMMY CARTER

I n 1976 American society was shaken and disillusioned by the failure to achieve political goals and maintain moral foundations in the Vietnam War. The mood was reinforced by the Watergate scandal, leading to the resignation in disgrace of President Richard Nixon, and by revelations of CIA involvement in assassinations and other immoral covert action. Jimmy Carter, former governor of Georgia, won the Democratic nomination and the presidential election by condemning past sins and promising moral rebirth. "We've lost the spirit of our nation . . . We're ashamed of what our government is as we deal with other nations around the world, and that's got to be changed, and I'm going to change it."[1]

Carter's initial philosophy of foreign policy was spelled out most clearly in his address at Notre Dame University in May 1977. In sentences soon to become famous and eventually to be used against him, Carter declared: "We are now free of that inordinate fear of communism which once led us to embrace any dictator in that fear . . . For too many years, we've been willing to adopt the flawed and erroneous principles and tactics of our adversaries, sometimes abandoning our values for theirs."[2] Here was a direct condemnation of the argument we have called the Kennan Corollary to the Monroe Doctrine: that in order to stop Communism

in Latin America the United States must not shrink from supporting harsh and repressive regimes.

One aspect of the administration's philosophy was a conscious
decision to refrain from mentioning or thinking in terms of the
Monroe Doctrine. Carter's influential national security adviser,
Zbigniew Brzezinski, had written in 1970 that "it would be wise
for the United States to make an explicit move to abandon the
Monroe Doctrine and to concede that in the new global age geo-
graphic or hemispheric contiguity no longer need be politically
decisive. Nothing could be healthier for Pan-American relations
than for the United States to place them on the same level as its
relations with the rest of the world . . ."[3] At a high-level policy-
review session early in the new administration Brzezinski argued
against treating Latin American nations "paternalistically in terms
of a special hemispheric policy." He noted that most Americans
saw the Monroe Doctrine as "a selfless U.S. contribution to hemispheric security; but to most of our neighbors to the south it was
an expression of presumptuous U.S. imperialism."[4] Brzezinski's
insight was at least as old as Hiram Bingham's discussion of the
"obsolete shibboleth" in 1913. But it bore repeating, and repeat
it he did in an interview with James Reston of *The New York
Times*: "Americans tend to be very proud of the Monroe Doctrine.
To most Latin Americans it is a document expressing American
domination."[5]

The administration's approach was influenced by the work of
the Commission on United States–Latin American Relations, a
group of business and academic leaders which in 1975 issued a
widely read report entitled *The Americas in a Changing World*—
often called the Linowitz Report after the commission's chairman,
Sol M. Linowitz. The report cited the Monroe Doctrine in asserting "that the policies which the United States has inherited
from the past—including many of their most basic assumptions
and goals—are inappropriate and irrelevant to the changed realities
of the present and trends of the future." The report's recommendations constituted a sweeping critique of the policies of every

administration from Truman through Ford and a repudiation of most of the principles of Monroeism. It urged that the United States refrain from military interventions and end covert interference in the internal affairs of Latin American countries; normalize relations with Cuba and end the trade embargo; sign and ratify a treaty granting Panama eventual control of the canal; terminate military grants and advisory groups in Latin America; abandon the threat or application of economic coercion; pay more respect to the Organization of American States and be guided by the wishes and initiatives of Latin American governments; and target foreign aid to assist the poorest segments of the population.[6]

In place of an "inordinate fear of communism" Carter sought to elevate the support of human rights to first place in the conduct of foreign policy. This meant asking first whether governments upheld or violated the rights of their people, not where they stood in the contest between the United States and the Soviet Union. Depending on the seriousness of violations, the offending governments would then be approached through quiet diplomacy, subjected to public criticism, or punished with low-grade economic sanctions. Since the only Communist state in Latin America, Cuba, was already subject to extreme economic sanctions and immune from criticism, Carter's human-rights campaign in the hemisphere was directed against right-wing and mostly military regimes accustomed to parading their anti-Communist credentials—most notably Nicaragua, Argentina, Brazil, and Chile. The Carter human-rights officials believed that the ideological evil of those regimes was indigenous and did not originate from a foreign source. They denigrated the alarmist Monroeite/Cold War perception of the Soviet Union as the source of all instability as wrong and irrelevant.

The Carter Administration's first goal was to reach a peaceful settlement of the long dispute with Panama over the future of the canal. Carter's advisers told him that the stalemate over the canal could explode at any moment, with loss of life, serious damage to the waterway, and—worst of all—lasting injury to American relations with all Latin America. Carter was soon persuaded that exclusive American control of the canal and virtual sovereignty over the surrounding zone—dividing Panama with a swath of foreign territory—was an anachronism and morally wrong. He hoped that an American demonstration of good faith and sympathy for Panama through relinquishment of the zone and exclusive control of the canal would avert an imminent catastrophe and lay the foundation for a new era of inter-American relations.

By his readiness to "surrender" the canal, to use the favorite verb of the critics, Carter was attacking the Monroe Doctrine's emotional sibling. Find an American who believed the doctrine was as sacred as the Constitution and the Declaration of Independence and you found also someone who believed the canal was American and should remain American forever. A good example was the inveterate flag-waver Congressman Daniel Flood, tireless opponent of any compromise with Panama. Whenever Flood talked of the canal, he brought in the doctrine. Permanent American right to the canal, like the doctrine, defined national identity and preeminence in the hemisphere. The doctrine protected the canal, a vital element in American security, and the canal made it possible to deploy the naval power necessary to enforce the doctrine. For true believers, the canal and the Monroe Doctrine were inseparable.

Almost from 1903, when independent Panama came into existence, through a conspiracy supported in the United States, and signed the original canal treaty, Panamanian political leaders and commentators had complained about the grossly unfavorable terms. Well they might. The United States provided a down payment of $10 million and an annual payment of only $250,000 beginning in 1913, a year before the canal opened. The treaty also gave the United States the right to intervene in Panama's internal affairs, control her foreign policy, and take additional territory. In short, the idea that Panama was a sovereign state was an empty fiction. Under President Franklin Roosevelt, as part of the Good Neighbor Policy, these terms were eased—but not much. A 1936 treaty, ratified in 1939, increased the annual payment to $430,000 (but in devalued dollars) and modified the grounds justifying intervention in Panama's affairs.[7]

The fear of international Communism after 1945 caused the Truman and Eisenhower Administrations to be less than sympathetic to Panamanian concerns. For example, at an International Labor Organization (ILO) meeting in Mexico City in April 1946, the Panamanians raised a justified complaint against the racially discriminatory policies of the United States within the Canal Zone. Panama was supported by Lombardo Toledano, prominent Mexican labor leader and a dangerous red from the U.S. point of view. But the U.S. delegation, twisting arms, got the Panamanian issue deleted from the agenda. The success led the American labor attaché in Mexico to conclude "that on the main issue of the Conference, namely, Russian vs. American leadership in the western hemisphere, the U.S. not only maintained its position but strengthened and consolidated it."[8]

By the 1950s fear of Communist influence in Panama was the dominating American concern. President Truman and Secretary of State Acheson in 1952 even contemplated the need to take "emergency measures . . . to safeguard our national interests on the Isthmus."[9] In 1953 Panamanian President José Remón came to Washington seeking fundamental revision of the Canal Zone regime. He was rebuffed by Secretary of State John Foster Dulles and President Eisenhower. Dulles told Remón that the United States negotiated new treaties with Spain, but "the treaty involving the purchase of Florida was never touched; neither did any treaty with Russia having to do with the status of Alaska, which had likewise been purchased by the United States."[10] The Eisenhower Administration did, however, increase the annual payment to $1,030,000 in 1955 and extend a few other economic concessions to Panama.

Egypt's nationalization of the Suez Canal in 1956 and the ensuing crisis had an effect in both Washington and Panama City. Dulles accused Panama of "conniving with Nasser" and preparing to make "the nationalization or internationalization of the Canal a major issue." The American government denied that the Suez and Panama situations were in any way comparable and contemplated threatening Panama with a sea-level canal to be built through Nicaragua. This, in the words of the U.S. ambassador in Panama, "would bring about a realization among Panamanians that they would do well to accept graciously the many benefits they are now reaping." Eisenhower thought this a splendid idea and told Dulles to explore the question, adding that the Panama Canal was already too small for many modern vessels.[11] Over the next decade the prospect of a second canal to be dug with nuclear explosions —part of so-called Operation Plowshares, a favorite idea of physicist Edward Teller—was used to keep Panama in line. In 1964 Lyndon Johnson made it an official U.S. objective, but afterward the idea faded.

The Eisenhower Administration until 1960 remained adamantly opposed to any fundamental adjustment in the relationship with Panama. Every small disturbance in the normally turbulent pattern of Panamanian politics was routinely seen by the State Department as evidence of the Communist menace. Thus, Fidel Castro was wrongly accused of staging an invasion of Panama in April 1959, and the United States in a state of high alarm mobilized air and naval patrols and invoked the Rio treaty before the Organization of American States. The affair, in fact, was a minuscule comic-opera landing led by Roberto Arias, husband of the British ballerina Margot Fonteyn. But since one can't prove a negative, U.S. officials believed a "Fidelista" intervention had been thwarted.[12]

The President's brother, Milton, urged the United States to be more flexible—for example, by allowing the Panamanian flag to fly in the zone. In November 1959, when a group of Panamanians tried to do just that, a riot ensued and 120 people were wounded, several by American soldiers. The Defense Department argued for a hard line: "No concessions should be made which impinge upon the sovereignty we exercise over the Canal Zone. Concessions in this area are but the beginning of continuing demands by Panama which would seriously jeopardize the United States' position in the Canal Zone and it is doubtful if such concessions would improve Panama–United States relations."[13] The President, however, listened to his brother and decided to permit the Panamanian flag to fly in the zone on ceremonial occasions.

The stage was set for bloodshed and death. On January 9, 1964, a riot broke out between Panamanian and American high-school students in the zone when the latter tried to prevent a display of the Panamanian flag. Huge crowds demonstrated against the United States, first in Panama City and then throughout the country; the offices of American companies were burned; gunfire filled the air as the U.S. Army exchanged fire with Panamanian snipers. President Roberto Chiari broke diplomatic relations with the United States. When the violence subsided, twenty-four Panamanians and four Americans were dead and many wounded on both sides.

CIA cables, arriving almost hourly, warned of a Communist coup. In his memoirs Lyndon Johnson states accurately his belief at the time: "Fidel Castro, working closely with the Panamanian Communist Party, had been sending guns, money, and agents into Panama . . . We expected the canal and the zone to become special targets."[14] Johnson was in a difficult position. The political right in the United States warned against concessions to a puny third-rate country, and public opinion in general had little sympathy for Panama. Johnson was much impressed with a report from political analyst Richard Scammon that the public's approval of better relations with the Soviet Union flowed from fear of nuclear war "and does not extend to getting pushed around by a small country about an area which every grade school history book features with an American flag, a snapshot of Teddy Roosevelt, and an image of gallant engineers overcoming the mosquito." Scammon said Panama could be a winning issue for Republicans.[15]

Johnson handled the issue shrewdly from the point of view of his personal political interests. He opened discussions with President Chiari but also brandished the old Eisenhower threat of a sea-level canal in Nicaragua or elsewhere outside Panama. Then he deliberately slowed the pace until after his election. On December 18, 1964, Johnson said there should be an "entirely new treaty." But a secret National Security Action Memorandum declared that no joint United States–Panamanian management of the canal could take effect until a new sea-level canal was open.[16] This proviso could delay a settlement indefinitely and, as Johnson's negotiators told him, lead to another round of violence in Panama. Johnson agreed to waive the requirement of a new canal before an agreement was made and in September 1965 announced that the United States and Panama had agreed to abrogate the 1903 treaty, acknowledge Panama's sovereignty over the Canal Zone, and share responsibility for operating the canal. "In about fifteen minutes, President Johnson had turned history around. The old game was over," wrote an American journalist/diplomat deeply involved in Panamanian negotiations.[17]

But the new game dragged on and on—in large part because of the American military's extreme reluctance to give up exclusive control of the canal. Not until June 1967 were three treaties ready for signature. One provided for joint administration of the canal until 1999, a second gave the United States the right to dig a new sea-level canal, and the third gave the United States the right to defend the canals for one hundred years. But opposition to the treaties was too great in both Panama and the United States for approval. Johnson—with time and attention dominated by Vietnam—abandoned them, as did President Marco Robles of Panama. But the treaties did make new arrangements thinkable.

In 1968 Arnulfo Arias, grand old man of Panamanian politics, won the presidential election for the third time. He was inaugurated on October 1 and overthrown eleven days later in a coup led by Colonel Omar Torrijos. A month later Richard Nixon was elected President of the United States. He and Henry Kissinger were deeply involved in dramatic events on the world stage which would lead to the President's trip to China, the brief period of détente with the Soviet Union, and the end of American military involvement in Vietnam. Even in the context of Latin American policies, Panama was not a high priority. Nixon, more sensitive to the American right than to Panama, withdrew some of what Johnson had conceded and the negotiations collapsed. Torrijos warned that Panama might have to take with violence what could not be gained by diplomacy. But instead of inciting violence, Torrijos decided "to make the problem international."

It happened that the African members of the United Nations had persuaded the Security Council to hold one meeting in Addis Ababa, Ethiopia, to discuss colonialism and racism. Aquilino Boyd, the Panamanian ambassador to the UN, delivered a spectacular speech tying colonial domination of Africa in the past to American domination of Panama in the present. Next Panama succeeded in getting the Security Council, over American objections, to hold a six-day meeting in Panama City in March 1973 to discuss "problems of colonialism and dangers to peace in Latin America"—which meant, of course, the Panama Canal. Torrijos grabbed the world attention he sought, but touched the raw nerve of Monroeism by bringing the United Nations into what the United States considered almost a domestic problem. Panama had done the intolerable by invoking outside interference in an issue of purely hemispheric concern. The enthusiastic support of Panama in the Security Council discussions from the Soviet Union, Cuba, and Third World states drove home the point and increased American indignation. The one specific task of the Panama meetings was to vote on a resolution concerning the canal. Negotiations for wording acceptable to the United States failed, as Torrijos intended. The resolution was highly favorable to Panama and critical of the United States. President Nixon ordered a veto, only the third by the United States in the history of the Security Council. Britain abstained. The vote was 13–1–1.[18] No longer, as had been the case during the Guatemalan affair of 1954, could the United States exclude the United Nations from hemispheric affairs.

The Nixon Administration was now convinced of the need to

be serious about reaching a settlement, and in February 1974 Secretary of State Henry Kissinger and Panama's Foreign Minister, Juan Tack, initialed an eight-point framework agreement which met in principle but not detail Panama's demand for acquiring sovereign control of the canal. But the prospect of relinquishing the canal stirred powerful congressional opposition. One congressman called "our sovereignty over the Canal Zone as legitimate as our owning New York City," and won House approval of an amendment denying funds to the State Department for the purpose of negotiating the "surrender" of the canal.[19] Meanwhile, Nixon had resigned the presidency over the Watergate coverup and Gerald Ford was President. As the 1976 election approached, Ford was challenged by Ronald Reagan for the Republican nomination. With Reagan making opposition to concessions on the canal a central part of his campaign (the canal is "ours and we intend to keep it"), Ford put the negotiations into icy stalemate. Ford won the nomination, but lost the election to Jimmy Carter.

Between the election and the inauguration, the Commission on United States–Latin American Relations (Linowitz Commission) released a second report highlighting the urgent need to resolve the Panama issue quickly before disaster struck. Carter agreed and made the negotiation and ratification of a settlement with Panama the first priority and touchstone of Latin American policy. Sol Linowitz agreed to serve as co-negotiator with veteran diplomat Ellsworth Bunker. By August 1977 they had agreed with the Panamanians on two treaties. The first provided for shared responsibility in operating the canal, but with an ever larger Panamanian role, through 1999. The second gave the United States the right to protect the security of the canal after that year.

By thus shucking off a relic of an unhappy, imperial past, Carter believed the United States would regain some of the moral purity lost in the era of Vietnam and dubious covert action by the CIA. Peaceful concessions would prevent violence and bloodshed and keep the canal from being sabotaged. And, the President hoped, all of Latin America would take notice and look warmly on the

United States for the first time in generations. But in his determination to push forward where his predecessors had pulled back,
Carter was attacking a symbol—American ownership of the
canal—as filled with emotion as the Monroe Doctrine, to which
it was so closely related.

When the treaties were presented to the Senate, there followed
one of the most intense legislative-executive battles over foreign
policy of the century. President Carter ordered that his administration spare no effort to win. Public opinion never was persuaded
that relinquishing the canal was in the American interest, but the
Senate by the narrowest of margins supported the President and
the treaties.[20] For Ronald Reagan opposition to the treaties and to
the weakness he said they symbolized became a road to the 1980
Republican nomination and the White House. His familiar refrain,
repeated in many a speech, was "When it comes to the Canal, we
built it, we paid for it, it's ours, and we should tell Torrijos and
company that we're going to keep it."[21]

The Senate vote of approval on the two treaties, with two votes
to spare, came in March and April 1978—a victory for good sense
in international relations but a concrete step toward writing the
obituary of a principle intimately tied to the modern Monroe
Doctrine. But good sense was a political disaster for President
Carter and the senators who supported him. Public opinion, as
judged by polls, had never supported the treaties. And in the 1980
elections half the Democratic senators who had voted for the treaty
and who were up for election lost, plus "one President," as Carter
himself noted with bitter humor.[22]

Sol Linowitz and other advisers who advocated a new start in
Latin America urged that the Carter Administration work for the
re-establishment of normal ties with Cuba. It seemed anomalous
to keep on isolating Cuba even as Soviet-American relations were
moving from "Cold War to accommodation." The Linowitz
Commission recommended that the United States take the initiative: "While emphasizing that progress toward improved rela-

tions requires positive action on both sides, the Commission urges that the United States act now to end the trade embargo."²³ The effort began well. Cuban and American delegations met in New York in March 1977—specifically to deal with fishing rights and maritime boundaries—and resumed in Havana in April. And on September 1 the two governments opened "interest sections" in their former embassy buildings in Washington and Havana respectively. Technically American diplomats in Havana were attached to the Swiss embassy; Cuban diplomats in Washington were attached to the Czech embassy. This was a device for having diplomatic relations—and pretending you didn't.²⁴

This promising start soon tripped over several obstacles. National Security Adviser Brzezinski was obsessed with a vision of Soviet domination of Africa, aided by Cuban troops in Angola and Ethiopia. In November 1977 he publicly said that the recent steady Cuban military buildup in Africa made normalization "impossible." Brzezinski's facts were wrong. There had been no buildup. But Brzezinski saw what he wanted to see, and the Cuban participation in defending Ethiopia against Somali attack in 1978 confirmed him in his views. Castro's pride, Cuba's military involvement in Africa, and above all strident anti-Castro voices and votes in the United States prevented fundamental change. Instead, the Cuban problem led to one of the Carter Administration's worst embarrassments, brought the Monroe Doctrine back to the front page of *The New York Times*, and ended the administration's hope of reducing the doctrine to a mere historical memory.

The specific circumstance was the apparent discovery and public revelation of a Soviet "combat brigade" in Cuba—in apparent violation of the Kennedy-Khrushchev understandings of 1962. Suddenly, in September 1979, the missile crisis was being replayed—in miniature and as farce. In fact, there were no Soviet combat forces in Cuba, only the training group present since the early 1960s. The contrary American perception resulted from National Security Adviser Brzezinski's determination to find evidence of Soviet hostile intent, defective and misinterpreted intelligence

data, and the effort of two senators—Richard B. Stone of Florida
and Frank Church of Idaho—to demonstrate their patriotic vigilance. Both put the administration under pressure to demonstrate
its own patriotic vigilance. The larger context was the Carter
Administration's faltering effort to win Senate approval of the
SALT II nuclear arms control treaty with the Soviet Union.[25]

Senator Stone, with a large Cuban-American constituency, was
required, along with every Florida politician, to demonstrate his
anti-Castro credentials. In return for supporting the Panama Canal
treaties in 1978, he had secured a letter from President Carter
affirming that "it has been and will continue to be the policy of
the United States to oppose any efforts, direct or indirect, by the
Soviet Union to establish military bases in the Western Hemisphere." The intelligence report on the "combat brigade" pointed,
or so it seemed, to precisely such a base. Senator Church's role
was particularly discomforting. He was in a losing campaign for
re-election and eager to find any device to overcome an image of
liberal naïveté about the Soviet Union. Therefore, the moment he
was told confidentially in his capacity as chairman of the Foreign
Relations Committee of the intelligence report, he called a press
conference and made his own alarmist announcement.

Secretary of State Cyrus Vance scrambled to protect the administration. A State Department team reviewed the applicability of
the Monroe Doctrine, the Rio treaty, and the OAS Charter—but
decided against citing the doctrine as such. The team did not really
see the troops, numbering about 3,000, as a threat in themselves.
The threat was to Senate approval of the SALT treaty. Vance
decided it was necessary to declare the presence of the troops a
serious matter and say that the status quo was "unacceptable . . .
counter to long-held policies." That was the closest he came to
the Monroe Doctrine, invoking a principle but not pronouncing
the name. National Security Adviser Brzezinski added his view:
"Cuba is an active surrogate for foreign policy which is not shaped
by itself, and is paid for by economic and military support on a
scale that underlines Cuba's status as a dependent client of the

Soviet Union."[26] So much for any hope of normalization of Cuban-American relations.

Congress was less hesitant about saying the words "Monroe Doctrine." In the midst of the furor, on September 11, the House of Representatives was debating export controls. Representative Peter A. Peyser introduced an amendment authorizing the President to "restrict exports to countries which violate the principles of the Monroe Doctrine." Peyser said, "The Soviets should have to choose between millions of bushels of wheat or the removal of their troops from the Western Hemisphere . . . Let us find out what really is important to the Russians."[27] The amendment passed unanimously, although it was dropped from the final bill by the House-Senate conference—much to Peyser's disappointment.

The noncrisis ended with Soviet assurances that there was no "combat" unit—only the same military advisory and training forces present since the end of the missile crisis. The administration boasted of its heightened state of awareness, announced the establishment of a special Caribbean military command, and turned back to working for the approval of SALT II. Cuban-American relations deteriorated further in the remaining sixteen months of the Carter presidency when Castro permitted an uncontrolled emigration of Cubans, including ordinary criminals, to the United States.

After the crisis over the nonexistent combat brigade, there were no more administration efforts to write the obituary of the Monroe Doctrine. Carter in that regard had been no more successful than Nikita Khrushchev. The doctrine remained available for Ronald Reagan to apply to Nicaragua and more broadly to Central America and the Caribbean. The stage for that effort was further set by events of the Carter years.

Nicaragua, the country which would become an American obsession in the 1980s, drew the attention of the Carter Administration because of the regime's appalling violations of human rights. President Anastasio Somoza, son of the founder of the family dynasty, had carried corruption to a level comparable to that of Batista in Cuba in 1958 or Trujillo in the Dominican Republic in 1961. The human-rights activists in the administration hoped to make Nicaragua a showcase of American success in persuading or coercing reform.

The obstacles were large. President Somoza was a worthy successor to his father, about whom the State Department in 1946 had written: "He has maintained himself in office by repression and trickery. He has constantly tried to convince the Nicaraguan people that we support his continuance in office . . . [and this] had tended to turn many of the better element against us. Somoza runs the country for his own financial benefit and has suppressed freedom of speech, press and assembly."[28]

In 1972 an earthquake destroyed much of Managua, the capital city. Somoza's greed in profiting personally from the relief efforts stimulated broad opposition. Soon a tiny radical group, the Frente Sandinista de Liberación (FSLN), began to win attention and adherents in the manner of Fidel Castro on the eve of Batista's collapse in Cuba. By calling themselves "Sandinistas" the group excited the romantic memories of the left wing in Nicaragua and in the United States. Augusto Sandino was a legendary guerrilla leader who had survived military attack by the United States in the 1920s and had been betrayed and murdered by the first Somoza regime in 1934. The Somoza of the 1970s responded to the Sandinistas with what one American critic called a "war of extermination" with truly horrendous human-rights violations.[29]

But Somoza had powerful allies in Congress and he was adept at getting Washington to ease the pressure by pretending to institute reforms. The result was a jerky sequence of aid denied, aid extended, promises made and broken in Managua, and rising violence. The January 1978 assassination by the Somocistas of Pedro Chamorro, leader of the nonradical opposition and editor/publisher of La Prensa, was a dark moment. Carter officials were divided over how much pressure to put on Somoza, but none described the problem in terms of the principles of the Monroe

Doctrine. They were right. What was happening in Nicaragua had little to do with external influence, Communist or otherwise. But by treating Nicaragua realistically, the Carter Administration would open the way, as we shall see, to a powerful Monroeite attack from Ronald Reagan and his supporters.

Carter rejected the advice of President Carlos Andrés Pérez of Venezuela that Somoza be ousted by some sort of military joint action. Instead, the administration did what predecessors had done in Cuba before the fall of Batista and in the Dominican Republic before the fall of Trujillo: they looked for a moderate middle force to replace Somoza and keep out the radical Sandinistas, who were now receiving military equipment from Venezuela. Sandinista power was dramatically demonstrated in August 1978, when they seized the National Palace in Managua and held hundreds of officials hostage for two days. The Sandinistas released the captives in return for the freeing of political prisoners, a cash ransom, and safe conduct out of the country.

The U.S. search for a moderate alternative was pursued through 1978 and into 1979. National Security Adviser Brzezinski hoped that there were enough Nicaraguans committed to a democratic transition to assure that there was "no repetition of the Castro situation."[30] Brzezinski's deputy David Aaron proposed the creation of a peacekeeping force to maintain stability after Somoza's departure and "keep the situation from being dominated by the Sandinistas."[31] As the fighting in Nicaragua grew ever more fierce, the United States in February 1979 cut off all aid to Somoza. But Carter was soon buffeted with criticism from both right and left. Three of Somoza's friends in Congress—Larry P. MacDonald, John M. Murphy, and George Hansen—urged all-out support for Somoza and raised the specter of Communism. "Cuba was surrounded by water; Nicaragua is not, and a Communist take-over would be a disaster not only to the Nicaraguan people, but to their neighbors in Central America, and indeed to the Western Hemisphere." The trio unwittingly were introducing an amendment to the principles of the Monroe Doctrine: the danger is dire only when foreign influence touches the mainland. Meanwhile, from the liberal side, Congressman Tom Harkin said that the United States by trying to preserve the National Guard was showing "absolutely no commitment to the Nicaraguan people's right of self-determination."[32]

The deteriorating situation convinced the administration in June 1979 that Somoza must go. The appalling nature of his regime was brought home to the American public that month when ABC-TV news correspondent Bill Stewart was murdered by Somoza's soldiers in a scene shown on camera. "Mr. Stewart, 37 years old, was ordered to his knees and then told to lie down before a soldier fired a single shot into his head at close range." So reported *The New York Times*.[33]

Brzezinski persuaded Carter that the United States should propose an OAS peacekeeping force to supervise the transition so as to keep the Sandinistas from power. This idea had zero chance of acceptance by the OAS. But Vance made the pitch at an emergency OAS meeting in Washington on June 21. He called for "an interim government of national reconciliation acceptable to all major elements of the society," an end to arms shipments, a cease-fire, and a peacekeeping force "to assist the interim government in establishing its authority."[34] Vance received not one word of support.

The next day Brzezinski said the United States should be ready to send in troops. The man who had repeatedly deplored thinking in terms of the Monroe Doctrine now spoke of "the major domestic and international implications of a Castroite take-over in Nicaragua." The United States "would be considered . . . incapable of dealing with problems in our own backyard and impotent in the face of Cuban intervention. This will have devastating domestic implications, including for SALT."[35] His voice now carried the accent of Monroeism.

On July 17 Somoza flew to the United States for temporary asylum. The long family regime was over. Last-minute American efforts to install a moderate successor failed. The Sandinistas took over. Although the Carter Administration had never disguised its ideological animosity to the Sandinistas, it did extend emergency economic assistance and tried to avoid a confrontation lest Nicaragua turn completely to Cuba for support.

The United States said from the outset that good relations depended on Nicaragua refraining from interfering in the internal affairs of its neighbors—which meant, specifically, El Salvador. The guiding assumption in Washington was that "a strategy of patience, assistance, and restraint was more likely to produce a friendly, non-Communist regime than a strategy that ignored, threatened, or attacked the new government."[36] Under Secretary of State Warren Christopher told a congressional committee the same thing: "We're realistic. We recognize that some elements of the present Government might prefer a closed, Marxist society. We recognize that Cuba is already providing substantial advice and assistance to Nicaragua. But the situation . . . remains fluid . . . If we walk away we will almost assure what we don't want, a Communist or Cuban regime."[37] That same day in Paraguay, where he would soon be assassinated, Somoza said, "It wasn't unhappiness and poverty in Nicaragua that forced me to leave, but an international Communist plot, blessed by the greatest killer, Carter."[38] Back in the United States, Carter's critics on the right would soon pick up that theme.

The strategy of "assistance and patience" failed for many reasons. The ascendancy of Zbigniew Brzezinski over Cyrus Vance as the most influential foreign policy adviser to Carter led to a more truculent reaction to real or perceived Soviet activity all over the world. The mini-storm over the nonexistent combat brigade in Cuba was part of the new climate. The hard line would be confirmed in December 1979 with the Soviet invasion of Afghanistan and the shelving of the SALT II treaty. The seizure and long imprisonment of American hostages in Tehran had nothing to do with the Soviet Union, but it did drain what little was left of a tolerant attitude toward revolutionary regimes. And even had the administration wanted to launch a major showcase effort in Nicaragua, which it did not, Congress was suspicious and tight-fisted toward the Sandinistas.

Two other obstacles to the strategy of assistance and patience came from the behavior of the Sandinistas themselves. Those who wanted a Marxist regime were more powerful than the State Department had believed. In the months after the fall of Somoza they forced or maneuvered the non-Sandinista leaders out of the governing group. The highly publicized visit to Moscow of a Sandinista delegation did not help. The two governments signed a trade agreement and issued a joint communiqué that echoed Khrushchev's ridicule of the Monroe Doctrine: "They also condemn attempts by some states to dominate others by arbitrarily declaring entire regions of the world to be spheres of their 'vital interests' and by exerting direction, military, political and economic pressure."[39]

A second major obstacle was the assistance provided by the Sandinistas to the leftist insurgency in nearby El Salvador, an issue which needs to be explained with some historical background. The Salvadoran government from 1932, the year thousands of Communist-inspired peasants were massacred when they sought better pay and working conditions, until the 1980s ranked high by the standards of the Kennan Corollary for harsh, effective control of the left. The Communist Party was illegal. The Army was efficient in dealing with discontent. The famous "fourteen families" grew ever wealthier. But U.S. officials repeatedly complained that the Salvador government was complacent about the Communist danger or sluggish when asked to cooperate with the United States. For example, in 1953 Assistant Secretary of State John M. Cabot asked El Salvador to support action against the Arbenz regime in Guatemala. But the Salvadoran Foreign Minister said the United States would have to act alone. Cabot was angry. He thought El Salvador above all countries should be in the lead, but "they did not seem interested in putting a stop to Guatemala's gross attempts at subversion."[40] Cabot was further frustrated when El Salvador failed to supply concrete evidence of Guatemalan Communist infiltration. Cabot was sure the infiltration had occurred. There had been rumors of Spanish Communists with Guatemalan passports. But the Salvadorans were asleep at the switch.[41]

Even the vociferously anti-Communist José María Lemus, President from 1956 to 1960, fell short of American standards. On the eve of his 1959 visit to Washington, the State Department briefing for President Eisenhower warned that the Salvadoran government had "a tendency to underestimate the potential threat inherent in Red influence in university and labor circles." Eisenhower raised the issue with Lemus.[42] Lemus seems to have listened, because in 1960 he discovered a "Communist plot" and sent soldiers into the university, where they raped women and killed a librarian. Moderate officers feared a civil war and overthrew Lemus in October. The CIA saw the sinister hand of Communism and the United States withheld recognition.[43] The comments of the British ambassador, Geoffrey Kirk, were accurate. The U.S. embassy, he said, "regard everyone left-of-centre as a communist or at least a potentially dangerous fellow-traveller, and feel that the only chance of preventing a 'Cuban situation' developing in El Salvador is for the right to regain power, if necessary by a military coup."[44] The extreme right did what the United States wanted and pushed out the younger officers in late January 1961. Washington was happy and extended recognition.

The Kennedy and Johnson Administrations decided to make El Salvador a showcase for the Alliance for Progress, and supplied more economic aid to the country than to any other in Central America—but wealth remained badly distributed and a population explosion undercut many of the economic gains. In 1969 El Salvador won the brief "soccer war" against Honduras, but afterward Honduras expelled many thousands of Salvadoran peasants. Their return added to social and economic pressures in El Salvador. Rising opposition to the military and wealthy families was met with harsh repression. By 1977 the country was close to civil war.

The inauguration of Jimmy Carter in Washington coincided with the normal, i.e., fraudulent, election of General Carlos Humberto Romero as President of El Salvador. The Carter Administration gave Romero its standard lecture on the primacy of human rights, but at the same time maintained aid. Assistant Secretary of State Terence Todman, no enthusiast for the human-rights crusade, further reduced American influence by acknowledging El Salvador's need to combat "terrorism."[45] For General Romero all opposition was terrorism. In November 1977 Romero declared a Law of Defense and Guarantee of Public Order, which effectively ended all protections of individual rights—very much the kind of legislation the United States had been urging on various regimes in the spirit of the Kennan Corollary for years. Romero proceeded with ever-bloodier repression. Institutionalized violence became a way of life.

In October 1979 some young officers overthrew Romero and promised a more liberal regime with civilian participation. In early 1980 José Napoleón Duarte, head of the Christian Democratic Party, joined the junta but had no power. American officials rejoiced and thought that the middle way—so elusive in the past in Cuba, the Dominican Republic, and Nicaragua—was now truly opening. They were wrong. Brutal repression was still in the saddle as "death squads" associated with the Army and the far right operated ever more brazenly.

In March 1980 a death squad murdered Catholic Archbishop Oscar Romero (no relation to the general) while he was saying Mass. The month before, the archbishop had sent a personal appeal to Carter to suspend aid to the Salvadoran military. His views were dismissed as "naïve" by the National Security Council staff's Latin Americanist. After the murder of the archbishop, conditions grew bloodier by the month. Mass killings drove more and more Salvadorans into the opposition. More opposition led to more killings—including the much publicized murder of four American nuns in December 1980 and two American agricultural experts in January.

From the moment of Somoza's overthrow, the United States had warned the Sandinistas against supplying arms to the insurgents in El Salvador. The Sandinistas said they had no such intention, but American officials and many in Congress remained deeply suspicious.[46] In November 1980, however, the Sandinistas decided to heed the plea of the Salvadoran guerrillas and sent some arms, most of which came from Cuba. U.S. intelligence had conclusive evidence of the arms flow. In response, Carter at the end of 1980 authorized the CIA to provide political assistance to the anti-Sandinista opposition, the first seed of what would grow under Reagan into the contra war.[47] The administration also resumed arms deliveries to El Salvador, notwithstanding the murder of the nuns. So much for the primacy of human rights.

CHAPTER 8

A TALE OF THREE
DOCTRINES: REAGAN, BREZHNEV,
AND MONROE

R onald Reagan rode to victory in the 1980 presidential race
against Jimmy Carter on a prancing white horse of American patriotism. In his memoirs Reagan described himself
as the spiritual heir of James Monroe in opposing "conspiracies
and machinations by distant powers in the western hemisphere."
He noted that "the Soviet Union had violated the Monroe Doctrine
and gotten away with it twice, first in Cuba, then in Nicaragua."
He believed in a great threat in the hemisphere and was fond of
quoting an alleged remark of Lenin's: "Once we have Latin America, we won't have to take the United States, the last bastion of
capitalism, because it will fall into our outstretched hands like
overripe fruit."[1]

The keepers of the sacred flame of Monroe were delighted.
William F. Buckley, Jr., conservative commentator and longtime
leader of the right, had in 1962 been co-founder of a Committee
for the Monroe Doctrine—in his disgust with Kennedy's failure
to exclude the Soviets from Cuba.[2] But the committee had slight
influence, and the doctrine, said Buckley, had become "a fugitive
term, used only with some embarrassment by historians required
to teach atavistic United States diplomacy." But here was Ronald
Reagan, whose "re-baptism of the Monroe Doctrine is nothing
less than a spiritual experience." Buckley offered some advice: "By
reaffirming the Monroe Doctrine, President Reagan is bound to

repudiate, or—a better word—announce the expiration of, any commitments respecting Cuba entered into by President Kennedy."[3]

Although Reagan saw himself as heir to James Monroe, he and his administration departed from the original character of the doctrine in a significant respect. Monroe in 1823 invoked the obligations of "candor" for the American government in contrast to the secrecy, intrigue, hypocrisy, and lying of European monarchies. For 125 years candor remained at the heart of the Monroe Doctrine and its applications. Sometimes there was partisan political disagreement over how the doctrine was used. Latin American nations generally resented, criticized, or opposed what the United States did in the doctrine's name. But neither Americans nor foreigners were misled.

John Foster Dulles in 1954 undermined truthfulness as a vital element of the Monroe Doctrine when he and his brother engineered the overthrow of the Arbenz regime in Guatemala and lied about it. The Reagan Administration showed equal contempt for truth, but was less successful in concealing its hand. It thereby lost another traditional element of the Monroe Doctrine: public trust.

While seeking the presidency, Reagan had denounced Carter's abandonment of American permanent control over the Panama Canal and failure to sustain a friendly government in Nicaragua against attack by Communist tools of Cuba and the Soviet Union. He so admired Jeane Kirkpatrick's attack on Carter, in the article "Dictatorships and Double Standards," that he nominated her as ambassador to the United Nations. The argument of this famous essay would play an important role in Reagan policies toward Latin America. The gist was that there is a profound difference between autocratic regimes in traditional societies and modern totalitarian dictatorships. The first are often vehicles for the ambitions of an individual such as Anastasio Somoza in Nicaragua or the Shah of Iran. Autocratic dictatorships come and go. Their respect for human rights may offend American moralists, but they

employ repression for specific purposes and not out of philo-
sophical conviction. Totalitarian regimes, including obviously
Communist ones, employ repression and terror because it is their
very essence. They are not limited by the life of an individual or
a dynasty but are dedicated to ideological expansion and have
no compunctions about the means. Worst of all, they are
permanent—unless overthrown with outside assistance. "Although there is no instance of a revolutionary 'socialist' or Communist society being democratized, right-wing autocracies do
sometimes evolve into democracies—given time, propitious economic, social, and political circumstances, talented leaders, and a
strong indigenous demand for representative government."

Kirkpatrick's view was that contemporary authoritarian regimes
are almost always anti-Communist and friendly to the United
States—again Somoza and the Shah as examples. The great flaw
in Carter's use of human rights as a guiding principle, Kirkpatrick
argued, was that he did not distinguish between the two types of
dictatorship. Carter did criticize both kinds, but he used power
only against authoritarian regimes—and brought them down. The
result was not democracy but the establishment of totalitarian
regimes implacably hostile to the United States—a Communist
one in Nicaragua and an Islamic fundamentalist one in Iran. Furthermore, the Carter Administration's "crowning achievement has
been to lay the groundwork for a transfer of the Panama Canal
to a swaggering Latin dictator of Castroite bent."[4] The lesson—
which Kirkpatrick helped apply during the Reagan Administration—was that the United States should support friendly
autocracies.

Kirkpatrick's views were less stark than George Kennan's corollary. At least she affirmed that America's ultimate purpose should
be the encouragement of democracy. But with Latin American
and other "traditional" societies this meant at most the use of
gentle persuasion and a recognition that democratic institutions
could take centuries to develop. Adopting Kirkpatrick's point of
view, the Reagan team extended the hand of friendship to the

military governments of Argentina and Chile, replacing the icy disapproval shown by the Carter Administration and ignoring their brutal violations of human rights.

The Kirkpatrick thesis that totalitarian regimes of the left will never voluntarily evolve toward democracy fed readily into what would soon be hailed as the Reagan Doctrine. The Truman Doctrine had said it should be the policy of the United States to help free people under attack from armed minorities. The Reagan Doctrine said it should be the policy of the United States to assist armed minorities in their attacks on Communist governments. The Reagan Doctrine was descended from John Foster Dulles's concept of "rollback" or "liberation" of people from Communist bondage, rather than being content with cowardly, passive "containment." The only place "liberation" was applied in the Dulles-Eisenhower years was against the Arbenz regime of Guatemala, a Communist regime only in the eyes of Dulles and his circle. Where there were genuine efforts by the people to overcome a Communist regime—in East Germany, Poland, and above all Hungary in 1956—the United States never went beyond rhetoric.

Reagan and his supporters were determined to do better. They warned of a new Communist offensive sweeping out of Cuba, controlling Nicaragua since the collapse of the Somoza regime in 1979, threatening El Salvador, next the remainder of Central America, ultimately the United States itself. President Reagan himself in March 1983 declared: "It isn't nutmeg that's at stake in the Caribbean and Central America. It is the U.S. National Security." The Soviets and their proxies are striking "at the heart of the Western Hemisphere," threatening us directly but also attempting "to destroy our capacity to resupply Western Europe in case of an emergency. They want to tie down our attention and forces on our own southern border and so limit our capacity to act in more distant places, such as Europe, the Persian Gulf, the Indian Ocean, the Sea of Japan."[5] Here was what could be called the "Reagan Corollary" to the Monroe Doctrine. The original doctrine made exclusion of foreign political-military influence a goal in itself. Behind the defensive shield the American continents could enjoy peace and safety in isolation. The Reagan Corollary set that concept on its head by declaring that the capacity of the United States to be militarily involved all over the world was paramount. Therefore, exclusion of alien force from the hemisphere was necessary to prevent American power from being tied down close to home. Behind the President's alarmist hyperbole was a specific goal: to overthrow the Sandinista government in Nicaragua by paying, training, equipping, and directing opposition military forces known as "contras" (for counterrevolutionaries). Officially the Reagan Administration said its goals were to end Sandinista support for the armed opposition in El Salvador and to work for a restoration of political pluralism in Nicaragua, but not to overthrow the Nicaraguan government. The goal of the Reagan Doctrine was to create or support armed opposition to Communist regimes all over the world—in Afghanistan, Angola, Cambodia, and above all in Nicaragua. President Reagan, before the American Legion in February 1983, declared that the United States must abandon a policy of merely reacting to "the offensive actions of those hostile to freedom and democracy" and go on the offensive itself—above all in Central America. "The spectre of Marxist-Leninist controlled governments in Central America with ideological and political loyalities to Cuba and the Soviet Union poses a direct challenge to which we must respond."[6] The fullest public elaboration was delivered by Secretary of State George P. Shultz two years later. The United States, he said, must support "popular insurgencies against communist domination" and "where dictatorships use brute power to oppress their own people and threaten their neighbors, the forces of freedom cannot place their trust in declarations alone . . . For many years we saw our adversaries act without restraint to back insurgencies around the world to spread communist dictatorships . . . any victory of communism was held to be irreversible. This was the infamous Brezhnev doctrine, first proclaimed at the time of the invasion of Czechoslovakia in 1968."[7]

The Brezhnev Doctrine, so oppressive to would-be dissidents within the Communist world, was magnificently useful for American propaganda—and the Reagan Administration made the best of it, ignoring its unfortunate symmetry with the unvarnished version of the Monroe Doctrine. Just as the principles of Monroeism were based on an American assumption of hegemony in the hemisphere and limited sovereignty for the other republics, the Brezhnev Doctrine declared that the preservation of "socialism" had priority over an individual country's sovereign right to chose an alternative.

The roots of the Brezhnev Doctrine go back to the Bolshevik revolution and more recently to the 1956 Soviet military intervention in Hungary, before being explicitly articulated to justify the intervention in Czechoslovakia in August 1968. There, after the liberal reforms of the "Prague spring" had exceeded the Kremlin's tolerance, Secretary General Leonid Brezhnev sent Soviet troops into Czechoslovakia to crush the reforms. But just as the United States in 1965 had covered the intervention in the Dominican Republic with the veneer of OAS resolutions and several OAS governments had contributed troops, so in Czechoslovakia the intervention was sanctioned by the Warsaw Pact. Soviet troops were joined by token contingents from Poland, East Germany, Hungary, and Bulgaria. Soviet Foreign Minister Andrei Gromyko told the United Nations that the intervention was fully congruent with Article 51 of the charter, providing for collective self-defense against aggression[8]—ironically the very article whose inclusion in the charter had satisfied Senator Arthur Vandenberg's determination in 1945 at San Francisco to protect the principles of the Monroe Doctrine from UN obstruction. But that article and the principles it represented had dismayed Leo Pasvolsky and his fellow American universalists. They had feared precisely the sort of use to which the Soviet Union applied it in 1968.

A full explication of the Soviet doctrine came in Brezhnev's November 1968 speech in Poland. While affirming the devotion of the Soviet Union to the "sovereignty and autonomy of socialist countries"—shades of Theodore Roosevelt's preamble to the Roosevelt Corollary—Brezhnev then declared that a "deviation" threatening socialism in one country was the "concern of all socialist countries." Then the heart: "It is quite clear that an action such as military assistance to a fraternal country to end a threat to the socialist system is an extraordinary measure, dictated by necessity; it can be called forth only by the overt actions of enemies of socialism within the country and beyond its boundaries, actions that create a threat to the common interests of the socialist camp."[9]

In the 1930s the Japanese had explicitly claimed a "Monroe Doctrine" for themselves, simultaneously recognizing an American sphere of influence in the Western Hemisphere and infuriating Americans by the comparison. Soviets in the Brezhnev era did not draw the comparison. Khrushchev had declared the Monroe Doctrine dead and Brezhnev certainly was not going to revive it. This lack of comparison worked to Reagan's advantage in the war of words. For Reagan, the Monroe Doctrine was based on freedom; the Brezhnev Doctrine represented oppression by the evil empire. And the Reagan Doctrine represented an active commitment to liberate those held captive under the Brezhnev Doctrine. When the Reagan Doctrine involved supporting anti-Communist insurgents in Afghanistan, it had no relation to the Monroe Doctrine. But when the United States acted in the Western Hemisphere, and specifically in Nicaragua, the Reagan Doctrine and the Monroe Doctrine merged into a single attitude and policy.

In 1983 President Reagan, following a suggestion from Senator Henry "Scoop" Jackson, called on former Secretary of State Henry A. Kissinger to chair a "bipartisan commission on Central America" in the expectation that the commission's report would win public support for the administration's policies. The commission was to "study the nature of United States interests in the Central American region and the threats now posed to those interests." The twenty-three members and "senior counselors" of the commission covered the political spectrum from center to right. There were four senators and four representatives, equally divided between Republican and Democratic; a retired Supreme Court Justice; a retired governor of Texas; the president of the AFL–CIO; the mayor of San Antonio; a scattering of leaders from law, business, and universities; and Jeane Kirkpatrick. The majority of the group, like Kissinger, had very slight prior experience with Latin America; however, Harry Shlaudeman, the executive director, was a senior diplomat with Latin American experience. The appointment of the commission was something quite rare in the administration's toolbox for Central America: an open activity honestly seeking public support.

The commission's report, submitted January 10, 1984, had something to please or anger everybody. It extolled the Monroe Doctrine as the idealistic foundation of American policy, while admitting that the doctrine was not without critics. "The Monroe Doctrine has sometimes been challenged by our neighbors to the south—especially in some of its unilateral interpretations. But they have never questioned its central inspiration: the vision of a hemisphere united by a core of common commitment to independence and liberty, insulated from other quarrels, free to work out its own destiny in its own way, yet ready to play as constructive a role in world affairs as its resources might permit." It echoed the Linowitz reports and the Alliance for Progress by taking account of Central America's desperate indigenous social, economic, and political problems, and recommending large-scale American aid for the eradication of poverty and support of democracy. But its major emphasis was on the necessity of barring "the Soviet Union from consolidating either directly or through Cuba a hostile foothold on the American continents in order to advance its strategic purposes."

In Kissingerian prose the concept of the Reagan Corollary was fully laid out. After recalling that it was British seapower which had allowed the United States "to uphold the Monroe Doctrine with minimal effort for more than a century—until the intrusion of communism into Cuba," the report went on:

The ability of the United States to sustain a tolerable balance of power on the global scene at a manageable cost depends on the inherent security of its land borders. This advantage is of crucial importance. It offsets an otherwise serious liability: our distance from Europe, the Middle East, and East Asia . . .

To the extent that a further Marxist-Leninist advance in Central America leading to . . . a further projection of Soviet and Cuban power in the region required us to defend against security threats near our borders, we would face a difficult choice between unpalatable alternatives. We would either have to assume a permanently increased defense burden, or see our capacity to defend distant troublespots reduced, and as a result have to reduce important commitments elsewhere in the world. From the standpoint of the Soviet Union, it would be a major strategic coup to impose on the United States the burden of defending our southern approaches, thereby stripping us of the compensating advantage that offsets the burden of our transoceanic lines of communication.[10]

The "compensating advantage," of course, depended on the fact that the Soviets had to defend land borders on all sides.

Before turning to the climax of the Reagan Administration's efforts to act on the principles of the Monroe Doctrine in Central America, we must look at two island episodes early in the administration, both of which hold an important place in the history of the doctrine: the war between Great Britain and Argentina over the Falklands and the invasion and temporary occupation of Grenada by the United States.

Argentina's armed seizure of the British-held Falkland (Malvinas) Islands in April 1982 raised the issue of the Monroe Doctrine in an ironically embarrassing manner for the United States government. Buenos Aires claimed that British intransigence justified seizing what rightfully belonged to Argentina. In London the government of Prime Minister Margaret Thatcher declared that Argentine aggression would not be tolerated and prepared an expedition to retake the islands.[11] As the crisis escalated toward war between Britain and Argentina, members of the Organization of America States voted in effect that British use of force to retake the islands would violate the principles of the Monroe Doctrine as embodied in the Rio treaty of 1947. Twice the United States abstained when seventeen Latin American governments reaffirmed Argentine sovereignty over the islands, declared British action an unacceptable "intervention of extra-continental . . . armed forces" against a nation of the hemisphere, and asked member states to give Argentina "any assistance they may be capable of providing." What explains this extraordinary reversal of roles, with the United States supporting a European power in war against an American republic and rejecting the applicability of the Monroe Doctrine against the near-solid opinion of Latin American governments that the principles of the doctrine were under serious attack? The answer goes back more than two centuries.

Located in the stormy South Atlantic, two hundred miles east of Tierra del Fuego, the Falkland Islands have been known to mariners since the sixteenth century. They consist of two main islands and dozens of smaller ones totaling 4,700 square miles. The population in 1982 was 1,800, most of whom were engaged in raising sheep. In 1770 Britain and Spain came close to war over possession of the islands. The dispute was not formally settled. In 1774 the British withdrew but did not relinquish a formal claim. Spain took over administration of the islands, and in 1820 Argentina, having won independence, inherited the Spanish title and soon established a small colony.[12] The islands in the meanwhile had attracted numerous vessels of many flags engaged in whaling and hunting seals.

Enter now the United States. In 1831 the Argentine governor of the islands, Louis Vernet, seized three American sealing vessels on the charge of violating an Argentine prohibition against foreign participation in the "fishery"—including sealing. A headstrong U.S. consul in Buenos Aires enlisted Captain Silas Duncan of the United States frigate *Lexington* to punish this alleged outrage. Duncan was a typical specimen of American naval bluster and the bullying style of Jacksonian diplomacy. He sailed to the Falklands, destroyed the insignificant Argentine fortifications, and ousted the garrison. Argentina broke diplomatic relations with the United States, and Great Britain saw its chance. In January 1833 two British warships expelled the last of the Argentinians, and the British flag went up. Settlers followed and in 1840 the islands formally were declared a British crown colony. Powerless Argentina spluttered, and the United States government made no protest against what Dexter Perkins, the premier historian of the early Monroe Doctrine, called a "clear violation."[13] On the contrary, American maritime interests were pleased to have the British arrive, replacing the "piratical" representatives of Argentina. For the rest of the nineteenth century, and until the opening of the Panama Canal in 1914, the islands were a useful refuge and repair station for shipping battered in the great storms of nearby Cape Horn.

After the Second World War the Argentine government of Juan Perón made the return of the islands a high national priority—and sought to enlist the support of the United States in its futile negotiations with Great Britain. For example, the negotiators of the Rio treaty in 1947 agreed that the region covered was bounded on the east by a mid-ocean line from the North to the South Pole. Within the region the parties to the treaty agreed that an armed attack on any American state would be considered an attack on all. The Falklands fell within the region, but was it territory of an American state? Argentina said yes and reaffirmed its view that the British colony was illegal. The United States said nothing in the Rio treaty affected the existing, i.e., British, sovereignty of the islands.[14]

The Argentines were not put off. In 1948, with rumors of war between the Soviet Union and the West in the air following the

Communist coup in Czechoslovakia, Argentine Foreign Minister Juan Atilio Bramuglia tried to play the Russian card with the pro-Perón, and rather gullible American ambassador, James Bruce. In time of war, said Bramuglia, Argentina will be at the side of the United States, but Britain would be unable to defend the islands against the Soviet Union. Therefore, the islands should revert immediately to Argentina for the strategic security of the world. Bramuglia asked for American support. Britain, he said, is in a sad state, run by socialists "contrary to all our principles, dependent for existence on the generosity of the United States." One word from the United States would determine Britain's position on the islands. Bruce told Secretary of State George C. Marshall that the Argentine argument made considerable sense. He recommended that the United States "give them every possible consideration." Marshall found the Argentine approach and Bruce's endorsement appalling. He sent back a terse instruction, tinged with reprimand. He defended Britain as a staunch, strong ally of the United States against all "totalitarian and anti-democratic elements." The United States would do nothing to weaken Anglo-American collaboration. As for the Falklands, the United States supports neither Britain's nor Argentina's claim of sovereignty and wishes only that the dispute be settled by peaceful means.[15] Marshall professed neutrality on the merits of the dispute, but by giving such emphasis to maintaining Anglo-American accord the practical result of his position was to favor British possession. In 1982, when Argentina moved beyond the use of peaceful methods, the American position was the same, and its implications led to support for Britain in war.

Rebuffed by the United States in March 1948, Argentina's next step was to join Guatemala, which had a parallel dispute with London involving British Honduras (subsequently Belize), in rallying support for the principle of decolonization among the governments soon to assemble in Bogotá for the founding conference of the Organization of American States. Latin American governments were enthusiastic. The United States saw the decolonization issue as nothing but an invitation to trouble with France and the Netherlands as well as Great Britain. At Bogotá the United States opposed the resolution and carefully avoided "taking any position that would favor either party to any existing disputes over European possessions."[16] But the resolution asserting "the just aspiration of the American Republics that colonialism and the occupation of American territories by extra-continental countries be brought to an end" passed with only the United States and the Dominican Republic abstaining. The resolution also established a decolonization committee—to which the United States refused to send a representative. For the next quarter century the decolonization issue occasionally produced minor ripples, but never serious enough to come to the attention of high officials in Washington. The Latin Americans were left with their decolonizing rhetoric and European nations were free to keep their colonies or grant independence without interference from the United States. By 1982 the only European territories in the region of concern to the Latin American republics were some French and Dutch islands, French Guiana, and the Falklands. Even in 1823 the United States had not claimed that the Monroe Doctrine called for the end of existing colonies. There was no chance that the United States would apply a new, irritating principle to its European allies in the Cold War.

Given the consistent American refusal to champion decolonization in the Western Hemisphere and refusal to side with Argentina on the Falklands dispute, it might seem odd that the Argentine junta of 1982 launched an attack whose ultimate success depended at least on American impartiality. The explanation lies in miscalculation flowing from the way the Reagan Administration had embraced the authoritarian Argentine junta, abandoning the ostracism and criticism employed by the Carter Administration as a protest against the junta's violations of human rights, and enlisting Argentine assistance in the covert war against the Sandinistas in Nicaragua. Throughout 1981 high officials of both governments visited each other's capital and exchanged the usual banalities about unity in the worldwide fight against international Communism. And more important, the two governments became clandestine collaborators in the effort to overthrow the Sandinista government of Nicaragua by training and equipping the contras. There was a U.S.–Honduran–Argentine partnership in the arrangement. Honduras provided the territorial base, Argentina the military training of the contras, and the United States the money and overall guidance. The warmest American supporter of the junta and of the anti-Sandinista partnership was UN ambassador Jeane Kirkpatrick, who had gained her appointment on the strength of the famous 1979 article attacking Carter's human-rights policy for undermining right-wing regimes. On the very day of the Argentine attack on the Falklands, Kirkpatrick was guest of honor at a dinner at the Argentine embassy in Washington. Haig's shuttle diplomacy failed and soon Britain and Argentina were at war—the first use of force by a European power against a Latin American state since 1902, when a German gunboat lobbed a few shells against Venezuela. And here was the United States on Europe's side. Where indeed was the Monroe Doctrine?

The Argentine move precipitated an argument between Secretary of State Alexander Haig, whose experience and outlook stressed the primacy of Europe in American foreign policy, and Kirkpatrick over the stance the United States should take. Kirkpatrick and those who advocated sympathetic consideration of Argentina's case never had a chance. The fact that Argentina had been the first to use force, President Reagan's close relationship with British Prime Minister Margaret Thatcher, Britain's importance as a NATO ally, and American public admiration of Britain and hostility toward the Argentine junta all meant a pro-British "neutrality." The die was cast with the first statement from the White House, on April 2, within hours of the Argentine attack, deploring the use of force and calling for an immediate cease-fire and withdrawal of Argentine forces, followed by negotiations. The next day the United Nations Security Council took the same position in Resolution 502.

Between April 8 and 19, Secretary of State Haig set a new mileage record for shuttle diplomacy: Washington–London–Buenos Aires–London–Washington–Buenos Aires–Caracas–Washington. He repeated the old formula that the United States took no position on the disputed issue of sovereignty and said he was acting as friend to both sides. In practice, the demand that Argentine forces withdraw as a precondition for negotiations was unacceptable to Buenos Aires. The Argentine military were confident that their occupation could never be dislodged by Britain, whose forces had to operate at the end of a 8,000-mile supply line. Haig's efforts at peacemaking were futile from start to finish.

With the collapse of Haig's efforts and British naval forces assembling for a counterattack, Argentina went to the Organization of American States, invoking Article 6 of the Rio treaty concerning threatened aggression, and requested a meeting of the Foreign Ministers of the American republics. The OAS Permanent Council granted the request, with the United States abstaining. In 1954 the United States suppressed Guatemala's appeal to the UN Security Council by arguing that the OAS was the appropriate organ for a hemispheric question. In 1962 the United States did the same when Cuba appealed to the Security Council. But now the United States argued that the issue should remain within the UN, under Resolution 502, and that it was most inappropriate to invoke the Rio treaty. The OAS then voted 17–0, with the United States abstaining, that sovereignty over the islands belonged to Argentina. The resolution urged a cease-fire and peaceful negotiations, but not an Argentine withdrawal.[17]

On April 30 the United States abandoned all pretense of impartiality by imposing economic sanctions on Argentina and announcing direct military assistance—short of the participation of American forces—to Britain. The predictable Argentine protest accused the United States of aiding British aggression and played on the theme of betrayal of hemispheric solidarity. "The Argentine people will never understand or forget that at one of the most critical moments in their history, in contrast to the solidarity that they received from all corners of the hemisphere, the United States preferred to take the side of an extra-hemispheric power."[18] On May 1 a British long-range jet bomber attacked the Argentine airfield at Port Stanley, and on May 2 the naval phase of the war began when the British sank the Argentine cruiser *General Belgrano*, cruising far from the Falklands, with heavy loss of life. With a British landing imminent, UN Secretary General Javier Pérez de Cuéllar made an energetic effort to arrange a peaceful solution. He failed. The land phase of the war began on May 21 and concluded with Argentine surrender on June 14 after heavy fighting. During this phase the OAS Foreign Ministers met again and passed a stronger condemnation of Britain, urging member states to assist Argentina (none did). The vote again was 17–0, with four abstentions, including the United States.

American support of Britain in the Falklands dispute ended the covert cooperation with Argentina against the Sandinistas and angered the Honduran government. General Gustavo Álvarez, Argentine-trained head of the Honduran forces, was especially angry. He asked U.S. ambassador John Negroponte how the United States could tolerate a British force on the Malvinas. "Where is the Monroe Doctrine? Look at the geography. Is South America part of Europe? Who is the next one you betray? Honduras? El Salvador? Guatemala? Costa Rica?"

Negroponte said the U.S. position was based on the fact that Argentina had been the first to use force.

Álvarez replied: "One hundred years ago, England used force to take the island. Argentina has been claiming sovereignty for 130 years."[19]

The war over the Falklands had many consequences. Argentine resentment of the United States, in the short term, was deep. As Mario del Carril, Argentine journalist, told a congressional hearing in July: "In 1982, as in 1831, the United States in continuous violation of its own Monroe Doctrine has once again helped Great Britain retake the Malvinas. Washington has always refused to honor the Argentine claim to the islands, and it has avoided taking sides on the legal issues of sovereignty. But materially the U.S. Government has helped Great Britain both in the 19th century and today." Robert Leiken, an American scholar who shared the outlook of Ambassador Kirkpatrick, told the same hearing that from the Latin American perspective U.S. aid to Britain was a renunciation not only of treaty obligations under the Rio Pact but "a betrayal of the spirit of American unity . . . And the anger focused on and felt toward the United States, as a hemispheric country, as the promoter of the Monroe Doctrine . . . was infinitely greater than the feelings of antagonism toward England." Leiken urged the United States to "dissociate itself from British plans" to rebuild the islands. "The United States should support its allies when they are victims of aggression, but should not also support their colonial ambitions." Leiken foresaw "two, three, many Falklands" in the future unless disputes over decolonization were quickly resolved.[20] But members of Congress and editorial writers, who could be counted on to invoke the Monroe Doctrine against Communism, now praised Britain's triumph over naked aggression. The most important consequence of the Falklands War was the humiliation and collapse of the military government of Argentina and its replacement in 1983 by a democratically elected government respectful of human rights. The new government held fast to the ancient goal of regaining the islands, and within a few years Britain and Argentina resumed a dialogue. Anti-American feeling in Argentina, as related to the Falklands, subsided. In Britain Prime Minister Thatcher won the popularity which enabled her to remain in office another decade, the longest time in office of any British Prime Minister in the twentieth century.

The policy followed during the war by the Reagan Administration was sound from the point of view of American national interest and principles of international law, but it placed an embarrassing strain on the Monroe Doctrine. By openly supporting a European power in a war against an American republic for the only time in American history, by denying the applicability of the Rio treaty, by reversing the long practice of excluding the UN

Security Council from hemispheric issues, by saying that the Organization of American States was not the appropriate forum, the United States abandoned many of the specific policies which it had been using to sustain the Monroe Doctrine since 1945. These actions, however, were entirely consistent with the larger principle that since 1945 the Monroe Doctrine had meaning only as it applied to the confrontation with the Soviet Union and the dread specter of "international Communism."

One year after the British regained possession of the Falkland Islands, with significant American assistance, the Reagan Administration used military force to overthrow and briefly occupy the Caribbean micro-state of Grenada—population 100,000, size about that of Martha's Vineyard. "I probably never felt better during my presidency than I did that day," Reagan wrote.[21] For Secretary of State Shultz American success in Grenada "was a shot heard round the world . . . Some Western democracies were again ready to use the military strength they had harbored and built up over the years in defense of their principles and interests."[22]

For Reagan, Shultz, and all supporters of the administration, the Grenada operation met the needs of the three doctrines: the Brezhnev Doctrine was defeated with the eradication of a Communist state, the Reagan Doctrine was applied with exemplary speed and effectiveness, and the Monroe Doctrine was vindicated. Furthermore, the United States would not have to allocate scarce defense resources to counter a new Soviet-Cuban base in Grenada. The Reagan Corollary had been upheld.

Located at the southern end of the island chain curving a thousand miles from Puerto Rico to Venezuela on the South American continent, Grenada received full independence from Great Britain in 1974—but the new country lacked prosperity and security for human rights. The problem was Eric Gairy, a bizarre and corrupt politician who dominated Grenada both before and after independence. While repressing the opposition with beatings, imprisonment, and an occasional killing, Gairy built a private fortune and behaved generally in a manner which reminded one observer of "Papa Doc" Duvalier in Haiti. He proclaimed his anti-Communism, caused no trouble for the United States, and admired the Pinochet regime in Chile. Gairy was also a nut. He believed in UFOs, witchcraft, and his own divinity. He made a habit of regularly addressing the UN General Assembly on the dangers of creatures from outer space.

In March 1979, while Gairy was in New York, the opposition New Jewel Movement (NJM) seized power in a coup. A crowd sang in celebration, "Freedom come, Gairy go, Gairy gone with UFO." The NJM Prime Minister was Maurice Bishop, a populist nationalist and man of the left. The deputy prime minister was Bernard Coard, self-proclaimed Marxist. Bishop immediately established diplomatic relations with Cuba and welcomed assistance from Fidel Castro. "A Cuban octopus is loose in the Caribbean," said one alarmed National Security Council staff member in Washington.[23] U.S. Ambassador Frank Ortiz traveled to Grenada (his base was in Barbados and rarely did an American official appear in Grenada) and met Bishop on April 10. Ortiz offered good relations and some economic aid—but Bishop seized on what he understandably read as a threat. Frank Ortiz warned that military ties between Grenada and Cuba would complicate relations with the United States. "No one," Bishop said in a speech a few days later, "no matter how mighty and powerful they are, will be permitted to dictate to the government and people of Grenada who we can have friendly relations with and what kind of relations we must have with other countries. We are not in anybody's back yard."[24]

The Carter Administration applied a political and economic freeze—withholding aid, rejecting overtures for better relations, refusing to receive Bishop's choice for ambassador to Washington, and engaging in considerable public denunciation. Wayne Smith, head of the U.S. "interests" office in Havana, did meet informally with the Grenadian ambassador to Cuba, but his conversations were first discouraged by Washington and later positively forbidden by the Reagan Administration.[25] As an American official later wrote, such behavior made the United States look like a bully and Bishop like a hero to himself and the people of Grenada.[26] Relations deteriorated in 1980. Grenada voted against a United Nations General Assembly resolution condemning Soviet aggression in Afghanistan. The State Department noted the presence in Grenada of Cuban military advisers and construction workers building an ominously large airport and suggested to Congress that the Soviets were behind the Cuban effort.[27]

Mutual accusations increased with the coming of the Reagan Administration. Bishop repeatedly charged that the United States was preparing to invade his country. In mid-1982 he went to Moscow and signed an economic-aid agreement with the U.S.S.R. President Reagan on a visit to Barbados in April 1982 declared that Grenada had joined the Soviet Union, Cuba, and Nicaragua in promoting international Communism throughout the Caribbean region. "That country," he said, "bears the Soviet and Cuban trademark, which means that it will attempt to spread the virus among its neighbors."[28] His use of the infectious-disease metaphor was in the long, cliché-ridden tradition of anti-Communism and the Monroe Doctrine.

The airport under construction at Point Salines attracted ever more alarmist comment from Washington. Although the long runways were indispensable for the development of tourist trade, the United States saw only a military threat. This facility, said the State Department, "adds a new and serious dimension to our security concerns. It is difficult, if not impossible, to identify any economic justification for the enormous investment being undertaken in the construction of this airfield."[29] And in March 1983, in the same speech announcing the Strategic Defense Initiative, Reagan imitated Adlai Stevenson displaying photographs of the Soviet missile sites in Cuba by showing aerial photographs of the Point Salines field. "Grenada doesn't even have an air force. Who is it intended for?" The answer, said Reagan, was that the airfield was part of a global Soviet military effort. It could threaten "our international commerce and military lines of communication" in the region through which "more than half of all American oil imports now pass."[30]

In the midst of the war of nerves against Grenada, American attention was suddenly caught by events in Suriname, formerly Dutch Guiana. What the United States failed to do in relation to Suriname had a direct impact on the decision to intervene the following year in Grenada. Suriname, with an extraordinarily mixed population of 400,000, is tucked between Guyana and French Guiana on the north coast of the South American continent. It acquired independence from the Netherlands in 1975 but retained loose ties with the mother country.

This was not the first time the United States government saw a security threat developing in the small jungle-grown countries emerging from colonial status on the northeast shoulder of South America. Suriname's neighbor Guyana, formerly the colony of British Guiana, had three times figured in the history of the Monroe Doctrine. First, of course, when Britain's boundary dispute with Venezuela in 1895 brought forth the Olney dictum that the will of the United States was law in this hemisphere. In 1953, when the British disallowed the election of Cheddi Jagan, a Marxist, and brought in troops, suspended the constitution, and ruled directly until 1957 in order to "prevent communist subversion," the United States supported and praised the British. But several Latin American governments questioned the imposition of military rule in a colony on the road to independence. The United States told the other American republics that "in our view the establishment of a communist bridgehead in British Guiana would be a matter of deep concern." The hemisphere "should regard the measures taken by the British with deep satisfaction."[31]

Eight years later, in 1961, the constitution had been restored and Jagan was running again for election as Prime Minister. Again the United States viewed a Jagan victory with high alarm and accused the British of complacency for the view that Jagan was more interested in economic development than in ideology.[32]

The United States almost certainly provided covert financial assistance to Jagan's opponents. Washington also solicited support from Canada, in the light of the large operations in British Guiana of the Aluminium Company of Canada. The American embassy in Ottawa was instructed to tell the Canadian government that the United States was "seriously concerned at the possible emergence in British Guiana of a Communist or Castro-type regime" and disagreed with the British view that Jagan was "salvageable."[33]

No help in blocking Jagan's election seems to have come from Canada and he was duly elected. There followed a period of rioting and instability—again with a likely CIA role. British troops returned and altered the voting system—which assisted in Jagan's defeat in 1964 elections by Forbes Burnham of the People's National Congress. Burnham enjoyed American support and Washington's fears abated. In 1966 the country became fully independent, with the name Guyana.

Thus, the U.S. government was not entirely unfamiliar with problems of the region when, on December 8, 1982, the unsavory military dictatorship of Lieutenant Colonel Desi Bouterse in Suriname, in power since a 1980 coup, murdered fifteen leaders of the political opposition and intensified a reign of terror over the population. Bouterse was an unstable leftist with ties to Cuba and Bishop in Grenada. The murders alarmed the State Department and the CIA. Secretary Shultz believed Bouterse was "taking Suriname on a forced march toward Cuba-style Communism and that Suriname stood at the edge of becoming the first Communist state on the mainland of South America."[34] The same thing had been said repeatedly about British Guiana under Jagan.

The United States urged the Netherlands to take military action and promised to provide a naval force to block potential Cuban counterintervention. The Dutch said no. The CIA then proposed using a hit squad of Koreans to take out Bouterse. Shultz rejected this "harebrained idea."[35] Next the CIA suggested preparing Surinamese exiles for a Bay of Pigs–type operation. The House and Senate intelligence committees, secretly informed, registered strong objections and said the CIA had failed to provide convincing evidence of a Soviet-Cuban threat.[36] And so nothing was done. Bouterse remained. Reagan and Shultz were angry and frustrated. A year later they would remember Suriname.

The American intervention in Grenada need be only briefly outlined. On October 12, 1983, Maurice Bishop was imprisoned during a coup led by his ultra-leftist deputy Bernard Coard. At the National Security Council in Washington the newly appointed Latin American specialist, Constantine Menges, saw a possible civil war in Grenada as a good pretext for organizing a military intervention to sweep away Communism. Menges, a fervent Reaganite who had just moved over from the CIA, was not so affectionately known as "Constant Menace" for his extreme views. He put together a plan for an invasion by the U.S. military together with token representatives from the nearby micro-states of the eastern Caribbean, followed by temporary supervision of the country's transition to democracy. He argued that such action would liberate the people of Grenada, safeguard American citizens, and send a positive signal of general American resolve. But the most pressing reason for action was to forestall the possibility that the Soviets intended to place nuclear weapons in Grenada in retaliation for the imminent deployment of a new generation of American nuclear missiles in Europe. In this way, Menges said, the Soviets could threaten the United States without violating the longstanding agreement not to put offensive weapons in Cuba. For the next several days Menges peddled his plan in the NSC and to friends in the Defense and State Departments. He was told it had little chance of being accepted.[37]

On October 19 a crowd of supporters freed Bishop and four imprisoned cabinet ministers. Coard's troops recaptured the five and shot them, and also killed many in the crowd of civilians. The Coard Revolutionary Military Council then imposed a shoot-on-sight curfew. Menges, according to his own account, took the lead in organizing the American response. The U.S. government, with no representative stationed in Grenada, had only sketchy information—but feared chaos and possible loss of life among over 600 American students at an offshore proprietary medical school in Grenada. By coincidence a naval force carrying Marines to Lebanon had just departed Virginia. It was diverted toward Grenada. At the same time the United States encouraged a request from the Organization of Eastern Caribbean States (OECS), Grenada's neighbors, for assistance.

Reagan made the decision to land forces; they came ashore on October 25 and encountered heavier than expected resistance from the Cuban construction workers and some Grenadian forces. Remembering the lack of action in Suriname, the administration decided not to consult the British government in advance—even though Grenada was a member of the British Commonwealth and had a Governor General who was a representative of the crown. Prime Minister Margaret Thatcher was furious and sent President Reagan a stinging cable.[38] It took three days to bring the fighting to an end. None of the American medical students was hurt. The casualty figures showed eighteen Americans, forty-five Grenadians, and twenty-nine Cubans killed in the fighting. By early November the United States had returned the Cubans, plus all Soviets, East Germans, Bulgarians, North Koreans, and Libyans to their countries. Shortly thereafter the U.S. government published a selection of captured documents on the Bishop regime's contacts within the Communist bloc.[39] A side benefit, carefully noted by Secretary of State Shultz, was that Colonel Bouterse in Suriname immediately broke diplomatic relations with Cuba. He apparently did not want to be next.[40]

In the United Nations Security Council the United States vetoed a resolution deploring its invasion. The vote was 11–1 (the U.S.)—with Great Britain, Togo, and Zaire abstaining.[41] The Monroe Doctrine was alive and well. And the Reagan Administration turned, with a renewed sense of power, to its first priority in the hemisphere: removing the Sandinista government of Nicaragua.

CHAPTER 9

NICARAGUA:
THE SELF-INFLICTED
WOUND

⟶ ᦔ ⟵

The "liberation" of Grenada was the proudest achievement of the Reagan Administration in the Western Hemisphere. It fulfilled both the Monroe Doctrine and its newborn cousin, the Reagan Doctrine, and appeared to dispose of the pretensions of the Brezhnev Doctrine that "socialist" regimes were forever. Many observers in that autumn of 1983 believed that an American invasion of Nicaragua, the most populous Marxist state in the American continents, would follow shortly. The Reagan Administration refrained from direct military action, but pursued a covert effort to overthrow Nicaragua's Sandinista regime. In the process the administration inflicted serious wounds on itself and on the principles of the Monroe Doctrine. The follies of the administration combined with a transformation of Soviet-American relations and a new assertiveness on the part of Latin American governments made the Nicaraguan affair the last chapter in the history of the doctrine. The story, as with all other aspects of the Monroe Doctrine, had many ramifications.

Although Reagan saw himself as heir to James Monroe, he and his administration departed from the original character of the doctrine in one significant respect. Monroe in announcing the original doctrine stressed the obligation of "candor." For Monroe and his generation, candor distinguished the American approach to international affairs from the secrecy, intrigue, hypocrisy, and lying of

European monarchies. Truthfulness was part of the foundation on which the doctrine rested. John Foster Dulles in 1954 undermined that foundation when he and his brother Allen of the CIA engineered the overthrow of the Arbenz regime in Guatemala and lied about it. Lyndon Johnson eroded it further in his dealings with Brazil and the Dominican Republic. Richard Nixon and Henry Kissinger did the same over Chile. But the Reagan Administration washed away the foundation altogether.

Whereas an important influence on Jimmy Carter's approach to Latin America had been the reports of the Commission on United States–Latin American Relations chaired by Sol Linowitz, the ideas of the Reagan Administration came in large part from Jeane Kirkpatrick and from a group of conservatives called the Santa Fe Committee. The 1980 Santa Fe report, *A New Inter-American Policy for the Eighties*, warned that the Cold War had moved to the American continents and was getting hot. Cuba was spreading revolution throughout the Caribbean and Central America, but the Soviet Union was the real source of threat and power. The Linowitz reports called for the United States to attend to conditions in Latin America—the poverty, the unhappy legacy of political repression and violations of human rights, understandable resentment against the United States. The Santa Fe report made the life of the people of Latin America incidental to the Soviet offensive, an offensive aiming for the conquest of Central America, Mexico, and ultimately the United States.[1] The Santa Fe report was preaching to the choir—meaning President Reagan, Director of Central Intelligence William J. Casey, and Secretary of State Alexander M. Haig, Jr.—but it was useful for public argument and as a reservoir of specifics for policy.

Whereas the geographical entry point for the Carter Administration's effort to carry out the recommendations of the Linowitz reports and, in effect, to write the obituary of the Monroe Doctrine had been Panama and the canal, the Reagan Administration's entry point for the doctrine's reassertion was El Salvador. The immediate purpose was to provide all necessary military and economic support to the Salvadoran government for a victory against the guerrilla insurgency of the Farabundo Martí National Liberation Front (FMLN) and its allied groups. That was in the tradition of the Monroe Doctrine and the Kennan Corollary: support for an existing harsh, repressive regime against leftist attack perceived as originating outside the hemisphere. But behind that open purpose was a larger, covert determination to destroy the existing Sandinista regime in nearby Nicaragua by creating and supporting a civil war. The second purpose expressed the Reagan Doctrine: that the United States would seek to overthrow leftist regimes in the Third World. So obsessed did Reagan become with this objective that he permitted policy to be set by people ignorant or contemptuous of the Constitution and law, people without judgment or accountability. Their behavior when fully exposed was so scandalous as to threaten the administration itself.

Administration spokesmen from the outset reasserted the principles of the doctrine with a stridency not heard since the days of John Foster Dulles, perhaps even of Richard Olney and Theodore Roosevelt. An alien threat of international Communism carried by Soviet power and applied through proxies was depicted by the White House and State Department in rhetoric more alarmist, even apocalyptic, than at any time since the brief and very real crisis of 1962 over nuclear missiles in Cuba. Why? The answer lies in the way Reagan and his advisers exploited, exaggerated, and aggravated Soviet-American tension in order to gain domestic political advantage. As Lawrence A. Pezzullo, a Carter appointee as ambassador to Nicaragua, told a journalist after Reagan's election, "This is a new Administration, there are going to be tradeoffs, and you've got to feed your right-wing somewhere . . . That's just the way I tend to think things will go, just feed it to the lions."[2]

Whether President Reagan, Secretary of State Haig, CIA Director William Casey, and a succession of militant national security advisers to the President really believed in the horrendous perils described in their public statements cannot be conclusively determined. Perhaps some believed from the beginning while others dutifully voiced the administration line. The first law of propaganda, however, is that the most vulnerable audience for propaganda is the authors. Another law is that a contrived crisis must always be presented as getting worse; any lessened description of the peril, without an obvious victory, will throw doubt on the whole fabrication.

None of those in the administration who made high policy toward Central America knew very much about the region, nor did they consider such knowledge relevant or necessary. In that sense they were true heirs to the original Monroe Doctrine. Never had policies developed in the doctrine's name been concerned with real Latin American conditions, but only as they were perceived as inviting or blocking extra-hemispheric intervention threatening the United States. Career people in the Department of State who had significant experience and understanding of Latin America were largely ignored; some were replaced by Reaganites. And if the newly appointed strayed from the Reaganite line, they were replaced in turn. Conveniently for the strategy of the administration, violence in El Salvador was intense in the winter of 1980–81. The Salvadoran FMLN launched a "final offensive" in January. The government and its allied death squads in response showed no mercy and little discrimination about whom they killed. Ambassador Robert E. White, appointed by Carter as a symbol of the importance of human rights, was openly critical of the Salvadoran government and had been verbally and physically attacked by the right wing in El Salvador. The administration in Washington fired him ten days after Reagan's inauguration, a clear signal that suppression of the insurgency would not be obstructed by a too nice concern for human rights. The Reagan Administration shifted the blame for the violence to the insurgents, and behind them Nicaragua, Cuba, and ultimately the Soviet Union. We have, said the State Department in a much publicized "white paper" on El Salvador, "definitive evidence of the clandestine military support given by the Soviet Union, Cuba, and their Communist allies to Marxist-Leninist guerrillas fighting to overthrow the established Government of El Salvador." Here is "a textbook case of indirect armed aggression by Communist powers through Cuba." The fact that the weapons available to the Salvadoran insurgents were largely American, and not of Communist origin, was explained as an example of the enemy's cleverness in covering up their involvement. The emphasis on Cuba reflected the views of Secretary of State Haig. His public comments were pithy: "The problem must be dealt with at the source . . . Cuba"; and "We consider Cuban interventionism in this hemisphere on our own doorstep as no longer tolerable."[3] Haig also said that the Soviet Union had a "hit list" in the Western Hemisphere. First was Nicaragua, already taken, followed by El Salvador, Honduras, and Guatemala.[4] This was another aspect of Monroeite thinking: the ascription to a foe (the Soviet Union) of a precisely calculated plan and high determination, where neither existed.

Soviet policy, as Russian scholars and former Soviet officials have persuasively argued, accorded Latin America a low priority, was held back by inertia, and lacked coherence. There was no master plan, no goal even remotely resembling the imaginary bogey of the Reaganites. As Kiva Maidanik, a senior Latin Americanist during the Soviet regime, has written: "Our innate passivity was balanced by the intensity of pressure from the Latin 'machos' . . . fighting for life-and-death issues, for their people. On occasion, our aging leaders and solemn functionaries could not resist youthful Latin enthusiasm, often reminiscent of our own past . . . However, ideology was more important than the economic, political, or military dimensions of our policy."[5]

Haig found no support within the administration for "going to the source" with a military attack or naval and air blockade, whatever he had in mind. To have abandoned the Kennedy-Khrushchev accord over Cuba would have been far too dangerous. The focus of American pressure, therefore, moved to the next link in the perceived chain of "textbook" aggression: Nicaragua. Publicly Washington declared that the only thing sought from Nicaragua was cessation of aid to the guerrillas. State Department officials on the Latin American desk and in the field sincerely accepted that goal and tried to maintain some bargaining power in Managua. When Washington cut off the last amount of Carter-era aid to Nicaragua, Ambassador Pezzullo said the United States was throwing away its bargaining chips. But bargaining was not the objective. CIA Director Casey, advisers within the National Security Council staff, and perhaps President Reagan from the beginning wanted to overthrow the Sandinista regime. Casey himself went to Managua in March 1981 and met with Ambassador Pezzullo and the CIA station chief, Nestor Sánchez, in order to explore what it would take to "knock off" the Sandinistas. Pezzullo, a believer in the limited goal of a negotiated settlement, warned Casey that the Sandinista revolution enjoyed deep popular support; the more it was attacked by the United States, the stronger it would become; the United States would find itself with more than it bargained for should it begin an intervention.[6]

The CIA and the Defense Department moved eagerly ahead. President Reagan authorized the CIA to begin training opposition forces—the "contras"—and conduct covert activity for the purpose of blocking the flow of arms to guerrillas in El Salvador, Honduras, and Guatemala. The most important preparations took place in Honduras, where the military government provided the sites, Argentina provided training for about a thousand contras, and the United States provided the money. Over the next five years Honduras became an American military base. The Honduran military was handsomely rewarded with dollars and weapons. Roads, bases, and airfields were constructed. A quip at the time was that the U.S.S. *Honduras* had become the largest aircraft carrier in the world. Gigantic "maneuvers" were held. Off the adjacent Nicaraguan shores powerful naval squadrons steamed back and forth. When Nicaragua complained, the U.S. government said all this was just routine peacetime training activity.

The limited objective of stopping the arms flow was quite easily achieved by tough talk from Assistant Secretary of State Thomas

O. Enders, a self-confident career diplomat with a reputation, earned in Southeast Asia, for understanding the uses of power. Enders went to Managua in August 1981 with this message: "You can do your thing, but do it within your borders, or else we're going to hurt you."[7] But Enders was a negotiator in an administration that did not believe in negotiation. Whether or not Nicaragua kept its revolution within its own borders was not the issue to Casey, Haig, or President Reagan.

Nor did the flow of arms, or its absence, have much effect on the insurgents in El Salvador. Most of their arms were of U.S. origin, captured or otherwise acquired within the country. The United States, therefore, loaded the Salvadoran military with staggering quantities of modern weapons and provided training for Salvadoran forces in the country, in Honduras, and in the United States. Total aid, most of it military, reached $4.7 billion between the start of the Reagan Administration and the end of the fighting in El Salvador in 1992—third worldwide behind Egypt and Israel. Under pressure from Congress, however, the number of uniformed American advisers in El Salvador was limited to fifty-five and they were not supposed to engage in combat—although over the years a few were killed while offering advice in combat conditions.

Public and congressional doubts about supporting the war in El Salvador were generated primarily by the appalling violations of human rights inflicted by the Army and the death squads. But since the administration's objective was to exclude the left from El Salvador, and not necessarily to advance human rights, such concerns were off the mark in the White House. As George Kennan had said years before, harsh repressive measures were a protection of the Monroe Doctrine, not a threat to it. The murders were a problem only because they made it difficult to sell Congress and the public on support for the Salvadoran military. The result was a charade. Congress made each release of funds for El Salvador contingent on the Secretary of State certifying every six months that the government was making progress toward democracy and respect for human rights. There was no progress, but the administration said what it had to say, while hundreds of people disappeared and dead bodies were collected from along the roads where they had been dropped by the death squads. Approximately nine thousand people were killed in the conflict in both 1981 and 1982.

Secretary of State George P. Shultz considered the certifying requirement an obstacle. The uncertainty over whether the Salvadoran military would receive the next six-month installment, he argued, led them to conserve rather than use their weapons—thus failing in the counterinsurgency and leading Congress to argue that the aid was wasted.[8] Furthermore, Shultz had to testify to human-rights "progress" against articulate and well-informed critics who had ample evidence that he was not describing reality. Truth was a casualty. Finally, the abuses were so flagrant that Secretary Shultz concluded that he could no longer sign the certification. President Reagan, therefore, simply vetoed a bill which continued the requirement. This, said a liberal critic, destroyed any hope that the United States could bring effective pressure to end the death squads. By that time the estimated number of Salvadorans killed by the security forces and death squads had reached 37,000.[9] The veto temporarily removed a legal annoyance, but in 1984 a federal appeals court overturned Reagan's action and the administration returned to the biannual charade, only to find public and congressional doubts were fueled by another concern. Just as Presidents since 1964 had feared another Cuba, many Americans feared another Vietnam. Secretary Shultz, especially, believed that this "syndrome" was a serious threat to national security. "We knew that any covert action by the CIA would be severely scrutinized, probably disallowed by the Congress, and that any direct military action would require that the president enter the as-yet-uncharted thicket of the War Powers Act, passed in 1973 over the veto of a weakened President Nixon . . . So the American agonies subsumed under the terms Vietnam and Watergate had us tied in knots."[10] The argument, in short, was that the Congress and the

American people themselves had become a hindrance to fulfilling the obligations and principles of the Monroe Doctrine.

President Reagan called those who would deny El Salvador military aid because of human-rights abuses "naïve or downright phony." Adopting the Kirkpatrick thesis, he said that curtailing aid on human-rights grounds would "lead to the overthrow of less-than-perfect democracies by Marxist dictatorships." And: "If we don't give friends so close to home the means to defend themselves against Soviet-supported insurgents, who will trust us anywhere in the world, especially in the faraway Middle East and Europe?"[11] Here was the old Vietnam credibility argument in the clothes of the Monroe Doctrine and the Reagan Corollary.

President Reagan prevailed. Congress continued military aid for El Salvador but did keep a lid on the number of American uniformed advisers permitted in the country. On the political front José Napoleón Duarte won a relatively honest election as President in May 1984. Duarte was a man of goodwill, but he lacked the stamina or political base to prevail against the far right. He never succeeded in eradicating the death squads or making the military respect human rights.

The war in El Salvador continued—until 1991. But the Reagan Administration's primary focus, and that of its critics, turned to Nicaragua. Secretary Shultz deplored congressional barriers to covert action, but—as the well-known tale of Iran-contra demonstrates—the administration was not deterred. It simply used subterfuge to violate the Constitution and the intent of Congress.[12] We need touch only on the low points. The contras under training in Honduras carried out their first attacks in 1982. In March they blew up two large bridges in northern Nicaragua. The Sandinistas responded by declaring a state of emergency. In the same year the U.S. government introduced a new public goal which, behind a benign outward appearance, aimed at removing the Sandinistas. No longer would the Sandinista government be able to "do their own thing" within the country. Now it had to introduce democracy. As Assistant Secretary of State Enders said in a September speech, "Unless Nicaragua permits the development of democratic or, at least pluralistic, institutions in which power is allocated by free elections, its neighbors will never trust it to keep the peace."[13] Superficially such a demand seemed peaceful and reasonable. But since the United States would be the judge of whether the regime had met these standards, it amounted to no less than a concealed demand for the end of the regime.

At the end of 1982 the mounting U.S.–supported violence became headline news in the United States. "America's Secret War—Target: Nicaragua" was the title of a cover story in *Newsweek* in November. The long, accurate account, complete with color photographs, contained warnings from unnamed critics in the administration. "This operation's just about out of control and people are getting panicky," said one.[14]

The violence of the "operation" was in Nicaragua, but the politics were in Washington. In reaction to the *Newsweek* revelations, Congressman Edward P. Boland, chairman of the House Select Committee on Intelligence, introduced and Congress passed (411–0) an amendment to a defense appropriations bill which prohibited the use of funds for the purpose of overthrowing the Nicaraguan government by any U.S. agency connected with intelligence. The life of the amendment was one year. During that year the administration denied that it was even thinking about anyone overthrowing the Sandinistas—and the level of contra attacks escalated and so did operations carried out directly by the CIA. Peter Kornbluh, in a well-documented study, summarizes the action: "CIA pilots bombed Nicaraguan communications towers, frogmen raided port facilities, and commandos planted mines—all missions deemed too sophisticated for the contras. In September 1983 the CIA attacked Puerto Sandino and in October destroyed huge petroleum supplies in the port of Corinto. The contras, on orders from Washington, took credit for the attacks in order to provide cover for the U.S."[15]

The political war in the United States was simultaneously waged between the administration and Congress, and within the administration between the State Department on the one hand and the

CIA and White House on the other. The Department of State was effectively excluded from control over policy toward Nicaragua. Secretary of State Shultz was astounded by CIA Director Casey's obsession. "We're in danger of losing on what is by far the most important foreign policy problem confronting the nation," Casey said to Shultz in December 1982. "You shouldn't be traveling around Europe. You should be going around the United States sounding the alarm and generating support for tough policies . . . Force is the only language the Communists understand."[16] Shultz, believing that force and negotiation had to go together, was increasingly derided by those who shared Casey's outlook in the CIA and the National Security Council. William Clark, President Reagan's national security adviser in 1983, torpedoed a promising Shultz initiative to involve Mexico in a constructive solution to Central America.

Shultz was unable to limit what he considered the excessive militarization of policy. For example, he was not even informed in advance of a huge six-month exercise called "Big Pine II" involving naval and military war games on the borders of Nicaragua. He correctly saw the maneuvers heightening the "worst fears" of people at home and abroad "in ways that would only further deprive the United States of the necessary range of options."[17] He was even more opposed to the mining of Nicaraguan harbors by the CIA, but could only delay that operation briefly. Unlike Shultz, Casey, Clark, et al., did not want a range of options. They wanted military victory.

Congressional restrictions were easily circumvented. The difficulty with the Boland Amendment was that it dealt with the imponderable of intent, not with measurable consequences. As the Reagan Administration argued, it was irrelevant that the contras wanted to overthrow the Sandinista regime as long as American purpose was to assist the contras in order to bring pressure on the Sandinistas to stop supporting the insurgents in El Salvador. Should the Sandinistas just happen to be overthrown, that indeed would achieve the purpose of ending aid to the revolution in El

Salvador.[18] Arguments like that make ordinary hypocrisy look good.

The Boland Amendment was not renewed in December 1983. In its place Congress limited to $24 million the amount the United States could spend "supporting, directly or indirectly, military or paramilitary operations in Nicaragua by any nation, group, organization, movement, or individual." Although the administration complained endlessly about these restrictions, they were not a burden. Money spent on military aid for Honduras was not within the limits—even though the Honduran military buildup, the maneuvers, and the construction of bases were all focused on Nicaragua.

A very low point came early in 1984, when the CIA planted mines in Nicaraguan harbors and rivers, causing considerable damage to Nicaraguan and foreign shipping and some loss of life. Senator Barry R. Goldwater, veteran conservative and chairman of the Senate Select Committee on Intelligence, had not learned in advance of this operation, as was the intent of the law on covert operations. Goldwater had no sympathy for the Sandinistas. He had run for President in 1964 as an uncompromising anti-Communist. But the mining caper filled him with anger. His letter to CIA Director Casey, often quoted, needs to be quoted again: "The President has asked us to support his foreign policy . . . But mine the harbors of Nicaragua? This is an act violating international law. It is an act of war. For the life of me, I don't see how we are going to explain it."[19]

The issue of international law—of no concern to Director Casey—soon gained world attention. In response to the rising level of attacks, the government of Nicaragua turned to the United Nations Security Council, as Guatemala under Arbenz had done in 1954. On six occasions within three years Nicaragua provided extensive and quite accurate details of contra operations and U.S. support and direct involvement. Unlike in 1954 the United States did not try to keep complaints from being heard, but Ambassador Jeane Kirkpatrick's response was snide and condescending. In 1982 she accused the Sandinistas of engaging in what psychologists call "projection"—denying a trait (i.e., committing aggression against neighboring countries) in oneself while claiming to find the trait in another. In 1983 the ambassador's line was that Nicaragua was seeking to establish a new "right"—the right to repress its own people—and had come to the Security Council for protection of that right against the "frustration and bitterness" of the Nicaraguan people. She did not deny American support for the contras, but cast it entirely in terms of assistance to a repressed people.

The climax of Nicaragua's efforts before the Security Council came in March 1984 in protest against the mining. The Nicaraguan account of these attacks on its ports was minutely detailed and impressive to every member of the Security Council except the United States. Ambassador Kirkpatrick ignored the specific charges and repeated that it was Nicaragua, not the United States, that was seeking to destabilize neighbors. "Nicaragua comes to this Council to seek protection while it undermines and over-throws neighboring Governments and represses its own people."[20] Nicaragua asked for a resolution condemning and demanding an immediate end of the mining. Thirteen nations voted in favor, Great Britain (perhaps as an expression of gratitude for American support during the Falklands War) abstained, and the United States cast a veto. The resolution, therefore, failed.[21] The American veto ended Nicaragua's chance for action by the Security Council.

Five days later, on April 9, Nicaragua filed a complaint against the United States before the International Court of Justice (ICJ) —popularly known as the World Court—at The Hague. The complaint, based on the same detailed evidence presented to the Security Council, charged the United States with supporting the contras in their military action and with mining Nicaraguan waters. Nicaragua asked for $370 million in damages.

The ICJ, successor to the interwar Permanent Court of International Justice, is the judicial organ of the United Nations. In 1946 the United States agreed that it would accept "compulsory jurisdiction" of the ICJ in disputes of a legal nature "in relation to any other state accepting the same obligation." In the 1920s and 1930s the Senate had declared that the United States, should it join the World Court of that era, would not accept any decision affecting the Monroe Doctrine. The issue was moot, because the United States did not join.

In 1946, when the United States accepted compulsory jurisdiction, Senator Vandenberg safeguarded the principles of the Monroe Doctrine—embodied in his mind in the inter-American treaty soon to follow from the American promise at Chapultepec—with a reservation that jurisdiction was not accepted for "disputes arising under a multilateral treaty unless (1) all parties to the treaty affected by the decision are also parties to the case before the Court, or (2) the United States of America specifically agrees to jurisdiction."[22] Just as Vandenberg's fight for regional treaties at San Francisco in 1945 gave John Foster Dulles an argument for blocking the Guatemalan complaint before the Security Council in 1954, his ICJ reservation of 1946 gave the United States an argument that the court lacked jurisdiction to hear the Nicaraguan complaint, since, it could be argued, the dispute fell within the ambit of the Rio pact, a multilateral treaty. The Monroe Doctrine was not mentioned by the United States in 1984 in arguing against the ICJ's jurisdiction—but its spirit was clearly present.

The United States used four arguments why the ICJ should reject jurisdiction. First was the claim that Nicaragua's acceptance of compulsory jurisdiction was defective. The Court did not find it so. Second was that the complaint dealt with political, not legal matters, and therefore should be heard by the Security Council. The fact that the United States had already blocked Security Council action with the veto made this argument appear hypocritical in the extreme. Again, the Court dismissed the American argument, as they did the third argument that other parties to a multilateral treaty (specifically Honduras and El Salvador) would be affected by a decision. The fourth and capstone argument was that Nicaragua was the aggressor by its assistance to the guerrilla forces in El Salvador and that whatever the United States was doing (although nothing was admitted) was justifiable individual and collective self-defense under Article 51 of the UN Charter. Had the United States wished to cite a precedent, it could have recalled that the Soviet Union had invoked Article 51 to justify the 1968 intervention in Czechoslovakia.

In November 1984 the Court voted 14–3 that it had jurisdiction. The United States called the vote "erroneous as to both fact and law" and declared it would "not participate in any further proceedings in connection with this case." In the meantime, the government of Nicaragua retained Abram Chayes, professor of international law at Harvard and legal adviser to the State Department in the Kennedy years, as counsel. Chayes's role enhanced the attention the case received throughout the United States. In October 1985 the United States withdrew its general adherence to the compulsory jurisdiction, effective in six months. In June 1986 the Court rendered its decision. By a 14–3 vote it declared the United States in violation of its obligations under international law by illegally aiding the military activities of the contras and the mining of harbors. The Court ordered the United States to pay reparations. The United States government made no response, but one of three dissents to the decision came from Justice Stephen Schwebel, an American citizen. Schwebel said the American claim of self-defense was well founded and accused the Court of extreme bias in favor of Nicaragua and uncritical acceptance of unreliable evidence. "Nicaragua's unclean hands require the Court to reject its claims."[23] Meanwhile, Congressman Boland and many other Democrats, notably Clement Zablocki of Wisconsin, concluded by mid-1983 that it was useless to bar U.S. military aid to the contras if the purpose was only to overthrow the Sandinistas. The administration would simply go on denying such an intent—no matter how obvious it was. Boland and Zablocki believed that aid to the contras would have to be barred altogether, regardless of its stated purpose. As they worked during 1983 and 1984 for a second amendment, the Congress divided along party and ideological lines. The right said that Boland and his allies were doing the enemy's work. Congressman Don Ritter brought up the Monroe and Brezhnev Doctrines:

> If the essence of the Brezhnev Doctrine is to prohibit nations in the Soviet sphere of influence from escaping superpower domination, the essence of the Monroe Doctrine is to prevent superpowers from subjugating less powerful countries . . . Boland-Zablocki, in essence, supports the Brezhnev Doctrine and refutes the Monroe Doctrine, turning history upside down in our own backyard. Boland-Zablocki, by cutting off all our support, covert or overt, to those fighting the Cuban-Soviet sister regime in Nicaragua, makes the United States the enforcer of the Brezhnev Doctrine . . . I predict there are just not enough Democrats in the House who will vote for Leonid Brezhnev over James Monroe.[24]

In October 1984 Congress passed the second Boland Amendment, which prohibited the Department of Defense or any agency of the U.S. government engaged in intelligence from supporting the contras or anybody else engaged in paramilitary or military operations in Nicaragua for a year. The congressional restriction produced one of the remarkable documents in the last chapter of the Monroe Doctrine, the December 1984 memorandum from CIA deputy director Robert Gates to Director Casey.

"It is time to talk absolutely straight," Gates wrote. The contras, he said, were fading and ineffective. Soviet and Cuban support for Nicaragua was increasing, leading toward "the establishment of a permanent and well armed ally of the Soviet Union and Cuba on the mainland of the Western Hemisphere. Its avowed aim is to spread further revolution in the Americas." After reviewing what he considered a sorry American record of half measures, indecision, and congressional obstruction to support of the contras, Gates asked, "Can the United States stand a second Cuba in this Hemisphere?" The only way to prevent such a dire outcome, he argued, was overt effort to bring down the Sandinista regime,

an effort involving recognition of a government-in-exile and cul-
minating in American air strikes against the Sandinistas. "The fact
is that the Western Hemisphere is the sphere of influence of the
United States. If we have decided totally to abandon the Monroe
Doctrine, if in the 1980's taking strong actions to protect our
interests . . . is too difficult, then we ought to save political capital
in Washington, acknowledge our helplessness and stop wasting
everybody's time."[25]

Of course, Gates was directing sarcasm against the supporters
of the Boland Amendments in suggesting that the Monroe Doctrine might have to be abandoned. He would no more advocate
rejecting the Monroe Doctrine than he would suggest the United
States surrender to the Soviet Union. The two possibilities were
the same in the mind of Robert Gates. Like Casey and Reagan,
Gates was a true believer. He also knew how to appeal to leaders
born in an earlier generation. Casey was seventy-one in 1984 and
Reagan seventy-three.

Gates did not get his overt war in 1984. But neither did Boland
II bring an end to the covert war conducted through the contras
and by American paramilitary personnel pretending to be private
citizens. The next two years saw the climax of illegal fund-raising,
arms supply, entanglement with the arms-for-hostages debacle
with Iran, and evasion of congressional intent which will be forever
associated with the name of Lieutenant Colonel Oliver North, but
which were ultimately directed by CIA Director Casey and the
successive national security advisers to President Reagan, Robert
C. McFarlane and Admiral John Poindexter. Historians may never
be able to determine the degree of President Reagan's personal
knowledge of how policy was implemented, but his overall encouragement is beyond question. During these two years the last
traces of candor associated with the principles of the Monroe Doctrine were destroyed.

Within the United States Lieutenant Colonel North orchestrated
fund-raising appeals to wealthy individuals and groups on the far
right—people who believed that their contributions to the contras

were preserving traditional American values, including the Monroe Doctrine. In the State Department a special Office of Public Diplomacy was established to influence the American media by extending privileges to selected journalists, and placing articles, op-ed pieces, including ghostwritten pieces, over the signature of contra leaders. Working directly and through well-paid "consultants," the Office of Public Diplomacy put out many fabricated accusations—for example, that the Sandinistas were virulently anti-Semitic, that Soviet MIG jets had arrived in Nicaragua, or that U.S. reporters in Nicaragua received sexual favors from Sandinista women and men in return for favorable coverage.[26] In a typical week, in March 1985, the office boasted to the White House of having placed an op-ed piece in *The Wall Street Journal* over the signature of an allegedly impartial professor, shaped an NBC–TV story on the contras, prepared op-ed pieces for signatures by contra leaders Alphonso Rubello, Adolpho Callero, and Arturo Cruz, contacted the *MacNeil-Lehrer Newshour* about the availability of Mr. Rubello, and planted some distorted information about the experiences of a visiting congressman in Nicaragua.[27] This particular activity was not lethal and some of it was silly, but it contributed to the erosion of candor which ultimately would undermine the administration's entire Central American policy.

Abroad, the United States solicited secret cash gifts to support the contras from Saudi Arabia and other governments. And, of course, there were the notorious "diversions" from the "profits" gained by overcharging Iran for arms secretly sold by the United States in contravention of law and official policy, transactions designed to yield the release of Americans held hostage by Islamic groups in Lebanon. The diversion also produced substantial commissions to American and foreign private arms dealers working with "the enterprise"—as Oliver North called it. The absurdity of defending the principles of the Monroe Doctrine by entangling the United States in commitments and corrupt dealings in the Middle East never occurred to Oliver North or his superiors.

Secret American operations in and around Nicaragua included training the contras in assassination, staging ever larger and deliberately intimidating maneuvers with American troops in Honduras, and operating clandestine airdrops of arms with planes based in Honduras, El Salvador, and, for a time, Costa Rica. These operations were conducted by a network of shadowy "private" companies employing aviators of fortune, many of them veterans of similar activity in Southeast Asia. In reality the activity was directed by Oliver North out of the National Security Council staff offices with "deniable" involvement by the CIA.

In May 1985 the U.S. government imposed a trade embargo against Nicaragua. Legally this required the President to declare a state of national emergency. He did so on the grounds "that the policies and actions of the Government of Nicaragua constitute an unusual and extraordinary threat to the national security and foreign policy of the United States."[28] Thereafter, the United States government treated Nicaragua as it had been treating Cuba for a quarter century—doing everything possible to exclude Nicaragua from aid and trade. The consequence was to force Nicaragua to rely even more on assistance from the Soviet Union.

The second Boland Amendment expired in December 1985 and the administration redoubled its pressure on Congress. The Senate approved a requested $100 million military-aid program for the contras, but in March the House said no, 222–210. After months of lobbying and arm twisting by the administration, about a dozen conservative Democrats changed their votes, and in June 1986 the House approved the $100 million by a vote of 221–209. The press and the administration believed the tide had turned and President Reagan had regained the momentum. They were wrong. This would turn out to be the last military aid voted for the contras.

In October 1986 a C–123 with an American crew, carrying small arms, military boots, and other equipment from El Salvador, was hit over Nicaragua by a hand-held Sandinista rocket. The pilot and co-pilot were killed. The third crew member, Eugene

Hasenfus—a soldier of fortune with ties to the CIA in the days of the Vietnam War—parachuted to the ground and was captured. He sang like a cage full of canaries. He said he was part of a regular CIA operation flying arms into Nicaragua. A collection of documents recovered from the plane substantiated his story and pointed to connections with the CIA and the White House. State Department, White House, and CIA spokesmen stated categorically that the operation had absolutely no connection with the U.S. government. Some officials suggested that a private group headed by retired Major General John Singlaub was involved. Singlaub denied it. Soon official statements shifted from denial of any connection to denial of command and control, with the admission that the White House (read Oliver North) had provided guidance for activities carried out by private individuals and financed to some degree by foreign governments. These events coincided with the resignation of Bernard Kalb as chief State Department press spokesman, because he was unwilling to be part of a system of deliberate lying to the press and people. Kalb was reacting specifically against the "disinformation" put out over the air attack on Libya. But the Hasenfus affair confirmed his point.

The Nicaraguan government, in turn, scored an easy propaganda victory. It published a photograph of Hasenfus, a bear of a man, being led on a thin little rope by a teenage captor. The picture appeared around the world and in Nicaragua was featured on billboards everywhere. This author was in Nicaragua at the time and noticed a curious discrepancy. The photograph as published in Nicaragua showed a crucifix around the neck of the boy—nothing remarkable in Nicaragua. But in American newspapers the crucifix was missing—possibly airbrushed away by someone who did not want the American public confused about the godless Sandinista Communists. Daniel Ortega, head of the Nicaraguan government, told Mike Wallace of CBS that Hasenfus would probably be home by Christmas, because he was merely a victim, while the United States was the real criminal.

The ease with which Nicaragua could reach the American public added to Washington's problem and illustrated an important characteristic of the political war in the United States. Thousands of Americans—almost all highly critical of the Reagan policies—traveled regularly to Nicaragua. Some stayed for years as peace activists, journalists, health workers, engineers, and missionaries of various sorts. Many American cities were linked as "sister cities" with Nicaraguan counterparts. Church groups were particularly active. The Sandinistas naturally welcomed these people and the opportunity to shape American opinion through them. The right wing in the United States denounced the visitors to Nicaragua as naïve at best, disloyal at worst. But even accounting for their bias, they reported first-hand experience which contradicted the horror stories out of the Office of Public Diplomacy and other propaganda mills.[29]

The well-publicized turning point in the war against Nicaragua came with the disclosure in November 1986, initially by an obscure Beirut newspaper, of the arms-for-hostages game with Iran. That disclosure soon led to the discovery of the illegal diversion of some of the "profits" on the sale of arms to Iran. Oliver North and National Security Council adviser John Poindexter were fired and the nation was soon treated to congressional and judicial investigations dragging on into the 1990s. Iran-contra was a death knell for President Reagan's war against the Sandinistas. The tide of congressional support turned permanently against the contras, toward skepticism of the administration's dire warnings that the Russians were coming, and in favor of nonmilitary solutions.

The malfeasance involved in Iran-contra was at least as serious as that involved in Watergate a decade before. But there never was a serious possibility that President Reagan would face impeachment or be forced to resign. Instead, the President retained his broad popularity to the end of his final term and Vice President George Bush was able to win an easy victory over Michael Dukakis in the 1988 election. The kind of backlash that helped elect Jimmy

Carter in 1976 never materialized. The reasons are to be found partly in Ronald Reagan's benign and friendly personality, but more in the global initiatives of Soviet Secretary General Mikhail Gorbachev toward ending the Cold War. President Reagan, to his lasting credit, recognized Soviet efforts to reduce the danger of nuclear war, cut military spending, and reach worldwide accommodation with the United States as genuine—and not just a trick designed to tempt America into lowering its guard. As the revelations about the connected Iran-and-contra affairs further tainted all those implicated, President Reagan turned his primary attention to a series of summit meetings with Gorbachev, summits which led to dramatic agreements on arms control and were greeted with enormous public acclaim and relief.

Meanwhile, the architects and implementers of the war against Nicaragua disappeared from the administration. Jeane Kirkpatrick had resigned in 1985 as UN ambassador, to be replaced by Vernon Walters, a far more discreet and balanced figure. There was considerable talk, promoted by fellow conservatives, that Kirkpatrick might return as national security adviser or even Secretary of State, but that did not happen. Constantine Menges, arch foe of negotiations on the NSC staff, had been eased out in May 1986. Lieutenant Colonel North and his boss, John Poindexter, were fired as soon as the scandals began to unravel in November 1986. CIA Director William Casey had a brain tumor operation in December 1986 and died five months later. The only prominent advocate of the old line remaining in office was Assistant Secretary of Inter-American Affairs Elliott Abrams, a neo-conservative with views close to those of Jeane Kirkpatrick. Secretary of State Shultz downgraded Abrams's role in favor of the remarkable negotiating talents of veteran diplomat Philip Habib. Abrams, however, had the distinction of giving the last full-blown tribute to the living Monroe Doctrine by a high government official—before the James Monroe Freedom Award Dinner at the State Department on April 28, 1987. Answering a resounding "no" to the question whether the doctrine had become "irrelevant and anachronistic," Abrams reminded his sympathetic audience that "there is still one European power whose intentions toward Latin America are not benign, indeed, a power that seeks to implant its alien system in the Americas. The czars are gone, but their despotism and colonialist impulses live on in the Soviet Government today."[30] The evidence of these assertions existed primarily in Abrams's mind. Meanwhile, at a higher level, Reagan, Shultz, Gorbachev, and Soviet Foreign Minister Eduard Shevardnadze were making giant strides toward dramatic nuclear-arms reduction agreements.

After the arms-for-hostages and contra scandals, Secretary of State Shultz for the first time was able to play the leading role in Central American affairs. In 1987 the United States gave a substantive and not merely hypocritical welcome to the diplomatic efforts of the Latin American governments themselves to work out a political settlement of the violence in Central America. The efforts began in January 1983 with a meeting on Contadora Island, Panama—hence "Contadora process"—of diplomats from Mexico, Colombia, Venezuela, Panama, plus Costa Rica, Honduras, El Salvador, Guatemala (the "core four"), and Nicaragua. Argentina, Brazil, Uruguay, and Peru were associated with Contadora as the "support group." These governments issued a Document of Objectives in September 1983, calling for democratic, pluralistic regimes, reduction in the level and flow of arms, and the prevention of all efforts by "persons, organizations or groups seeking to destabilize" governments. The last point was directed at the contras and the United States. Officially the United States welcomed the Contadora process. In reality, Washington hoped the effort would fail—and it did.

The initiative then shifted to President Oscar Arias of Costa Rica. Arias took office in May 1986 and was the prime mover of a summit meeting of Central American heads of government at Esquipulas, Guatemala, that month. At the same time, the first Latin American Secretary General of the United Nations, Javier

Pérez de Cuéllar, and the Secretary General of the Organization of American States, Baena Soares, became actively involved—independent of Washington but without American obstruction. In August 1987, in Guatemala City, the heads of government reached a major agreement—known as Esquipulas II. It provided for cease-fires throughout the region, amnesties, free elections, arms reduction, and the end of foreign support for military activity. The opponents of negotiation in the CIA and NSC were no longer able to block American support for peaceful settlement. Elliott Abrams did not like what was happening and told Secretary of State Shultz that "Communists win these kinds of negotiations. This could be the end of our policy."[31] Shultz disagreed. Even the White House now was on the side of negotiations, more eager to reach an understanding with House Speaker Jim Wright (D-Texas), who was backing a program similar to Esquipulas II, than to go on with the fight.

In October 1987 President Arias won the Nobel Peace Prize. But no American ideologues in the government complained that this was an unacceptable intrusion by the Stockholm committee into the affairs of the American continents and an affront to the Monroe Doctrine—as they might have done at an earlier time. In February 1988 the House turned down President Reagan's last and minuscule request for military aid to the contras and settled in March for a small, terminal appropriation for "humanitarian" support. There was one last little military flurry when Sandinista forces crossed briefly into Honduras in pursuit of some contras and the United States rushed 3,000 troops to Honduras. But nothing more happened. There were many stumbles, setbacks, and delays in the implementation of Esquipulas II. But when U.S. aid dried up, the contra leadership agreed to serious talks with the Sandinistas.

The Nicaraguan election anticipated in Esquipulas II took place in February 1990 and the Sandinistas lost to a coalition headed by Violeta Barros de Chamorro, widow of the *La Prensa* publisher murdered in 1979 by agents of Somoza. And on New Year's Day

1992 the Farabundo Martí National Liberation Front and the government of El Salvador signed a peace treaty negotiated with the indispensable assistance of a United Nations mediator. The bloody twelve-year Salvadoran war was over. Eight days before, for reasons entirely unconnected with the Monroe Doctrine, the Soviet Union had ceased to exist.

CHAPTER 10

FADE AWAY

arly during the administration of President George Bush the Mexican novelist Carlos Fuentes spoke of a visit he had made in 1968 to Prague in company with Gabriel García Márquez and Julio Cortázar. It was the cold winter of Soviet intervention following the democratic hopes of the previous spring. "While we couldn't refer directly to the Brezhnev Doctrine," Fuentes recalled, "we could talk about the Monroe Doctrine, so that when we mentioned U.S. intervention in Latin America, everyone understood that we were talking about Soviet intervention in Eastern Europe." Fuentes lamented that the demise of the Brezhnev Doctrine in 1990 was "not being echoed by the demise of the Monroe Doctrine in the other theater of the cold war, the U.S. sphere of influence in Central America and the Caribbean." And he praised Soviet Foreign Ministry spokesman Gennadi Gerasimov for saying that the "Sinatra Doctrine" now was the rule for Eastern Europe—"I'll do it my way."[1]

Fuentes was writing in the immediate aftermath of the American attack on Panama and the removal of General Manuel Antonio Noriega to the United States for trial. Fuentes was correct that the United States was still quite capable of intervening in the affairs of Latin American states—but he was quite wrong to see such intervention as related to the Monroe Doctrine, i.e., motivated by the reality or perception of an extra-hemispheric threat which demanded that the United States restrict the right of other countries to "do it their way."

In the same month that Fuentes's article appeared, the Sandinistas were defeated in a free Nicaraguan election—although the Bush Administration was not happy that newly elected President Violeta Barros de Chamorro allowed Sandinistas to retain important posts in the government, including chief of the armed forces. The FMLN had not taken over El Salvador. The Soviet Union had lost interest in Latin American clients. Castro's Cuba was isolated. But purely regional issues such as the illegal trade of narcotic drugs into the United States and uncontrolled migration confronted Washington with real and intractable difficulties. The situation led Mark A. Uhlig, an experienced American observer, to write: "The newly resonant chords of the Monroe Doctrine seemed to be laced with a mocking descant from Oscar Wilde: 'When God wants to punish you, he gives you what you want.' "[2] In short, there was no longer even a perception of external threat, but the United States had no grounds for celebration.

Were Fuentes and Uhlig right? Nostalgic celebrants could, admittedly, argue that the Monroe Doctrine had triumphed and rather than fading away was merely going into honorable retirement, ready to return, if needed, to active duty should another threat to the American continents arise. After all, by 1994 the Soviet military presence in Cuba was no more. The Soviet Union itself was gone. A radical nationalist political foe of Boris Yeltsin, Vladimir Zhirinovsky, said Russia should take back Alaska— shades of the days of James Monroe—but hardly anyone took him seriously. A few pessimists saw a potential Adolf Hitler, most saw only a buffoon. No one invoked the Monroe Doctrine against a new Russian threat.

The issue of whether the Monroe Doctrine was gone or merely in retirement involved far more than a semantic quibble. It was part of the larger question of why the Cold War ended and whether the United States had "won." American superpatriots claimed that, under Presidents Reagan and Bush, the United States stood tall against the "evil empire." By rebuilding military and especially nuclear strength and by challenging Soviet-supported regimes around the world through the Reagan Doctrine, the United States had forced the Kremlin to "cry uncle." Another view, with which this author agrees, was that Soviet and American militarism and confrontational politics had been a system of mutual support, prolonging the Cold War and serving the political, bureaucratic, and personal interests of powerful people and groups in both countries.

The truculent reassertion of the principles of the Monroe Doctrine in the 1980s, according to this alternative view, was the indispensable fuel for a decade of tragic violence in Central America. The crimes committed in the doctrine's name deprived the Reagan Administration of political support at home and abroad and compelled a sensible abandonment of reliance on force and covert operations. The fading of the Monroe Doctrine, not its enforcement, then made possible the political settlement of the early 1990s. Similarly, on the larger stage, President Reagan's wise decision to accept Mikhail Gorbachev's offers to reduce nuclear weapons, rather than to maintain a threatening posture when the Soviet Union was in domestic difficulty, ended the Cold War.

This argument depends on defining the essence of the Monroe Doctrine as behavior driven by the perception that a hostile political-military force would conquer the American continents unless the United States took all necessary steps to prevent it. The heart of the Monroe Doctrine is defiant unilateralism, distrust even of allied governments such as the British when they hint at criticism, a determination to exclude the United Nations from any role, and contempt for the Organization of American States except when it is obedient to proposals from Washington. The simple use of American power, even the invasion of other countries—to fight a war on narcotics or interdict "illegal" would-be immigrants—is not action under the Monroe Doctrine. The essential ingredient is the belief in an immense external threat so great that no limitations on American freedom of action could be tolerated in the Western Hemisphere. By that definition, the Monroe Doctrine and many of its corollaries and tools employed since 1945 disappeared. They did not end, bang, at a single moment or within a single year, but faded piecemeal through the late 1980s and early 1990s.

Take, for example, the shift in policy toward Chile which took place even while the Reagan Administration was still pursuing a Monroeite victory in Central America. General Augusto Pinochet, whose military coup and complicity in the death of President Salvador Allende had been a cause of rejoicing for Richard Nixon and Henry Kissinger, was treated coldly by the Carter Administration. He epitomized the brutal dictatorship whose anti-Communist rhetoric had once produced an embrace from Washington. When Chile refused to extradite three men accused of the murder in Washington of former Allende Foreign Minister Orlando Letelier, the Carter Administration banned exports to Chile.[3] In 1981 the Reagan Administration welcomed Pinochet back into the fold, praising the revival of Chile's economy through the free market and defending the government against international censure for its human-rights record, lifting the ban on exports, and moving toward the resumption of arms sales. Pinochet's Foreign Minister René Rojas Galadames was warmly received in Washington in 1981, and in 1983 the United States denied Salvador Allende's widow an entry visa, saying her presence would be "prejudicial to U.S. interests." Meanwhile, Chile declared it would no longer cooperate with the Inter-American Human Rights Committee. Pinochet, having in 1980 been elected President for eight years under a new constitution which left supreme power in the hands of the military and allowed no effective opposition, seemed a permanent friend and fixture of the Reagan Administration.

But the harsh, repressive character of Pinochet's regime persisted and, in the face of popular protest, intensified. Many died or were injured as mass demonstrations against Pinochet became more frequent. In 1984 Pinochet declared a state of siege, imposed censorship, arrested thousands on mere suspicion, and closed the universities. For the first time since the Carter years, the United States said something critical: "We regret both the increasing violence of the nondemocratic left and the failure of the authorities to respond clearly to the desire of the vast majority of Chileans for a peaceful return to democracy. We are reviewing carefully how recent developments may affect U.S. interests."[4] The Kennan Corollary was beginning to slip, and it slipped further in 1985 as conditions in Chile grew worse. In 1986 the United States, for the first time under Reagan, criticized Chile in the United Nations by introducing a resolution of censure in the UN Human Rights Commission. There went the Monroeite principle that action by the United Nations in reference to anything on the American continents was inappropriate and to be resisted.

Secretary of State George P. Shultz directed the shift in American policy and selected Harry G. Barnes, Jr., a career diplomat noted for effectiveness in dealing with opposition groups, to go to Santiago as ambassador at the end of 1985. The following July the ambassador's presence at a funeral became a powerful symbol of repudiation, as far as Chile was concerned, of the Kennan Corollary. During an anti-Pinochet demonstration, a young U.S. resident and son of a Chilean exile, Rodrigo Rojas di Negri, was doused with gasoline and burned to death by uniformed men with painted faces—almost certainly belonging to Pinochet's security forces. Ambassador Barnes and his wife joined the funeral procession, which was disrupted by the police with tear gas and water cannons. In the United States, Senator Jesse Helms said Barnes had "planted the American flag in the midst of a Communist activity." Helms was a leading voice on the ultra-right, but Barnes was fully supported by the State Department and eventually by President Reagan himself. In 1988 the United States openly supplied funds to support democratic institutions in Chile and in October Pinochet lost a plebiscite which would have continued his rule indefinitely. In 1990 in free elections Chile returned to democracy.[5]

The fading Monroe Doctrine was especially evident in Central

America. Latin American issues were not prominent in the 1988 presidential campaign, contrary to what one might have predicted during the height of the Iran-contra controversy in 1986–87. Democratic candidate Michael Dukakis made no effort to use Iran-contra the way Jimmy Carter had used Watergate in 1976. Instead, the victorious Republican candidate, George Bush, stressed his qualifications to continue the positive relationship with the Soviet Union. Dukakis had nothing new to offer. President Bush and his Secretary of State, James A. Baker III, rejected the early Reaganite obsession with Central America and ritualistic invocation of the principles of the Monroe Doctrine. Their attention was on the dramatic events surrounding the end of the Cold War and on the collapse of Communism in Eastern Europe and eventually the Soviet Union. During 1990–91 they were also heavily occupied with the war to turn back Iraq's aggression against Kuwait.

Baker and Bush succeeded in erasing Nicaragua and El Salvador from the arena of political contention in the United States. They followed the very un-Monroeite tactic of encouraging the United Nations to play a sustained peacemaking role. John Foster Dulles and Arthur Vandenberg would have been appalled. Thus, in November 1989 the Security Council unanimously approved the creation of a UN Observer Force for Central America to manage the demobilization of insurgent forces. The force eventually numbered 600 and was active in Nicaragua and El Salvador. In an earlier era the United States would have either killed such an idea before it reached the Security Council or cast a veto had it come to a vote. A few months later, the UN and many other international observers helped with the free election in Nicaragua. With the inauguration of President Violeta Barros de Chamorro, President Bush terminated the 1985 embargo on trade with Nicaragua and extended reconstruction aid to the government.

In spite of the efforts of a UN mediating team, progress toward a peaceful settlement in El Salvador was slow—but the United States for the first time put real pressure on the Salvadoran government, now headed by President Alfredo Cristiani of the right-wing Arena Party, to repudiate the repressive practices that had taken so many lives and mocked human rights. In a gesture truly unthinkable a few years before, Secretary of State Shultz and Soviet Foreign Minister Eduard Shevardnadze in October 1990 established a joint Soviet-American working group to persuade the government of El Salvador and the FMLN to refrain from military action and get on with peacemaking.[6] No one worried in Washington over what this said about the Monroe Doctrine. A difficult year later the Salvadoran civil war finally ended. The FMLN agreed to a cease-fire and gained recognition as a legitimate political group. The formal proclamation that the civil war was over took place in San Salvador on December 15, 1992, in a ceremony involving government and FMLN leaders and watched by visiting heads of state from around the world.

Nowhere was change more evident than in Cuba. Fidel Castro remained—gray, living on heroic memories—while the Cuban people suffered the burden of economic and political isolation. Even Castro's daughter and granddaughter left the island in 1994 to seek a better life in the United States. The relationship between Fidel Castro and the Soviet government had never been easy—in spite of the endless American reiteration that Cuba was a Soviet proxy in the Western Hemisphere. And with the end of the Cold War the Soviet Union, never as aggressive in Latin America as Washington alarmists believed, stopped even its modest efforts. General Secretary Mikhail Gorbachev, faced with a catastrophic internal economic situation, needed to reduce the costs of Soviet foreign and defense policy. That meant withdrawing from Afghanistan, permitting the unification of Germany and the establishment of non-Communist regimes in Eastern Europe, and everywhere the abandonment of the Brezhnev Doctrine, including in Latin America, where it had never been applied unequivocally. The two doctrines, Brezhnev and Monroe, had been like exhausted heavyweight boxers leaning on each other's shoulders.

In 1960 American newspapers carried huge headlines reporting Nikita Khrushchev's declaration that the Monroe Doctrine was dead. The effect was to incite a chorus of American affirmations that the doctrine was as alive as ever. Thirty-two years later, on September 17, 1992, there appeared a two-inch story on page 15 of *The New York Times*. With a Havana dateline, it reported that Russia and Cuba had agreed that the former Soviet infantry brigade on the island since 1962 would be withdrawn during 1993. That minuscule notice was far more important in the history of the doctrine than Khrushchev's fulminations.

The United States government had papered over the breach in the Monroe Doctrine represented by the Soviet presence in Cuba by figuratively expelling Cuba from the hemisphere and locating her in the Communist bloc. But now there was no longer a Communist bloc. Where, then, was Cuba? The logical course would have been to welcome Cuba back into the Western Hemisphere. But three decades of sustained confrontation had created a powerful domestic political force in the United States: new Americans of Cuban origin who hated Castro, dreamed of his removal, and hoped themselves to return. Cuban-Americans, wooed by both the Republican and Democratic Parties, succeeded in sustaining economic sanctions. The instrument was the Cuban Democracy Act of 1992, which tightened the thirty-year embargo on trade with Cuba, increased sanctions which could be applied to other countries trading with the island, and made improved relations contingent on free and fair elections involving opposition parties and a free press, democratic constitutional reform, and progress toward a free-market economy. When President Bush signed the act in October 1992, Jorge Más Canosa, the most powerful Cuban-American political leader, stood at the President's side.[7] The economic and political war with Castro was still on—but it had now outlived the Monroe Doctrine, its original justification. President Bill Clinton during his first year in office, 1993–94, showed no desire to reach an accommodation with Castro and every intention to avoid political difficulties at home and let time do its work.

Ironically, at the very moment that the war in Nicaragua had ended, the political process in El Salvador was moving toward peace, and the Soviet Union was withdrawing support of Cuba, the United States sent the largest military force into combat since the Vietnam War and the largest force to be used in Latin America since the 1898 war with Spain. This operation—which achieved the objective of capturing General Manuel Antonio Noriega of Panama but at the cost of hundreds of Panamanian lives—had nothing to do with the Monroe Doctrine, except that it violently reversed a relationship once justified by the perceived need to stop the Soviet Union in Central America.

Omar Torrijos, the Panamanian ruler who had worked so effectively with Jimmy Carter in negotiating the canal treaties of 1977, died in a plane crash in July 1981 and was succeeded by General Noriega, his former chief of intelligence, and possibly the man responsible for the plane crash. Noriega was, in the vernacular, a "mean piece of work"—but he was smart. He exploited the CIA's eagerness for assistance in the war against the Sandinistas and pretended to cooperate in suppressing the narcotics trade. At the height of the covert American war in Nicaragua, he had a close relationship with Oliver North and William Casey, provided training facilities for the contras, and offered to send Panamanian hit squads into Nicaragua to deal with Sandinista leaders (an offer refused by Washington).[8] But in 1986 the truth about Noriega's involvement in the drug trade began to come out—just as the Reagan Central American policy was beginning to unravel. There was never any secret about his cruelty and oppression, including murder, of political opponents. In 1988 Noriega was indicted in a federal court in Florida on a charge of drug trafficking. American efforts to negotiate his retirement from Panamanian politics had failed miserably. The United States imposed severe economic sanctions, which certainly hurt the Panamanian economy but did nothing to dislodge Noriega.

When Noriega thugs beat two opposition candidates in the May 1989 elections into a bloody pulp in front of television cameras and Noriega annulled the elections, President Bush concluded that Noriega would have to be removed one way or another. Winning the war on drugs was a major issue for the President, and Noriega had been revealed as a major money launderer and friend of the Colombian "king pins." To have Noriega flaunt his former ties with the CIA was deeply embarrassing. The United States sent additional troops to its large "Southern Command" base in what had been called the Canal Zone. Week by week at the end of 1989 the situation grew ever more tense. American civilians and uniformed personnel were harassed. Noriega on December 15 declared that there was a "state of war" between Panama and the United States. On December 16 an off-duty Marine lieutenant was killed by Noriega troops. Bush ordered the invasion, "Operation Just Cause." On December 20 Stealth fighter bombers dropped 2,000-pound bombs, troops descended from helicopters, tanks rolled, neighborhoods in Panama City burned—and Noriega escaped to the papal nuncio's residence. The United States reported the action to the United Nations, declaring it was exercising the inherent right of self-defense under Article 51 of the charter. In January Noriega surrendered and was sent to Florida for trial, eventual conviction, and imprisonment. At the end there was one moment reminiscent of the old Monroe Doctrine. The United States vetoed a Security Council resolution deploring the invasion and was on the losing side of a 20–1 condemnation by the Organization of American States. But never throughout the entire affair was there a syllable out of Washington about the need to ward off a foreign threat to Panama or the canal—for none existed. There was no external dimension.

From 1945 into the 1990s, two Latin American nations with very close connections to the United States—Haiti and Mexico—avoided even the threat of American intervention under the Monroe Doctrine. But as the United States in the 1990s became more concerned with the internal rather than external problems facing the hemisphere, both rose high on the foreign policy agenda. This transformation illuminates how immediate issues in Latin American countries directly affecting conditions in the United States replaced fading fantasies of the hit lists of international Communism and thus rendered the Monroe Doctrine irrelevant.

Haiti, with its exclusively black population and its long history of intimate and often violent involvement with the United States, seldom appeared high on the list of American hemispheric concerns during the Cold War—despite its location in the strategic heart of the Caribbean. Secretary of State George P. Shultz expressed a widespread point of view: "Haiti was not part of the cold war context. Soviet and Cuban ambitions, so aggressive and confident in seeking to advance the Communist cause elsewhere in the hemisphere, seemed to lose heart in contemplation of the morass of problems in Haiti."[9] The State Department in 1954 commented to President Eisenhower that the government of General Paul Magloire "has been reasonably democratic, has opposed communism, has encouraged foreign investment, and has been very friendly toward the United States."[10] What more could Washington ask?

But by 1956 Magloire was out and the next year François "Papa Doc" Duvalier seized power in a normal, i.e., fraudulent, election. Haiti entered a period of economic decline and increasingly bizarre and barbaric government. Duvalier tried to ingratiate himself by offering the United States a military training camp and submarine base in Haiti. The "generous offer" was declined.[11] When Duvalier objected to criticism from Ambassador Gerald A. Drew and asked that he be withdrawn, Secretary of State Christian Herter said Drew was doing a fine job and should stay—"The situation there is essentially chronic."[12]

In the wake of the Bay of Pigs fiasco in Cuba and the rising influence of Fidel Castro, the Kennedy Administration debated the pros and cons of expressing stronger, more public American distaste for Duvalier. But Under Secretary of State Chester Bowles decided that maintenance of normal relations, without explicit endorsement of Duvalier, was the best course lest Duvalier exclude the American presence from Haiti and open the way for "Communists or other anti-U.S. factions getting control of the state."[13]

The policy enunciated by Bowles remained in force during the Johnson years. In 1964 the U.S. ambassador was told that wider U.S. relations with Latin America demanded the maintenance of productive relations with the government of Haiti no matter how egregious Duvalier's behavior. A State Department intelligence analysis of "Opportunities for Communist Exploitation in Latin America" saw little danger in Haiti, where Duvalier preserved stability through fear and superstition and killing his opponents or forcing them into exile.[14] In short, Washington's fear of Communism was Duvalier's guarantee of survival. No informed American official disagreed with the assessment of the Senate Foreign Relation Committee's Latin American staffer, Pat M. Holt, that "Haiti is about as hopeless as a country can get," with massive poverty, illiteracy, and soil erosion. "The country, in short, is one vast stinking slum with a few decent houses sticking out like pearls in a pigpen."[15] In similar vein, Thomas Mann, Assistant Secretary of State for Inter-American Affairs, told the Senate Foreign Relations Committee in Executive Session in 1965 that Haiti was more akin to the "most backward parts of Africa" than to Latin America. Mann was clearly at his wit's end in trying to develop a policy for Haiti and could think of no alternative but the use of military force under the OAS:

> We have tried nearly everything to get aid to the people, to help them get educated. If you put in an education program, then the teachers have to kick back to the government. If you try to build a dam, the trucks are taken away from hauling dirt and put to hauling people to political rallies. We have simply given up, Mr. Chairman, in trying to do anything.
> . . . There is some Communist infiltration, and we are afraid if we are pushed out without any ears or eyes, that before we get back in we may have a Communist in the presidential chair. I think the only way we deal with that kind of situation is by collective action, and we have never been able to get collective action. We have tried it since 1945 periodically. By

collective action, I mean the use of military force, because the force he [Duvalier] has and exercises in the island is total.[16]

In 1971 "Papa Doc" passed the dictatorship to his son, Jean-Claude or "Baby Doc." The Nixon and Carter Administrations maintained the basic policy of not provoking the Duvalier regime, although the Carter Administration raised a small voice on human rights and young Duvalier made a few cosmetic gestures toward reform—but not enough to stop the rise of an issue which was to define U.S.–Haitian relations into the 1990s: the flight of refugees and their treatment in the United States. In 1980, at a time when the United States was receiving tens of thousands of refugees from Southeast Asia and Cuba, thousands also sought to escape from Haiti. The Carter Administration deported most of them through an agreement with President Duvalier. One member of the Carter Administration raised a tormenting issue that would long persist. Richard Celeste, director of the Peace Corps, said that "regardless of diplomatic and domestic pressures, I believe we must be at least as generous to these refugees as we are to Southeast Asians, Cubans, Eastern Europeans, and Russians. This decade is likely to be remembered . . . as the decade of the refugee—with a movement of persons in every corner of the world unmatched in the past 100 years. We can, should, set an example of what should be done by a country of first asylum. This, I believe, is the least we can do for those Haitians who flee to our shores."[17] Ironically, it was the Reagan Administration, initially scornful of the Carter-era emphasis on human rights, that first brought effective pressure against "Baby Doc"—who in 1986 fled the country on an airplane provided by the United States government.

The next four years were hopeless from Washington's point of view—repression, blood in the streets, rival generals concerned only with their personal power, no possibility of democracy. There was a brief ray of hope in democratic circles with the December 1990 election of the Reverend Jean-Bertrand Aristide, a charismatic Catholic priest supported by the poor and detested by the Army. Aristide was overthrown by the Army in October 1991. The United States and eventually the UN Security Council imposed an economic blockade on the military regime in an effort to force Aristide's return. The principal diplomatic efforts were conducted not by the United States but by Dante Caputo, former Argentine Foreign Minister, now serving as special UN representative for Haiti. Again, Washington encouraged the United Nations to take an active role in a hemispheric problem. There was a glimmer of hope in July 1993, when the military, led by General Raoul Cedras, agreed at a meeting held on Governors Island, in New York Harbor, to Aristide's return by October 30. But Cedras broke his word. Mobs under his control raged against the United States and the UN and forced the withdrawal of an American vessel before it could land a contingent of U.S. and Canadian peacekeeping forces. The Security Council reimposed an embargo on the shipment of oil and weapons to Haiti, and American vessels stopped merchant ships heading for the country. The sanctions wounded an already crippled economy, but did not apparently shake the will of the military to relinquish its grip.

President Clinton fought off a congressional effort to ban the use of American forces in Haiti, but acted as if the ban were in effect. Publicly the United States demanded that Aristide be permitted to return, but behind the scenes American officials were divided. The Central Intelligence Agency, for example, had ties with the Haitian military and saw Aristide as emotionally unstable, a Catholic priest expelled from his order because of his political involvement, a figure espousing a chaotic leftist Haitian brand of liberation theology.

But Washington's immediate interest was less in the political outcome in Haiti than on the problem of uncontrolled Haitian immigration. Tens of thousands of desperate people crowded into small open sailboats for the dangerous passage to Florida, as they had been doing since 1980. Untold numbers perished in the sea. Thousands of others were intercepted by the U.S. Coast Guard and returned to Haiti or, for a time, interned in a sun-blasted camp at Guantánamo Bay, Cuba. A practice carried out vigorously by the Bush Administration was continued under President Bill Clinton—much to the disappointment of old-line liberals. Articulate human-rights advocates, echoing Richard Celeste of a decade before, sought through the courts to keep open the Haitians' right of asylum. The advocates were defeated when the Supreme Court ruled in June 1993 that the President had the authority to use the armed forces of the United States to intercept Haitians on the high seas and return them, without further proceedings, to Haiti. The refugees, having failed to reach American territory, were not entitled to due process on the issue of whether they were eligible for asylum becuase of a well-founded fear of political persecution.[18] This sad business illustrated that America's fear of impoverished blacks had replaced fear of subversive reds. Headlines now spoke of infection by the HIV virus (with which many Haitians were afflicted), not infection by the virus of international Communism. So far had the old doctrine faded.

Finally, a comment concerning Mexico, second-most-populous Latin American nation (after Brazil), the only country in the region with a land border with the United States, the only Latin American country with whom the United States has been formally at war, the source of millions of immigrants to the United States, more in the twentieth century than from any other country in the world, the country with more social and economic ties to the United States than all the rest of Latin America. President Dwight D. Eisenhower in 1960 told a group of advisers that if Communists took over Mexico, the United States would probably have to go to war.[19] Such a strong statement raises the question why Mexico was almost never discussed by American officials after 1945 in terms of the Monroe Doctrine and, accordingly, has scarcely been mentioned in this narrative so far.

The answer is not because Mexico supported the United States on international issues like a loyal neighbor and was so staunchly opposed to the left that Americans had nought of which to complain. On the contrary, the Mexican government was the only one in Latin America to maintain unbroken diplomatic relations with the Soviet Union after 1945, and the only one not to break relations with Castro's Cuba. Mexico almost never supported what the United States desired in the Organization of American States or the United Nations, and on Nicaragua was strongly sympathetic to the Sandinistas. Mexico opposed John Foster Dulles's anti-Communist resolution at the Caracas conference of 1954, condemned the Bay of Pigs invasion and the intervention in the Dominican Republic. When the Reagan Administration eliminated aid and imposed economic sanctions against Nicaragua, Mexico offered assistance and trade on favorable terms. In no other non-Communist Latin American country was condemnation of the United States from intellectuals and government officials alike so strident. History, geography, ideology, international politics —all would lead one to expect that the United States government would in the years after 1945 have devoted more effort under the Monroe Doctrine to excluding alien forces from Mexico than from Cuba, Central America, Brazil, or Chile. Why this was not the case tells us, like the famous dog that did not bark in the Sherlock Holmes story, a good deal about why the principles of the Monroe Doctrine were so fervently embraced in regard to other countries.[20]

The history of Mexican-American relations in the first part of the twentieth century would, at first glance, seem a prelude for trouble. President Woodrow Wilson sent troops into Mexico in 1914 and 1916, spilling Mexican blood on Mexican soil. In 1917 there was a clumsy German effort—the Zimmermann telegram incident—to enlist Mexico as an ally in a war against the United States and to receive the return of its lost territories as a reward for victory. British intelligence revealed the scheme and American outrage contributed to the April 1917 declaration of war against Germany.[21] Talk about a potential violation of the Monroe Doctrine!

The Mexican and Bolshevik revolutions took place in the same decade and were superficially similar in ideology. Conservative

Americans at the time saw little difference. They noted how rapidly the Mexican Communist Party, founded in 1919, appeared to be growing. During the civil war in Nicaragua in the 1920s, the leftist hero Augusto César Sandino looked to Mexico for help, and some in the U.S. State Department believed events in Nicaragua were part of a Bolshevik grand design to take over the Americas from a base in Mexico. In the 1930s Mexico nationalized its oil industry at the expense of foreign, largely American, companies. Although President Franklin D. Roosevelt and Ambassador Josephus Daniels accepted Mexico's right to control her own resources, other Americans looked on nationalization as akin to Communism and never forgave Mexico.[22]

Roosevelt's Good Neighbor Policy, exemplified by the tranquil acceptance of the oil nationalization, continued through the Second World War. But by 1945 the American ambassador in Mexico, George S. Messersmith, saw trouble ahead. He focused on the rising stature of Vicente Lombardo Toledano, charismatic labor leader and Marxist. Lombardo, reported Messersmith, was attacking the United States as the source of all evil in Latin America while extolling the Soviet Union as friend and model. He could well be a crucial agent in the fulfillment of Soviet objectives in the hemisphere.[23] Lombardo Toledano for the next two decades would be Washington's favorite Mexican bogeyman. Messersmith had a thin skin and a rather personal view of international politics. In 1946, when he was criticized by Mexican Communists at public meetings, he saw "an indication of the interest which Soviet Russia has in sowing discord in Mexico and in Latin America, and in developing resentment against us." He reported that Lombardo Toledano had made a bargain with the Soviets, during a visit to London in 1944, to be their agent in Mexico.[24] The FBI, which maintained a large staff in Mexico, found a sinister connection between Henry Wallace, whom President Truman had just dismissed from the cabinet because of his too tolerant attitude toward the Soviet Union, and Lombardo Toledano. When Wallace came to Mexico City, he met privately with the Mexican before the two

went together to a lunch in Wallace's honor.[25] Lombardo Toledano, however, had no chance of achieving power in Mexico. He
founded the Popular Party in 1948, largely because the Mexican
Communist Party was too slavish in following the Moscow line,
and lost badly in a 1952 run for the presidency.[26] Nevertheless,
he remained a favorite and convenient bogeyman for Washington
alarmists. In the years ahead, American conservatives and diplomats frustrated with Mexico's eternal criticism of the United States
would see rising Communist influence. But their complaints were
like the yapping of little dogs—noise but little else.

There were two reasons why high American officials took a
calm view of Mexico. First, they recognized the strength and
stability of the ruling party, the Institutional Revolutionary Party
(PRI). It had never lost an election and it was far more institutional
than revolutionary. No other Latin American government had
had a single party continuously in charge through all the years
since 1945 and was never threatened by even a hint of a coup. The
PRI leaders were strong and self-confident enough to permit a
large Soviet embassy, to be undisturbed by the presence of a small
Communist Party, and to provide asylum on occasion to the likes
of Jacobo Arbenz and Fidel Castro.

Second, the daily life of Mexico and the United States was too
mixed up together and involved too many significant economic,
social, environmental, and even criminal issues to permit a policy
based on ideological excess. Millions of Americans of Mexican
origin had political power. Hundreds of thousands arrived in the
United States each year as immigrants, legal and illegal. Mexican
workers picked much of the farm produce of the Western states.
Tariff relations between the two determined the profits for great
corporations and provided or hindered employment for millions.
And increasingly through the 1980s, Mexico was the transit point
for a flood of narcotics—cocaine, heroin, marijuana—crossing into
the United States. So important were these issues that the Presidents of the United States and Mexico met annually, and sometimes more often, from the 1970s onward. And in 1993 one of

the largest issues linking foreign and domestic policy for the United States was the fate of the North American Free Trade Agreement—signed in 1992 by the Presidents of the United States and Mexico and the Prime Minister of Canada, but awaiting approval or rejection when the Clinton Administration took office in Washington.

Opponents of the agreement charged that it would cost the jobs of millions of Americans as companies moved south to take advantage of cheap Mexican labor. Proponents said that any loss of jobs would be more than offset by the anticipated rise in American exports to Mexico once tariff barriers were down and by greatly improved North American competitiveness with the rest of the world. Furthermore, they argued that defeat of NAFTA would tell the world that the United States was returning to protectionism, the dread sibling of isolationism. The world might then degenerate into the selfish and destructive trade practices of the early 1930s, practices widely considered to be a cause of World War II. The approval of NAFTA was necessary not, in the classic sense of the Monroe Doctrine, in order to shield the American continents from the rest of the world, but to demonstrate the involvement of the United States in the world. On November 17, 1993, the Clinton Administration won congressional approval by a narrow margin and NAFTA provisions went into effect on January 1, 1994.

All this had absolutely nothing to do with the Monroe Doctrine, and to drive home the point, we close with a final vignette—about a genuine hostile penetration of American territory. In June 1993 an elaborate secret tunnel was discovered under construction in Tijuana, Mexico. It began in a warehouse, descended through solid rock for 65 feet, and at that depth extended for a more than a quarter mile under the international border with the United States. The tunnel was lighted, air-conditioned, and had wheeled carts for removing the diggings. The outlet on the American side—a warehouse in San Diego, California—had not yet been reached. The purpose of this penetration of the American frontier was to facilitate the movement of cocaine and other illegal drugs.[27] Here was a far more substantial and serious symbol of a problem facing United States and Latin American society than George Kennan's 1950 worry over the inability of democracies to resist Communism, John Foster Dulles's belief that Arbenz had been captured by a handful of Communists close to his government, Lyndon Johnson's fear that the Dominican Republic would become another Cuba, or Ronald Reagan's fantasy of a new airport on Grenada upsetting the strategic balance.

NOTES

ABBREVIATIONS

AFP: American Foreign Policy: Current Documents with year or years and document number

CR: Congressional Record with date and page

DSB: Department of State Bulletin with date and page

FO 371: Records of the British Foreign Office with document number

FRUS: Department of State, *Foreign Relations of the United States.* The abbreviation will indicate year and volume. Thus *FRUS50/2* means Volume 2 for the year 1950

NYT: The New York Times

PPP: Public Papers of the Presidents. Abbreviations will include name of President and year. Thus *PPP*: Reagan, 1981

1. WHATEVER HAPPENED TO THE MONROE DOCTRINE?

1. *NYT*, December 2, 1923.
2. *CR*, September 26, 1962, p. 20872.
3. Robert M. Gates memorandum to William J. Casey, December 14, 1984, *NYT*, September 20, 1991. The memorandum was made public by Senator Howard M. Metzenbaum (D–Ohio).
4. Note on morning meeting, January 4, 1950, *FRUS50/2*, p. 589n.
5. John P. Vloyantes, *Spheres of Influence: A Framework for Analysis*

(Tucson, AZ: Institute of Government Research, University of Arizona, 1970). I was directed to this book by the excellent essay by Walter LaFeber, "The Evolution of the Monroe Doctrine from Monroe to Reagan," in Lloyd Gardner, ed., *Redefining the Past: Essays in Diplomatic History in Honor of William Appleman Williams* (Corvallis: Oregon State University Press, 1986), pp. 121–41.

6. U.S. delegation to IADB memorandum, August 15, 1951, *FRUS*51/2, p. 1019.

7. Frederick M. Nunn, *Yesterday's Soldiers: European Military Professionalism in South America, 1890–1940* (Lincoln: University of Nebraska Press, 1983) shows how slight was the influence of the United States before World War II.

8. Report, April 27, 1947, *FRUS*47/1, pp. 725–26.

9. Secretary of War Robert P. Patterson to Acting Secretary of State, March 27, 1947, *FRUS*47/8, p. 108.

10. A long and representative State Department argument against arming Latin America, dated September 20, 1949, is in *FRUS*50/1, pp. 608–19.

11. 143rd meeting of the NSC, May 6, 1953, NSC summaries, Eisenhower Library.

12. C. W. Weedon to Group Captain Bayne, Air Ministry, January 7, 1954, FO 371 108755, Public Record Office.

13. Statement of Assistant Secretary of State Thomas Enders, September 30, 1982, *AFP*82, doc. 616.

14. Quoted from a *Newsmaker Sunday* television transcript by LaFeber, "Evolution," p. 125.

15. Memorandum, August 3, 1950, *FRUS*50/1, p. 643.

16. Memorandum, December 12, 1950, Edward G. Miller, Jr., papers, box 8, Truman Library.

17. Ivan White to Edward G. Miller, Jr., February 14, 1951, *FRUS*51/2, pp. 994–97.

18. Lincoln Gordon to Thomas Mann, March 4, 1964, National Security Files, Latin America, reel 4, Johnson Library.

19. Gordon Connell-Smith, *The Inter-American System* (London: Oxford University Press, 1966) remains a good factual description based on public documents.

20. Philip Agee, *Inside the Company: CIA Diary* (New York: Stonehill,

1975) presents a picture of the variety of daily low-level CIA activities in Latin America in the 1960s. See also Victor Marchetti and John D. Marks, *The CIA and the Cult of Intelligence* (New York: Alfred A. Knopf, 1974).
21. Discussion at 277th meeting of the NSC, February 27, 1956, *Declassified Documents* 1987, no. 441.
22. From NSC–5631, "Policy toward Latin America," September 12, 1956, *Declassified Documents* 1986, no. 447.
23. *PPP*: Kennedy, 1961, pp. 170–81.
24. Jerome Levinson and Juan de Onis, *The Alliance That Lost Its Way* (Chicago, IL: Quadrangle Books, 1970), p. 323.

2. THE HISTORICAL LEGACY

1. The distinguished historian Dexter Perkins devoted a career to tracing the history of the doctrine. See his *The Monroe Doctrine, 1823–1826* (Cambridge, MA: Harvard University Press, 1927); *The Monroe Doctrine, 1826–1867* (Baltimore, MD: The Johns Hopkins University Press, 1933); *The Monroe Doctrine, 1867–1907* (Baltimore, MD: The Johns Hopkins University Press, 1937); and the one-volume summary, *A History of the Monroe Doctrine* (Boston, MA: Little, Brown, 1955). Ernest R. May, *The Making of the Monroe Doctrine* (Cambridge, MA: Harvard University Press, 1975) stresses the domestic political context. Samuel Flagg Bemis, *John Quincy Adams and the Foundations of American Foreign Policy* (New York: Alfred A. Knopf, 1956) is the best account of Secretary of State Adams's substantial contribution. John A. Logan, Jr., *No Transfer: An American Security Principle* (New Haven, CT: Yale University Press, 1961) traces the history of an important cognate principle, often considered part of the doctrine itself. A useful if rather supercilious essay is Kenneth M. Coleman, "The Political Mythology of the Monroe Doctrine: Reflections on the Social Psychology of Hegemony," in John D. Martz and Lars Schoultz, eds., *Latin America, the United States and the Inter-American System* (Boulder, CO: Westview Press, 1981), pp. 96–114. The text of the relevant portions of the message has been reprinted uncounted times. See, for example, Ruhl J. Bartlett, *The Record of American*

Diplomacy, 4th ed. (New York: Alfred A. Knopf, 1964), pp. 181–83.

2. See the classic Felix Gilbert, *To the Farewell Address: Ideas of Early American Foreign Policy* (Princeton, NJ: Princeton University Press, 1961).

3. Bartlett, p. 344.

4. Ibid., p. 539.

5. Thomas L. Karnes, "Hiram Bingham and His Obsolete Shibboleth," *Diplomatic History* 3 (Winter 1979), pp. 39–57, discusses the writing and impact of Bingham's article and book and notes the author's retreat from his original idea after he became a United States senator.

6. Perkins, *Monroe Doctrine, 1867–1907*, pp. 282–83.

7. Perkins, *History*, p. 273.

8. The two-year attempt to fashion the Pan-American pact is generously documented in Charles Seymour, ed., *The Intimate Papers of Colonel House* (Boston, MA: Houghton Mifflin, 1926), vol. 1, pp. 207–34.

9. Bartlett, p. 454.

10. Ibid., pp. 455–57.

11. For text of the covenant, ibid., pp. 461–70.

12. Reservation No. 5, ibid., p. 471.

13. Perkins, *History*, pp. 306–8.

14. Excerpts from the *Congressional Record* are conveniently gathered in Bartlett, pp. 521–23.

15. Perkins, *History*, p. 311; also Robert Ferrell, *Peace in Their Time: The Origins of the Kellogg-Briand Pact* (New Haven, CT: Yale University Press, 1952).

16. Secretary of State Frank B. Kellogg draft to American diplomatic officers in Latin America, February 28, 1929, *FRUS29/1*, pp. 698–99.

17. Perkins, *History*, p. 345.

18. Bryce Wood, *The Making of the Good Neighbor Policy* (New York: Columbia University Press, 1961).

19. Bartlett, p. 421; George H. Blakeslee, "The Japanese Monroe Doctrine," *Foreign Affairs* 11 (July 1993), pp. 671–81.

20. *FRUS, Japan* 31–42/2, pp. 224–25.

21. Ibid., p. 284; Cordell Hull, *Memoirs* (New York: Macmillan, 1948), vol. 1, pp. 281–82; vol. 2, p. 959.

22. *FRUS40/2*, pp. 494–96; Hull, vol. 1, p. 817; Lothar Gruchmann, *Nationalsocialistische Grossraumordnung: Die Konstruktion einer "deutschen Monroe-Doktrin"* (Stuttgart: Deutsche Verlags-Anstalt, 1962).

23. Bartlett, pp. 556–57.

24. Stetson Conn and Byron Fairchild, *The United States Army in World War II: The Framework of Hemispheric Defense* (Washington, DC: Office of the Chief of Military History, 1960), p. 3.

25. OF 200, box 42, Franklin D. Roosevelt Library.

26. Conn and Fairchild, p. 12.

27. Perkins, *History*, pp. 358–59.

28. Ibid., pp. 385–86.

29. Conn and Fairchild, p. 114.

3. The Ghost at San Francisco

1. The indispensable source is Ruth B. Russell, *A History of the United Nations Charter: The Role of the United States, 1940–1945* (Washington, DC: The Brookings Institution, 1958).

2. Herbert Feis, *Churchill, Roosevelt, Stalin: The War They Waged and the Peace They Sought* (Princeton, NJ: Princeton University Press, 1957), p. 238.

3. Memoranda of conversations between Brazilian ambassador Martins and Norman Armour, September 12 and October 19, 1944, *FRUS44/1*, pp. 924, 932, 952.

4. George S. Messersmith to Secretary of State Edward R. Stettinius, Jr., January 25, 1945. George S. Messersmith papers, item 1672, University of Delaware Library.

5. Adolf A. Berle diary, entries for February 20, 21, and 27, 1945, Adolf A. Berle papers, Franklin D. Roosevelt Library. Some but not all of the quoted passages are printed in Beatrice Bishop Berle and Travis Jacobs, eds., *Navigating the Rapids, 1918–1971* (New York: Harcourt Brace Jovanovich, 1973).

6. U.S. Department of State, *Report of the Delegation to the Inter-American*

Conference on Problems of War and Peace, Mexico City, Mexico, February 21–March 8, 1945 (Washington, DC, 1946).

7. Russell, p. 562.

8. *DSB*, June 3, 1945, p. 1107. For a fuller treatment of the Argentine tangle, see Russell, pp. 569–71.

9. Arthur H. Vandenberg, Jr., ed., *The Private Papers of Senator Vandenberg* (Boston, MA: Houghton Mifflin, 1952), p. 182.

10. Meetings of delegation, April 16, 1945, *FRUS45/1*, pp. 302–6.

11. Henry L. Stimson diary, vol. 51, entries for April 26, 29, and May 2, 1945, Henry L. Stimson papers, microfilm, Yale University Library.

12. *FRUS45/1*, p. 591.

13. Arthur Hendrick Vandenberg, *The Trail of a Tradition* (New York: G. P. Putnam's Sons, 1926), p. 213. See pp. 241–43 for Vandenberg's comment on the League of Nations.

14. Arthur H. Vandenberg letter to Edward R. Stettinius, Jr., May 5, 1945, copy in the Hamilton Fish Armstrong papers, box 51, Seeley Mudd Library, Princeton University.

15. Russell, pp. 691–92.

16. *FRUS45/1*, p. 614.

17. Ibid., p. 594.

18. Ibid., p. 619.

19. Ibid., pp. 622–23.

20. Ibid., p. 624.

21. Ibid., pp. 635–36.

22. Ibid., p. 619.

23. Transcript of telephone conversation between Henry L. Stimson and John J. McCloy, Henry L. Stimson papers, box 420, Yale University Library.

24. Vandenberg, *Private Papers*, pp. 189–90.

25. *FRUS45/1*, pp. 659–60.

26. Ibid., pp. 666, 668.

27. Ibid., p. 693.

28. Arthur H. Vandenberg to N. J. Schorn, July 17, 1945, Arthur H. Vandenberg papers, box 2, folder 29, University of Michigan.

29. Alan Bullock, *Ernest Bevin: Foreign Secretary, 1945–1951* (London: Heinemann, 1983), pp. 193–95; Denis Smith, *Diplomacy of Fear* (To-

ronto: University of Toronto Press, 1988), p. 120, quoting report by Canadian diplomat Dana Wilgress of December 12, 1945, conversation with Bevin.

30. John Morton Blum, *The Price of Vision: The Diary of Henry A. Wallace* (Boston, MA: Houghton Mifflin, 1973), pp. 581, 665.

31. *NYT*, March 13, 1947.

32. *FRUS*47/8, p. 75.

33. Vandenberg, *Private Papers*, p. 371.

34. Policy statement, January 27, 1947, *FRUS*47/1, p. 1050.

35. PPS–31, "Antarctica," June 9, 1948, *FRUS*48/1, pp. 977–83.

36. The exchange of messages between Marshall and Lovett is in *FRUS*48/9, pp. 49, 53. For a vivid account, see Vernon A. Walters, *Silent Missions* (Garden City, NY: Doubleday, 1978), pp. 150–70. Walters, then a major in the United States Army, was at the conference as interpreter and aide to Secretary of State Marshall.

37. *NYT*, March 23, 1949.

38. Press conference, August 14, 1947, *PPP: Truman, 1947*, pp. 383–84.

39. Paper on Communism, the Monroe Doctrine, and European colonies, November 7, 1947, John M. Cabot papers, microfilm reel 1, Massachusetts Historical Society.

40. The neatly bound volumes of these reports are in Naval Aide Files, box 15, Truman Library.

41. Hoover's quarterly reports addressed to General Harry Vaughan, Truman's aide, are in PSF, FBI, box 168, Truman Library.

4. THE KENNAN COROLLARY AND GUATEMALA

1. *FRUS*50/1, pp. 245–301.

2. Truman to Dean Alfange, May 18, 1948, PSF, box 184, Truman Library.

3. Memorandum of telephone conversation between John Foster Dulles and President Eisenhower, February 26, 1953, Dulles files, telephone conversations, box 10, Eisenhower Library.

4. Memorandum of conversation between Eisenhower and Arturo

Frondizi, January 22, 1959, WHO, OSS, international series, Eisenhower Library.

5. The best study of Kennan's involvement in the conduct of policy is Wilson D. Miscamble, *George F. Kennan and the Making of American Foreign Policy, 1947–1950* (Princeton, NJ: Princeton University Press, 1992).

6. George F. Kennan to the Secretary of State, February 24, 1948, *FRUS*48/1, p. 509.

7. George F. Kennan to the Secretary of State, March 29, 1950, *FRUS*50/2, pp. 598–624. Except where otherwise noted, the following discussion draws on this document.

8. George F. Kennan, *Memoirs: 1925–1950* (Boston, MA: Little, Brown, 1967), p. 476.

9. *FRUS*46/6, p. 709; also Kennan, p. 559.

10. Edward G. Miller, Jr., speech before the Pan-American Society of New England, April 26, 1950, *DSB*, May 15, 1950, p. 769.

11. *FRUS*50/1, p. 244.

12. The term "Kennan Corollary" was not in use at the time. It was coined by the present author in "The Legacy of Monroe's Doctrine," *NYT Magazine*, September 9, 1984.

13. Piero Gleijeses, *Shattered Hope: The Guatemalan Revolution and the United States, 1944–1954* (Princeton, NJ: Princeton University Press, 1991) is the best book on the subject.

14. Robert H. Ferrell, ed., *Dear Bess: Letters from Harry to Bess Truman, 1910–1959* (New York: Norton, 1982), p. 431.

15. Memorandum of conversation, March 16, 1948, *FRUS* microfiche supplement, 1947–52, doc. 427.

16. Secretary of State to Ambassador Patterson, June 14, 1949, *FRUS*49/2, p. 650.

17. Edward G. Miller, Jr., to Richard C. Patterson, July 27, 1949, Edward G. Miller, Jr., papers, box 7, Truman Library.

18. Richard C. Patterson to Edward G. Miller, Jr., June 17, 1949, ibid.

19. Richard C. Patterson to Samuel Zemurray, September 2, 1949, and January 11, 1950, Richard C. Patterson papers, box 5, Truman Library. The second letter is marked "not sent." It reports what Patterson recommended to United Fruit officers in Guatemala.

20. Memorandum, April 19, 1950, *FRUS*50/2, pp. 880–84.

21. Kenedon P. Steins memorandum, May 17, 1950, ibid., pp. 889–96.

22. Memorandum, August 2, 1951, Edward G. Miller, Jr., papers, box 7, Truman Library.

23. Memorandum, February 18, 1952, ibid.

24. Memorandum, October 14, 1952, *FRUS*52–54/4, pp. 1046–48.

25. Memorandum of conversation between Dean Acheson and Guillermo Toriello, November 17, 1952, ibid., pp. 1050–52.

26. In a May 3, 1961, letter to Harry Truman, Acheson ridiculed the Bay of Pigs invasion as "asinine" and recalled how he and Truman had turned down similar proposals for Iran and Guatemala. David S. McLellan and David C. Acheson, *Among Friends: Personal Letters of Dean Acheson* (New York: Dodd, Mead, 1980), pp. 206–7. Contemporary evidence confirms Acheson's memory. See especially letter from Walter Bedell Smith, director of Central Intelligence, to Under Secretary of State David Bruce, December 12, 1952, *FRUS*52–54/4, pp. 1055–56.

27. Thomas Mann memorandum to Dean Acheson, October 3, 1952, ibid., pp. 1041–43.

28. 137th meeting of the NSC, March 31, 1953, NSC summaries, Eisenhower Library.

29. See Stephen Schlesinger and Stephen Kinser, *Bitter Fruit* (Garden City, NY: Doubleday, 1982), which emphasizes the role of the United Fruit Company, and Richard H. Immerman, *The CIA in Guatemala* (Austin: University of Texas Press, 1982), which, more convincingly, stresses the anti-Communist ideology of the Eisenhower Administration. The best work is Gleijeses, *Shattered Hope*.

30. John M. Cabot, *First Line of Defense* (Washington, DC: Georgetown School of Foreign Service, 1971), p. 87.

31. David Green, *The Containment of Latin America* (Chicago, IL: Quadrangle Books, 1971), pp. 263, 292.

32. Memorandum of conversation, November 18, 1953, Secretary of State's Memoranda of Conversations, November 1952–December 1954, *FRUS* microfiche supplement, 1992, doc. 293.

33. *FRUS*52/4, pp. 299–300.

34. *NYT*, March 16, 1954.

35. Roy Rubottom Oral History, Dulles Oral History Project, Seeley Mudd Library, Princeton University.

36. 189th meeting of the NSC, March 18, 1954, *FRUS52–54/4*, pp. 304–5.

37. State Department press release, May 17, 1954, *DSB*, May 31, 1954, p. 835.

38. Telephone conversation between John Foster Dulles and President Eisenhower, May 15, 1954, Dulles files, telephone conversations, box 2; memorandum for the President, May 22, 1954, Dulles files, WH memoranda, box 1, Eisenhower Library.

39. John Foster Dulles speech, June 10, 1954, Seattle, *DSB*, June 21, 1954, p. 938.

40. Transcript of conversation between John Foster Dulles and Deputy Under Secretary of State Robert Murphy, June 10, 1954, Secretary of State's Memoranda of Conversations, November 1952–December 1954, *FRUS* microfiche supplement, 1992, doc. 501.

41. United Nations, *Security Council Official Records*, 675th meeting, June 20, 1954, pp. 16, 33, 38.

42. Telephone conversation between John Foster Dulles and Henry Cabot Lodge, June 22, 1954, Dulles files, telephone conversations, box 2, Eisenhower Library.

43. Telephone conversation between John Foster Dulles and Henry Cabot Lodge, June 24, 1954, Secretary of State's Memoranda of Conversations, November 1952–December 1954, *FRUS* microfiche supplement, 1992, doc. 526.

44. Memorandum of conversation, June 25, 1954, FO 371 108743, Public Record Office.

45. Telephone conversation between John Foster Dulles and Henry Cabot Lodge, June 25, 1954, Dulles files, telephone conversations, box 2, Eisenhower Library.

46. Sir Pierson Dixon to Foreign Office, June 26, 1954, FO 371 108742, Public Record Office.

47. John Colville, *The Fringes of Power: 10 Downing Street Diaries, 1939–1955* (New York: Norton, 1985), p. 694.

48. *Annals of the Organization of American States*, vol. 6, 1954, p. 160.

49. Great Britain, *Parliamentary Papers: Report on Events . . . in Guatemala, 1954*, Cmd. 9277, October 1954.

50. Minute by C. S. Cope, September 11, 1954, FO 371 108945, Public Record Office.

51. Department of State Publication 5556, Inter-American Series 48, pp. 30–34.

52. John Peurifoy speech, August 28, 1954, *DSB*, September 6, 1954, p. 336.

53. Susanne Jonas, *The Battle for Guatemala: Rebels, Death Squads, and U.S. Power* (Boulder, CO: Westview Press, 1991).

54. The trip rates one of the chapters in Richard M. Nixon, *Six Crises* (Garden City, NY: Doubleday, 1962), pp. 183–234.

55. Memorandum, December 9, 1948, *FRUS48/9*, pp. 146–47.

56. Memorandum, February 29, 1952, *FRUS52–54/4*, p. 1602.

57. Rómulo Betancourt, *Venezuela, Oil and Politics* (Boston, MA: Houghton Mifflin, 1979), pp. 298–99.

58. Memorandum of discussion, 237th meeting of the NSC, February 17, 1955, *FRUS55–57/6*, p. 4.

59. Memorandum of conversation between Robert Cutler and George Humphrey, September 17, 1954, WHO, OSANAS, NSC series, briefing notes subseries, Eisenhower Library.

60. Nixon, *Six Crises*, pp. 229–30.

61. Memorandum of conversation between John Foster Dulles and Eisenhower, May 18, 1958, Dulles files, WH memoranda, box 6, Eisenhower Library.

5. AGROUND AND SHATTERED ON CUBA

1. John A. Logan, Jr., *No Transfer: An American Security Principle* (New Haven, CT: Yale University Press, 1961) traces the long American determination to keep Cuba out of the hands of a more powerful government than Spain.

2. Louis A. Perez, Jr., *Cuba Between Empires, 1878–1902* (Pittsburgh, PA: University of Pittsburgh Press, 1983); Frank Freidel, *The Splendid Little War* (Boston, MA: Little, Brown, 1958) is a popular and illuminating study.

3. Louis A. Perez, Jr., *Cuba under the Platt Amendment, 1902–1934* (Pittsburgh, PA: University of Pittsburgh Press, 1986).

4. Central Intelligence Agency, "Cuban Political Trends," March 26, 1948, PSF, Central Intelligence Reports, box 255, Truman Library.

The State Department said the CIA estimate of adverse impact on the United States of Cuban nationalism was exaggerated. CIA Situation Report 29, ibid., box 261.

5. Edward G. Miller, Jr., letter to Claude Bowers, March 27, 1952, Assistant Secretary Lot files, box 4, National Archives.

6. Memorandum of conversation between Willard Beaulac and Cuban Minister of State Miguel Angel de la Campa, March 22, 1952; Dean Acheson to Truman, March 24, 1952, *FRUS*52–54/4, pp. 869–71.

7. Earl Smith to Secretary of State, February 2, 1958, *FRUS*58–60/6, p. 21.

8. Memorandum from deputy director of Intelligence and Research, Department of State, April 1, 1958, ibid., pp. 77–78.

9. Ellis Briggs oral history interview, Columbia University Library, p. 118.

10. Philip W. Bonsal, *Cuba, Castro and the United States* (Pittsburgh, PA: University of Pittsburgh Press, 1971) is the ambassador's account.

11. Ibid., p. 59.

12. Richard Nixon, *RN: The Memoirs of Richard Nixon* (New York: Grosset & Dunlap, 1978), pp. 201–3.

13. State Department evaluation of Castro, April 23, 1959, Whitman file, Cuba, folder 1, Eisenhower Library.

14. Robert Kleberg memorandum, June 25, 1959, Whitman file, diary series, Eisenhower Library.

15. Christian Herter memorandum for the President, July 7, 1959, Whitman file, Herter series, Eisenhower Library.

16. *CR*, July 7, 1959, p. 12896.

17. Christian Herter memorandum for the President, November 5, 1959, WHO, OSS, international series, Eisenhower Library.

18. *U.S. News & World Report*, December 28, 1959; reprinted in the *CR*, January 7, 1960, pp. 104–5, at the request of Senator Prescott Bush.

19. For Bemis's extensive correspondence with Hosmer, Bush, and others similarly alarmed about Castro and the Monroe Doctrine, see Samuel Flagg Bemis papers, series II, box 52, Yale University Library.

20. *CR*, January 11, 1960, p. 273.

21. 432nd meeting of the NSC, January 14, 1960, *FRUS*58–60/6, p. 744.

22. Memorandum of conversation, January 26, 1960, WHO, OSS, international series, Eisenhower Library.

23. Arleigh Burke to Livingston Merchant, February 26, 1960, *FRUS58–60/6*, pp. 813–14.

24. Wayne S. Smith, *The Closest of Enemies: A Personal and Diplomatic History of the Castro Years* (New York: Norton, 1987), p. 55; Morris H. Morley, *Imperial State and Revolution: The United States and Cuba, 1952–1986* (Cambridge, England: Cambridge University Press, 1987), pp. 87–88; Robert S. Walters, "Soviet Economic Aid to Cuba, 1959–1964," *International Affairs* 42 (January 1966), pp. 74–86.

25. Bonsal, pp. 133–34.

26. "A Program of Covert Action Against the Castro Regime," March 17, 1960, WHO, OSS, international series, Eisenhower Library; also General Goodpaster memorandum, March 17, 1960, *Declassified Documents* 1991, no. 3407.

27. Wayne S. Smith, *Enemies*, pp. 52–57.

28. *NYT*, July 10, 1960.

29. Transcript of Khrushchev press conference of July 12, 1960, *NYT*, July 13, 1960.

30. Statement, July 14, 1960, *DSB*, August 1, 1960, pp. 170–71.

31. "Provocative Actions of Cuba Against the United States Which Have Served to Increase Tensions in the Caribbean Area," memorandum submitted to the Inter-American Peace Committee of the OAS, June 2, 1960, *DSB*, July 18, 1960, pp. 79–87.

32. United Nations, *Security Council Official Records*, 874th meeting, July 18, 1960, pp. 4, 13.

33. Synopsis of intelligence material, October 18, 1960, Whitman file, diary series, Eisenhower Library.

34. Memorandum of conversation, October 15, 1960, ibid.

35. Richard M. Nixon, *Six Crises* (Garden City, NY: Doubleday, 1962), pp. 351–56.

36. Samuel Flagg Bemis to Prescott Bush, December 17, 1960, Samuel Flagg Bemis papers, box 52, Yale University Library.

37. The best account is Peter Wyden, *Bay of Pigs* (New York: Simon & Schuster, 1979); see also Trumbull Higgins, *Perfect Failure* (New York: Norton, 1987).

38. Morley, pp. 146–55, 178–205.

39. *DSB*, February 19, 1962, p. 281.

40. On the thirtieth anniversary the CIA published *CIA Documents on the Cuban Missile Crisis, 1962* (Washington, DC: CIA History Staff, 1992). The theme of the documents is the prescience of Director McCone.

41. *PPP*: Kennedy, 1962, p. 654.

42. The Schlei memorandum and a 1968 letter from Schlei to Abram Chayes is in Chayes, *The Cuban Missile Crisis: International Crises and the Role of Law* (New York: Oxford University Press, 1974), pp. 108–34.

43. *The Wall Street Journal*, September 5, 1962.

44. *CR*, September 6, 1962, pp. 18728–29, 18774.

45. *Time*, September 17, 1962, pp. 17–21.

46. *Life*, September 21, 1962.

47. *Time*, September 17, 1960, p. 17.

48. "Today and Tomorrow," New York *Herald Tribune*, September 18, 1962.

49. *CR*, September 26, 1962, p. 20863.

50. Memorandum, October 16, 1962, meeting with the President, *CIA Documents*, doc. 47.

51. Robert F. Kennedy, *Thirteen Days: A Memoir of the Cuban Missile Crisis* (New York: Signet, 1969), pp. 37–39.

52. John McCone memorandum, October 19, 1962, *CIA Documents*, doc. 60.

53. Memorandum for the President, October 22, 1962, *Declassified Documents* 1975, no. 327D.

54. Memorandum of conversation between John McCone and Johnson, October 22, 1962, *CIA Documents*, doc. 73.

55. *DSB*, November 12, 1962, pp. 715–20.

56. Kennedy, *Thirteen Days*, p. 85.

57. Raymond L. Garthoff, "The Cuban Missile Crisis: An Overview," in James A. Nathan, ed., *The Cuban Missile Crisis Revisited* (New York: St. Martin's Press, 1992), p. 46.

58. Kennedy to Khrushchev, October 27, 1962, *DSB*, November 12, 1962, p. 743. The negotiations continued in secret correspondence into December. For an account and recently declassified texts, see

Philip Brenner, "The Kennedy–Khrushchev Letters," in Nathan, pp. 281–96.

59. Robert K. Murphy, *Diplomat Among Warriors* (Garden City, NY: Doubleday, 1964), p. 443.

60. Spruille Braden, *Diplomats and Demagogues* (New Rochelle, NY: Arlington House, 1971), pp. 430–31.

61. Gaddis Smith conversations at the time with Samuel Flagg Bemis.

62. Dean Acheson, "The Monroe Doctrine: Dead or Alive?" October 1963, quoted by Douglas Brinkley, *Dean Acheson: The Cold War Years, 1953–1971* (New Haven, CT: Yale University Press, 1992), p. 361 n. 24.

63. *PPP*: Kennedy, 1963, p. 891.

6. No More Cubas: The Monroe Doctrine under Johnson and Nixon

1. Morris H. Morley, *Imperial State and Revolution: The United States and Cuba, 1952–1986* (Cambridge, England: Cambridge University Press, 1987) provides a mass of detail especially on the political and economic efforts.

2. William Attwood, *The Twilight Struggle: Tales of the Cold War* (New York: Harper & Row, 1987), p. 263.

3. Victor Marchetti and John D. Marks, *The CIA and the Cult of Intelligence* (New York: Alfred A. Knopf, 1974), pp. 138ff.

4. David S. McLellan and David C. Acheson, *Among Friends: Personal Letters of Dean Acheson* (New York: Dodd, Mead, 1980), p. 74.

5. Vernon A. Walters, *Silent Missions* (Garden City, NY: Doubleday, 1978).

6. Military Intelligence Division of the War Department, "Reorganization of the Brazilian Armed Forces," August 8, 1946, Naval Aide Files, box 15, Truman Library.

7. Edward G. Miller, Jr., to Herschel Johnson, January 27, 1950, Edward G. Miller, Jr., papers, box 2, Truman Library.

8. I have relied on Thomas E. Skidmore, *Politics in Brazil, 1930–1964* (New York: Oxford University Press, 1967).

9. John M. Cabot to Senator J. William Fulbright, August 9, 1961,

J. William Fulbright papers, series 2:1, box 1, University of Arkansas Library.

10. Telegram to embassy, Rio, September 6, 1961, National Security Files, Latin America, microfilm reel 1, Kennedy Library.

11. Secretary of State Dean Rusk to Ambassador Lincoln Gordon, September 21, 1962, ibid., microfilm reel 2.

12. Lincoln Gordon telegram to Secretary of State, October 3, 1962, ibid.

13. Lincoln Gordon telegram to Secretary of State, January 14, 1963, ibid.

14. Lincoln Gordon telegram to Secretary of State, February 3, 1963, ibid.

15. Stephen Clissold, *Soviet Relations with Latin America, 1918–1968: A Documentary Survey* (London: Oxford University Press, 1970), doc. 85.

16. Department of State to embassy, Rio, August 19, 1963, National Security Files, Latin America, microfilm reel 3, Kennedy Library.

17. William H. Draper, Jr., to Kennedy, November 5, 1963, and Ralph Dungan to Benjamin Read, November 21, 1963, ibid., microfilm reel 2.

18. Lincoln Gordon to Department of State, March 27 and 29, 1964, National Security Files, Latin America, reel 4, Johnson Library.

19. U.S. consul in São Paulo telegram, March 30, 1964, *Declassified Documents* 1976, no. 49e.

20. CIA cables, March 30 and 31, 1964, National Security Files, Latin America, reel 4, Johnson Library.

21. The key document is the transcript of the March 31, 1964, teleconference between Washington and the embassy in Rio, National Security Files, Latin America, microfilm reel 5, Johnson Library. See also extensive cables in the same file.

22. Walters, p. 389. Walters protests at length that he had nothing to do with the coup and that his frequent contact with its leaders was simply in the ordinary performance of his duties.

23. CIA intelligence summary, July 29, 1964, National Security Files, Latin America, microfilm reel 5, Johnson Library.

24. Jack Valenti briefing paper, August 10, 1965, confidential file, CO 37, Johnson Library.

25. Ambassador George H. Butler to Secretary of State, October 30, 1946, *FRUS*46/9, p. 805.

26. *FRUS*51/2, pp. 1367–70.

27. Memorandum of conversation between Ambassador Ralph Ackerman and Trujillo, ibid., pp. 1370–74.

28. Policy memorandum, October 9, 1951, ibid., pp. 1386–87.

29. John M. Cabot, *First Line of Defense* (Washington, DC: Georgetown School of Foreign Service, 1971), p. 86.

30. Roy Rubottom memorandum to Secretary of State, February 20, 1957, *FRUS*55–57/6, p. 908. See pp. 877–908 for documentation on the Galíndez case.

31. Briefing book, White House Central Files, confidential file, box 42, folder 2, Eisenhower Library.

32. Edwin Norman Clark to Eisenhower, March 21, 1960, Whitman file, Dulles-Herter series, Eisenhower Library.

33. Christian Herter memorandum for Eisenhower, April 14, 1960, Whitman file, Dulles-Herter series, Eisenhower Library.

34. Arthur M. Schlesinger, Jr., ed., *The Dynamics of World Power: A Documentary History of United States Foreign Policy, 1945–1973*, vol. 3, *Latin America*, Robert Burr, ed. (New York: Chelsea House, 1973), pp. 448–51.

35. United Nations, *Security Council Official Records*, 895th meeting, September 9, 1960, pp. 1–6; see also Clissold, pp. 219–20.

36. This summary follows John Bartlow Martin, *Overtaken by Events: The Dominican Crisis from the Fall of Trujillo to the Civil War* (Garden City, NY: Doubleday, 1966).

37. Ibid., p. 601.

38. State Department, Bureau of Intelligence and Research memorandum, April 7, 1964, National Security Files, Latin America, microfilm reel 1, Johnson Library.

39. Gordon Chase memorandum for McGeorge Bundy, April 27, 1964, ibid.

40. Lyndon B. Johnson, *Vantage Point: Perspectives on the Presidency, 1963–1969* (New York: Holt, Rinehart & Winston, 1971), p. 197.

41. Pat Holt oral history interview, Hoover Library.

42. Jack Valenti notes of White House meeting, April 29, 1965; and May

2 meeting with congressional leaders, *Declassified Documents* 1982, no. 584.

43. General Bruce Palmer, Jr., *Intervention in the Caribbean: The Dominican Crisis of 1965* (Lexington: The University Press of Kentucky, 1989). General Palmer was commander of the American forces.

44. Embassy, Buenos Aires, to Secretary of State, December 13, 1965, National Security Files, Latin America, microfilm reel 4, Johnson Library.

45. Sol M. Linowitz, *The Making of a Public Man: A Memoir* (Boston, MA: Little, Brown, 1985), p. 21.

46. Raymond L. Garthoff, *Détente and Confrontation: American-Soviet Relations from Nixon to Reagan* (Washington, DC: The Brookings Institution, 1985), pp. 76–77.

47. Richard Nixon, *RN: The Memoirs of Richard Nixon* (New York: Grossett & Dunlap, 1978), p. 486.

48. Henry A. Kissinger, *The White House Years* (Boston, MA: Little, Brown, 1979), pp. 642–46; Nixon, *RN*, p. 487.

49. Kissinger, *White House Years*, pp. 650–51.

50. Nixon, *RN*, p. 490.

51. CIA Situation Report 9, September 1, 1947, PSF, Intelligence Files, box 259; Claude Bowers to Truman, July 18, 1950, PSF, box 172, Truman Library.

52. Claude Bowers to Edward G. Miller, Jr., October 7, 1952, Edward G. Miller, Jr., papers, box 4, Truman Library.

53. Report on Chile, November 23, 1955, Operations Coordinating Board Central Files, box 17, Eisenhower Library.

54. CIA Survey of Latin America, April 1, 1964, National Security Files, Latin America, microfilm reel 1, Johnson Library.

55. Gordon Chase to McGeorge Bundy, April 30, 1964, ibid.

56. Kissinger, *White House Years*, p. 653.

57. Ibid., p. 657.

58. Thomas Powers, *The Man Who Kept the Secrets: Richard Helms and the CIA* (New York: Alfred A. Knopf, 1979), p. 235; Nathaniel Davis, *The Last Two Years of Salvador Allende* (Ithaca, NY: Cornell University Press, 1985). Davis succeeded Korry as ambassador in 1971.

59. Henry A. Kissinger, *Years of Upheaval* (Boston, MA: Little, Brown, 1982), pp. 374–413.

60. Taylor Branch and Eugene M. Propper, *Labyrinth* (New York: Viking, 1982).

7. PREMATURE OBITUARY: THE DOCTRINE AND JIMMY CARTER

1. Gaddis Smith, *Morality, Reason, and Power: American Diplomacy in the Carter Years* (New York: Hill and Wang, 1986), p. 28.
2. *PPP*: Carter, 1977, pp. 955–62.
3. Zbigniew Brzezinski, *Between Two Ages: America's Role in the Technetronic Era* (New York: Viking, 1970), p. 288.
4. Zbigniew Brzezinski, *Power and Principle: Memoirs of the National Security Adviser, 1977–1981* (New York: Farrar, Straus and Giroux, 1983), pp. 134–35.
5. *NYT*, January 9, 1979.
6. Commission on United States–Latin American Relations, *The Americas in a Changing World* (New York: Quadrangle Books, 1975), pp. 11–61.
7. Walter LaFeber, *The Panama Canal: The Crisis in Historical Perspective* (New York: Oxford University Press, 1978) is an excellent survey.
8. *FRUS*46/9, pp. 47–52.
9. Dean Acheson memorandum for Truman, January 17, 1952, PSF, box 165, Truman Library.
10. Memorandum of conversation, September 28, 1953, Secretary of State's Memoranda of Conversations, November 1952–December 1954, *FRUS* microfiche supplement, 1992, doc. 236.
11. Julian F. Harrington to Assistant Secretary of State Henry F. Holland, August 24, 1956; memorandum of conversation between John Foster Dulles and Eisenhower, August 2, 1956, *FRUS*55–57/7, p. 30.
12. John M. Cabot, *First Line of Defense* (Washington, DC: Georgetown School of Foreign Service, 1971), p. 107. See also briefing paper, April 29, 1959, Whitman file, diary series, Eisenhower Library.
13. Deputy Secretary of Defense Thomas Gates to President Eisenhower, December 1, 1959, WHO, OSS, international file, Eisenhower Library.
14. Lyndon B. Johnson, *Vantage Point: Perspectives on the Presidency, 1963–1969* (New York: Holt, Rinehart & Winston, 1971), p. 180.

15. LaFeber, *Panama Canal*, p. 143.

16. Ibid., p. 146.

17. William J. Jorden, *Panama Odyssey* (Austin: University of Texas Press, 1984), p. 111.

18. Ibid., pp. 189–95.

19. LaFeber, *Panama Canal*, pp. 186–87.

20. Jorden is best on the negotiations. For the political struggle over approval of the treaties, see J. Michael Hogan, *The Panama Canal in American Politics* (Carbondale, IL: Southern Illinois University Press, 1986) and George D. Moffett III, *The Limits of Victory: The Ratification of the Panama Canal Treaties* (Ithaca, NY: Cornell University Press, 1985).

21. Moffett, p. 45.

22. Jimmy Carter, *Keeping Faith: Memoirs of a President* (New York: Bantam Books, 1982), p. 184.

23. *Americas in a Changing World*, pp. 29–30.

24. The essential source is the history/memoir of the diplomat sent to Havana as head of the interest section, Wayne S. Smith: *The Closest of Enemies: A Personal and Diplomatic History of the Castro Years* (New York: Norton, 1987).

25. This summary draws heavily on the superb case study by David D. Newsom, *The Soviet Brigade in Cuba* (Bloomington: Indiana University Press, 1987).

26. The Vance and Brzezinski press conference remarks are reprinted as Appendices B and C, ibid.

27. *CR*, September 11, 1979, p. 24031; *NYT*, September 12, 1979.

28. Secretary of State James F. Byrnes memorandum for the President, March 5, 1946, PSF, box 183, Truman Library.

29. William M. LeoGrande, "The Revolution in Nicaragua: Another Cuba?" *Foreign Affairs* 58 (Fall 1979), pp. 28–50.

30. Robert A. Pastor, *Condemned to Repetition: The United States and Nicaragua* (Princeton, NJ: Princeton University Press, 1987), pp. 60–61.

31. Ibid., pp. 86–89.

32. Larry P. MacDonald, John M. Murphy, and George Hansen to Carter, June 29, 1979; Tom Harkin to Carter, July 12, 1979, CO 114, box CO–46, Carter Library.

33. *NYT*, June 21, 1979.

34. *AFP*77–80, doc. 698.

35. Zbigniew Brzezinski diary, June 22, 1979, quoted by Pastor, *Condemned*, pp. 147–48.

36. Ibid., p. 195.

37. *NYT*, September 11, 1979.

38. Ibid., quoting interview in German magazine *Der Stern*.

39. Robert S. Leiken and Barry Rubin, *The Central American Crisis Reader* (New York: Summit Books, 1987), pp. 674–76.

40. Cabot, p. 87.

41. *FRUS*52–54/4, pp. 1007–8.

42. Briefing paper and memorandum of conversation between José María Lemus and Eisenhower, March 11, 1959, Whitman file, El Salvador, folder 3, Eisenhower Library.

43. Intelligence summary for the President, November 7, 1960, diary series, Eisenhower Library; Walter LaFeber, *Inevitable Revolutions: The United States in Central America*, 2nd ed. (New York: Norton, 1993), pp. 174–75.

44. Geoffrey Kirk to Foreign Office, January 6, 1961, FO 371 155728, Public Record Office.

45. James Dunkerley, *The Long War: Dictatorship & Revolution in El Salvador* (London: Junction Books, 1982), pp. 111–12.

46. Senator Richard Stone to Carter, August 10, 1979; J. Brian Atwood, Assistant Secretary of State for Congressional Relations, to Stone, October 9, 1979, White House Central Files, CO–9, box 9, Carter Library.

47. Peter Kornbluh, *Nicaragua: The Price of Intervention* (Washington, DC: Institute for Policy Studies, 1987), p. 19.

8. A Tale of Three Doctrines: Reagan, Brezhnev, and Monroe

1. Ronald Reagan, *An American Life* (New York: Simon & Schuster, 1990), pp. 471–74.

2. Gaddis Smith, "The Legacy of Monroe's Doctrine," *NYT Magazine*, September 9, 1984.

3. William F. Buckley, Jr., "The Monroe Doctrine, I Presume?" *National Review*, April 17, 1981, p. 446.

4. Jeane Kirkpatrick, "Dictatorships and Double Standards," *Commentary* 68 (November 1979), pp. 34–45.

5. Reagan speech to the National Association of Manufacturers, March 10, 1983, *AFP83*, doc. 614.

6. *AFP83*, doc. 1.

7. George P. Shultz, *Turmoil and Triumph: My Years as Secretary of State* (New York: Scribners, 1983), pp. 535–36.

8. Robert A. Jones, *The Soviet Concept of 'Limited Sovereignty' from Lenin to Gorbachev: The Brezhnev Doctrine* (London: Macmillan, 1990).

9. Arthur M. Schlesinger, Jr., ed., *The Dynamics of World Power: A Documentary History of United States Foreign Policy, 1945–1973*, vol. 2, *Eastern Europe and the Soviet Union*, Walter LaFeber, ed. (New York: Chelsea House, 1973), p. 815.

10. *The Report of the President's National Bipartisan Commission on Central America* (New York: Macmillan, 1984), pp. 109–10.

11. The best account of all aspects of the Falklands war is Lawrence Freedman and Virginia Gamba-Stonehouse, *Signals of War: The Falklands Conflict of 1982* (London: Faber and Faber, 1990).

12. The distant history is recounted in Julius Goebel, *The Struggle for the Falkland Islands* (New Haven, CT: Yale University Press, 1927; reprint, 1982).

13. Dexter Perkins, *The Monroe Doctrine, 1826–1867* (Baltimore, MD: The Johns Hopkins University Press, 1933), p. 7.

14. U.S. delegation to Secretary of State, August 29, 1947, *FRUS47/8*, p. 75.

15. James Bruce to Secretary of State Marshall, March 10, 1948, and Marshall to Bruce, March 17, 1948, *FRUS48/1*, pp. 966–68.

16. *FRUS48/9*, p. 16.

17. The various UN and OAS resolutions together with official U.S. statements are conveniently collected in *AFP82*, docs. 621–64.

18. Argentine Foreign Minister Nicanor Costa Mendez to Alexander M. Haig, Jr., May 2, 1982, *AFP82*, doc. 636.

19. Roy Gutman, *Banana Diplomacy: The Making of American Policy in Nicaragua, 1981–1987* (New York: Simon & Schuster, 1988), p. 105.

20. U.S. Congress, House, Committee on Foreign Affairs, Subcom-

mittee on Inter-American Affairs, *Latin America and the United States After the Falklands/Malvinas Crisis*, 97th Cong., 2nd sess. (Washington, DC, 1982), pp. 44–46, 68.

21. Reagan, p. 457.

22. Shultz, p. 340.

23. Wayne S. Smith, *The Closest of Enemies: A Personal and Diplomatic History of the Castro Years* (New York: Norton, 1987), p. 171.

24. An excellent account is Michael Massing, "Grenada Before and After," *The Atlantic Monthly*, February 1984, pp. 76–87. See also the long letter from Ambassador Frank Ortiz, ibid., June 1984.

25. Wayne S. Smith, *Enemies*, pp. 271–72.

26. Richard E. Feingold, *The Intemperate Zone: The Third World Challenge to U.S. Foreign Policy* (New York: Norton, 1983), pp. 198–99.

27. *AFP77–80*, doc. 714.

28. *PPP: Reagan*, 1982/1, p. 448.

29. Deputy Assistant Secretary of State Stephen Bosworth testimony, June 15, 1982, *AFP82*, doc. 687.

30. Reagan speech, March 13, 1983, *AFP83*, doc. 13.

31. Progress report on implementation of NSC–144, November 20, 1953, *FRUS52–54/4*, pp. 29–30.

32. "Record of Anglo–United States Talks at the State Department," February 9, 1961, FO 371 159674, Public Record Office.

33. Department telegram to U.S. consul in Georgetown (Melby), February 15, 1961; Secretary of State Dean Rusk to embassy, Ottawa, August 12, 1961, National Security Files, Latin America, microfilm reel 3, Kennedy Library.

34. Shultz, p. 293.

35. Ibid., p. 296.

36. *NYT*, June 1, 1983. This article by Philip Taubman is based on extensive interviews with unidentified committee members and is consistent with Shultz's account.

37. Constantine C. Menges, *Inside the National Security Council* (New York: Simon & Schuster, 1988), pp. 58–68.

38. Margaret Thatcher, *The Downing Street Years* (New York: HarperCollins, 1993), p. 331.

39. U.S. Department of State and Department of Defense, *Grenada Documents: An Overview and Selection* (Washington, DC, 1984).

40. Shultz, p. 344.
41. United Nations, *Security Council Official Records*, 2491st meeting, October 28, 1983, p. 5; *NYT*, October 29, 1983.

9. NICARAGUA: THE SELF-INFLICTED WOUND

1. *New Inter-American Policy for the Eighties* (Washington, DC: Council for Inter-American Security, 1980). See also Jeane Kirkpatrick, "U.S. Security & Latin America," *Commentary* 71 (January 1981), pp. 29–40; Roger Fontaine, Cleto DeGiovanni, and Alexander Kruger, "Castro's Specter," *Washington Quarterly* 3 (Autumn 1980), pp. 3–27.
2. Lawrence A. Pezzullo interview with Christopher Dickey, November 1980, quoted in Dickey, "Central America: From Quagmire to Cauldron?" *Foreign Affairs: America and the World, 1983* 62, no. 3, pp. 659–94.
3. U.S. Department of State, *Communist Interference in El Salvador: Documents Demonstrating Communist Support of the Salvadoran Insurgency* (Washington, DC, February 23, 1981). Poor translations from Spanish and bad arithmetic weakened the impact of this "white paper."
4. *DSB*, April 1981, pp. 13–20.
5. Kiva Maidanik, "On the *Real* Soviet Policy Toward Central America," in Wayne S. Smith, ed., *The Russians Aren't Coming: New Soviet Policy in Latin America* (Boulder, CO: Lynne Reiner Publishers, 1992), pp. 89–96. The essays in this book were written before the disappearance of the U.S.S.R.
6. Bob Woodward, *Veil: The Secret Wars of the CIA* (New York: Simon & Schuster, 1987), p. 121.
7. Roy Gutman, *Banana Diplomacy: The Making of American Policy in Nicaragua, 1981–1987* (New York: Simon & Schuster, 1988), p. 67.
8. George P. Shultz, *Turmoil and Triumph: My Years as Secretary of State* (New York: Scribners, 1993), pp. 290–91. For a long account of a massacre committed by American-trained Salvadoran troops in December 1981 and the subsequent efforts of the Reagan Administration to deny knowledge, see Mark Danner, "The Truth of El Mozote," *The New Yorker*, December 6, 1993, pp. 50–92.
9. Anthony Lewis, *NYT*, December 4, 1983.

10. Shultz, p. 294.
11. *NYT*, March 19, 1984.
12. A good starting point in the immense literature on the subject is Theodore Draper, *A Very Thin Line* (New York: Hill and Wang, 1991).
13. Thomas Enders speech before Inter-American Press Association, Chicago, September 30, 1982, *AFP82*, doc. 616. Only six weeks before, Enders had said, "It is, of course, for Nicaragua to decide what kind of government it has. No one challenges that. We don't. Its neighbors don't." Speech before the Commonwealth Club, San Francisco, August 20, 1982, ibid., doc. 693.
14. *Newsweek*, November 8, 1982.
15. Peter Kornbluh, *Nicaragua: The Price of Intervention* (Washington, DC: Institute for Policy Studies, 1987), p. 47.
16. Shultz, p. 285.
17. Ibid., p. 311.
18. Kornbluh, pp. 56–57.
19. Draper, pp. 20–21.
20. United Nations, *Security Council Official Records*, 2525th meeting, p. 41.
21. United Nations, *Security Council Official Records*, 2529th meeting, pp. 108–10.
22. *DSB*, September 8, 1946.
23. International Court of Justice, *Military and Paramilitary Activities In and Against Nicaragua* (mimeograph).
24. Op-ed piece, *NYT*, July 19, 1983.
25. Robert M. Gates memorandum to William J. Casey, December 14, 1984, *NYT*, September 20, 1991.
26. Kornbluh, pp. 163–65.
27. Jonathan S. Miller to Patrick Buchanan, White House Director of Communications, March 13, 1985 (declassified September 10, 1987). See also Samantha Power, "The Office of Public Diplomacy" (Senior essay, Department of History, Yale University, 1991). I am indebted to Ms. Power for the above document.
28. *AFP85*, doc. 554.
29. The most active of the sister-city relationships, still functioning in 1994, is between New Haven, CT, and León, Nicaragua. It had

offices in both cities and sponsored short- and long-term visits by hundreds of people—teachers, carpenters, church workers, doctors, day-care specialists, etc.—and sent large amounts of relief supplies. The author was a participant in the New Haven–León project.

30. Elliott Abrams, "The Spirit Behind the Monroe Doctrine," *Current Policy* 949 (Washington, DC: Department of State, 1987).
31. Shultz, p. 960.

10. FADE AWAY

1. Carlos Fuentes, "Time for *Our* Sinatra Doctrine," *The Nation*, February 12, 1990.
2. Mark A. Uhlig, "Latin America: The Frustrations of Success," *Foreign Affairs: America and the World, 1990/91* 70, pp. 101–19.
3. Taylor Branch and Eugene M. Propper, *Labyrinth* (New York: Viking, 1982).
4. State Department press briefing, October 30, 1984, *AFP84*, doc. 566.
5. This brief account is based on the *NYT* and George P. Shultz, *Turmoil and Triumph: My Years as Secretary of State* (New York: Scribners, 1993), pp. 969–75.
6. *AFP90*, doc. 633.
7. *NYT*, October 29, 1992.
8. Kevin Buckley, *Panama: The Whole Story* (New York: Simon & Schuster, 1991), pp. 44–46. I rely heavily on this excellent book for my brief treatment of the Noriega affair.
9. Shultz, p. 621.
10. Robert Murphy memorandum for President Eisenhower, May 28, 1954, Whitman file, Dulles-Herter series, Eisenhower Library.
11. Telegram to embassy, Port-au-Prince, September 22, 1959, WHO, OSS, international series, Eisenhower Library.
12. Memorandum of conversation among Secretary Herter, President Eisenhower, and others, July 13, 1960, Whitman file, diary series, Eisenhower Library.
13. Chester Bowles memorandum to Adolf A. Berle, May 25, 1961, Chester Bowles papers, file 299–0512, Yale University Library.

14. State Department intelligence analysis, April 7, 1964, National Security Files, Latin America, microfilm reel 1, Johnson Library.

15. Report to members of the Senate Foreign Relations Committee, November 9, 1966, Bourke Hickenlooper papers, box 120, Hoover Library.

16. Thomas Mann testimony, January 12, 1965, *Executive Sessions of the Senate Foreign Relations Committee (Historical Series)*, vol. 17 (made public September 1990), p. 148.

17. Richard Celeste to President Jimmy Carter, April 24, 1980, domestic policy staff files, box 178, Carter Library.

18. *NYT*, June 22, 1993.

19. Memorandum of conversation among Eisenhower, Under Secretary of State Douglas Dillon, and others, October 18, 1960, Whitman file, diary series, Eisenhower Library.

20. A unique two-way perspective on Mexican-American relations is offered in Robert A. Pastor and Jorge G. Castaneda, *Limits to Friendship: The United States and Mexico* (New York: Alfred A. Knopf, 1988).

21. Barbara Tuchman, *The Zimmermann Telegram* (New York: Viking, 1958).

22. E. David Cronon, *Josephus Daniels in Mexico* (Madison: University of Wisconsin Press, 1960).

23. George S. Messersmith to Secretary of State, February 11, 1945, doc. 1676, George S. Messersmith papers, University of Delaware Library.

24. George S. Messersmith to John Willard Carrigan, Mexican desk, Department of State, January 12, 1946, doc. 1763, ibid.

25. J. Edgar Hoover to George E. Allen for President Truman's attention, September 23, 1946, PSF, FBI, box 169, Truman Library.

26. Alan Riding, *Distant Neighbors* (New York: Vintage Books, 1986), pp. 145–46.

27. *NYT*, June 4, 1993.

BIBLIOGRAPHY

Primary Sources: Printed and Manuscript

The single most important printed source for this study is the Department of State's published collection of historical documents, *The Foreign Relations of the United States* (Washington, DC: U.S. Government Printing Office), published approximately thirty-five years after the date of the original material. The footnotes indicate year and number of the volumes cited. There is a microfiche supplementary publication of *FRUS* containing memoranda of the conversations of the Secretaries of State, 1949–60. Central Intelligence Agency, *CIA Documents on the Cuban Missile Crisis, 1962* (Washington, DC: CIA History Staff, 1992) is useful for that subject. Other valuable government publications are *The Department of State Bulletin*, a weekly and then a monthly, for most of the years of this study; the annual volumes of the Department of State, *American Foreign Policy: Current Documents*, covering the years since 1977, supplementing and then replacing *The Department of State Bulletin; Public Papers of the Presidents*, published and here cited by name of the President and year; and the *Congressional Record* cited by date and page number. Also of use were Arthur M. Schlesinger, Jr., ed., *The Dynamics of World Power: A Documentary History of United States Foreign Policy, 1945–1973*, vol. 3, *Latin America*, Robert Burr, ed. (New York: Chelsea House, 1973); United Nations, *Security Council Official Records*, cited by date and number of meeting; and the *Annals of the Organization of American States*.

Manuscript records, some on microfilm, from the following presidential libraries were essential: the Herbert C. Hoover Library, West Branch, Iowa; the Franklin D. Roosevelt Library, Hyde Park, New York; the Harry S. Truman Library, Independence, Missouri; the Dwight D. Eisenhower Library, Abilene, Kansas; the John F. Kennedy Library, Boston, Massachusetts; the Lyndon B. Johnson Library, Austin, Texas; the Gerald R. Ford Library, Ann Arbor, Michigan; and the Jimmy Carter Library, Atlanta, Georgia. The manuscript records of the Department of State in the National Archives, Washington, D.C., were an important supplement to *The Foreign Relations of the United States*—especially the lot files of the Assistant Secretaries of State for Inter-American Affairs. Additional documents can be found in the Carrollton Press microfiche compilation, *Declassified Documents*, cited by year of publication and document number. Records of the British Foreign Office, FO 371, in the Public Record Office, Kew, London, were important for the Guatemalan affair of 1954.

The manuscript papers of the following individuals contained useful material: Dean Acheson, Truman Library, Independence, Missouri; Hamilton Fish Armstrong, Seeley Mudd Library, Princeton University, Princeton, New Jersey; Samuel Flagg Bemis, Archives and Manuscripts, Yale University Library, New Haven, Connecticut; Adolph A. Berle, Franklin D. Roosevelt Library, Hyde Park, New York; Chester Bowles, Archives and Manuscripts, Yale University Library; Ellis Briggs oral history interview, Oral History Collection, Columbia University Library, New York; John M. Cabot, microfilm, Massachusetts Historical Society, Boston, Massachusetts; John Foster Dulles, Seeley Mudd Library, Princeton University; J. William Fulbright, University of Arkansas Library, Fayetteville, Arkansas; Bourke Hickenlooper, Hoover Library, West Branch, Iowa; Pat Holt oral history interview, Hoover Library; George S. Messersmith, Special Collections, University of Delaware Library, Newark, Delaware; Edward G. Miller, Jr., Truman Library; Richard C. Patterson, Truman Library; Henry L. Stimson, Archives and Manuscripts, Yale University Library; Arthur H. Vandenberg, University of Michigan Library, Ann Arbor, Michigan.

Books and Articles

Abbott, Elizabeth. *Haiti: The Duvaliers and Their Legacy*. New York: McGraw-Hill, 1988.

Agee, Philip. *Inside the Company: CIA Diary*. New York: Stonehill, 1975.

Allman, T. D. *Unmanifest Destiny: Mayhem and Illusion in American Foreign Policy—From the Monroe Doctrine to Reagan's War in El Salvador*. Garden City, NY: Doubleday, 1984.

Attwood, William. *The Twilight Struggle: Tales of the Cold War*. New York: Harper & Row, 1987.

Bartlett, Ruhl J. *The Record of American Diplomacy*. 4th ed. New York: Alfred A. Knopf, 1964.

Bemis, Samuel Flagg. *John Quincy Adams and the Foundations of American Foreign Policy*. New York: Alfred A. Knopf, 1956.

———. *The Latin American Policy of the United States*. New York: Harcourt, Brace and Company, 1943.

Berle, Beatrice Bishop, and Travis Jacobs, eds. *Navigating the Rapids, 1918–1971*. New York: Harcourt Brace Jovanovich, 1973.

Betancourt, Rómulo. *Venezuela, Oil and Politics*. Boston, MA: Houghton Mifflin, 1979.

Blachman, Morris J., William M. LeoGrande, and Kenneth Sharpe. *Confronting Revolution: Security Through Diplomacy in Central America*. New York: Pantheon Books, 1986.

Black, Jan Knippers. *United States Penetration of Brazil*. Philadelphia: University of Pennsylvania Press, 1977.

Blakeslee, George H. "The Japanese Monroe Doctrine." *Foreign Affairs* 11 (July 1933), pp. 671–81.

Blasier, Cole. *The Giant's Rival: The USSR and Latin America*. Pittsburgh, PA: Pittsburgh University Press, 1983.

———. *The Hovering Giant: U.S. Responses to Revolutionary Change in Latin America*. Pittsburgh, PA: University of Pittsburgh Press, 1987.

Blight, James G., and David A. Welch. *On the Brink: Americans and Soviets Reexamine the Cuban Missile Crisis*. New York: Farrar, Straus and Giroux, 1990.

Blum, John Morton. *The Price of Vision: The Diary of Henry A. Wallace*. Boston, MA: Houghton Mifflin, 1973.

Bonsal, Philip W. *Cuba, Castro and the United States.* Pittsburgh, PA: University of Pittsburgh Press, 1971.

Braden, Spruille. *Diplomats and Demagogues.* New Rochelle, NY: Arlington House, 1971.

Branch, Taylor, and Eugene M. Propper. *Labyrinth.* New York: Viking, 1982.

Brinkley, Douglas. *Dean Acheson: The Cold War Years, 1953–1971.* New Haven, CT: Yale University Press, 1992.

Brown, Cynthia. *With Friends Like These: The Americas Watch Report on Human Rights and U.S. Policy in Latin America.* New York: Pantheon Books, 1985.

Brzezinski, Zbigniew. *Between Two Ages: America's Role in the Technetronic Era.* New York: Viking, 1970.

———. *Power and Principle: Memoirs of the National Security Adviser, 1977–1981.* New York: Farrar, Straus and Giroux, 1983.

Buckley, Kevin. *Panama: The Whole Story.* New York: Simon & Schuster, 1991.

Buckley, Tom. *Violent Neighbors: El Salvador, Central America, and the United States.* New York: Times Books, 1984.

Burns, E. Bradford. *At War in Nicaragua: The Reagan Doctrine and the Politics of Nostalgia.* New York: Harper & Row, 1987.

Cabot, John M. *First Line of Defense.* Washington, DC: Georgetown School of Foreign Service, 1971.

Campbell, Thomas M., and George C. Herring, eds. *The Diaries of Edward R. Stettinius, Jr., 1943–1946.* New York: New Viewpoints, 1975.

Carter, Jimmy. *Keeping Faith: Memoirs of a President.* New York: Bantam Books, 1982.

Chayes, Abram. *The Cuban Missile Crisis: International Crises and the Role of Law.* New York: Oxford University Press, 1974.

Christian, Shirley. *Nicaragua: Revolution in the Family.* New York: Vintage Books, 1986.

Clissold, Stephen. *Soviet Relations with Latin America, 1918–1968: A Documentary Survey.* London: Oxford University Press, 1970.

Cockburn, Leslie. *Out of Control.* New York: Atlantic Monthly Press, 1987.

Coleman, Kenneth M. "The Political Mythology of the Monroe Doctrine: Reflections on the Social Psychology of Hegemony." In Martz, John D., and Lars Schoultz, eds. *Latin America, the United States and the Inter-American System*. Boulder, CO: Westview Press, 1981.

Colville, John. *The Fringes of Power: 10 Downing Street Diaries, 1939–1955*. New York: Norton, 1985.

Commission on United States–Latin American Relations. *The Americas in a Changing World*. New York: Quadrangle Books, 1975.

Conn, Stetson, and Byron Fairchild. *The United States Army in World War II: The Framework of Hemispheric Defense*. Washington, DC: Office of the Chief of Military History, 1960.

Connell-Smith, Gordon. *The Inter-American System*. London: Oxford University Press, 1966.

Crabb, Cecil V., Jr. *The Doctrines of American Foreign Policy*. Baton Rouge, LA: Louisiana University Press, 1982.

Cronon, E. David. *Josephus Daniels in Mexico*. Madison: University of Wisconsin Press, 1960.

Davis, Nathaniel. *The Last Two Years of Salvador Allende*. Ithaca, NY: Cornell University Press, 1985.

Detzer, David. *The Brink: The Cuban Missile Crisis, 1962*. New York: Crowell, 1979.

Dickey, Christopher. *With the Contras*. New York: Simon & Schuster, 1987.

Draper, Theodore. *A Very Thin Line*. New York: Hill and Wang, 1991.

Dunkerley, James. *The Long War: Dictatorship & Revolution in El Salvador*. London: Junction Books, 1982.

Feingold, Richard E. *The Intemperate Zone: The Third World Challenge to U.S. Foreign Policy*. New York: Norton, 1983.

Feis, Herbert. *Churchill, Roosevelt, Stalin: The War They Waged and the Peace They Sought*. Princeton, NJ: Princeton University Press, 1957.

Ferrell, Robert H. *Peace in Their Time: The Origins of the Kellogg-Briand Pact*. New Haven, CT: Yale University Press, 1952.

———, ed. *Dear Bess: Letters from Harry to Bess Truman, 1910–1959*. New York: Norton, 1982.

Freedman, Lawrence, and Virginia Gamba-Stonehouse. *Signals of War: The Falklands Conflict of 1982*. London: Faber and Faber, 1990.

Garthoff, Raymond L. *Détente and Confrontation: American–Soviet Rela-*

tions from Nixon to Reagan. Washington, DC: The Brookings Institution, 1985.

Gilbert, Felix. *To the Farewell Address: Ideas of Early American Foreign Policy*. Princeton, NJ: Princeton University Press, 1961.

Gleijeses, Piero. *The Dominican Crisis: The 1965 Constitutionalist Revolt*. Baltimore, MD: The Johns Hopkins University Press, 1978.

―――. *Shattered Hope: The Guatemalan Revolution and the United States, 1944–1954*. Princeton, NJ: Princeton University Press, 1991.

Goebel, Julius. *The Struggle for the Falkland Islands*. New Haven, CT: Yale University Press, 1927. Reprint, 1982.

Green, David. *The Containment of Latin America*. Chicago, IL: Quadrangle Books, 1971.

Gruchmann, Lothar. *Nationalsocialistische Grossraumordnung: Die Konstruktion einer "deutschen Monroe-Doktrin."* Stuttgart: Deutsche Verlags-Anstalt, 1962.

Gutman, Roy. *Banana Diplomacy: The Making of American Policy in Nicaragua, 1981–1987*. New York: Simon & Schuster, 1988.

Haig, Alexander, Jr. *Caveat: Realism, Reagan and Foreign Policy*. New York: Macmillan, 1984.

Higgins, Trumbull. *Perfect Failure*. New York: Norton, 1987.

Hogan, J. Michael. *The Panama Canal in American Politics*. Carbondale, IL: Southern Illinois University Press, 1986.

Hull, Cordell. *Memoirs*. 2 vols. New York: Macmillan, 1948.

Immerman, Richard H. *The CIA in Guatemala*. Austin: University of Texas Press, 1982.

Johnson, Lyndon B. *Vantage Point: Perspectives on the Presidency, 1963–1969*. New York: Holt, Rinehart & Winston, 1971.

Jonas, Susanne. *The Battle for Guatemala: Rebels, Death Squads, and U.S. Power*. Boulder, CO: Westview Press, 1991.

Jones, Robert A. *The Soviet Concept of 'Limited Sovereignty' from Lenin to Gorbachev: The Brezhnev Doctrine*. London: Macmillan, 1990.

Jorden, William J. *Panama Odyssey*. Austin: University of Texas Press, 1984.

Karnes, Thomas L. "Hiram Bingham and His Obsolete Shibboleth." *Diplomatic History* 3 (Winter 1979), pp. 39–57.

Kennan, George F. *Memoirs: 1925–1950*. Boston, MA: Little, Brown, 1967.

Kennedy, Robert F. *Thirteen Days: A Memoir of the Cuban Missile Crisis.* New York: Signet, 1969.

Kissinger, Henry A. *The White House Years.* Boston, MA: Little, Brown, 1979.

———. *Years of Upheaval.* Boston, MA: Little, Brown, 1982.

Kornbluh, Peter. *Nicaragua: The Price of Intervention.* Washington, DC: Institute for Policy Studies, 1987.

Langguth, A. J. *Hidden Terrors.* New York: Pantheon Books, 1978.

LaFeber, Walter. "The Evolution of the Monroe Doctrine from Monroe to Reagan." In Gardner, Lloyd, ed. *Redefining the Past: Essays in Diplomatic History in Honor of William Appleman Williams.* Corvallis: Oregon State University Press, 1986.

———. *Inevitable Revolutions: The United States in Central America.* 2nd ed. New York: Norton, 1993.

———. *The Panama Canal: The Crisis in Historical Perspective.* New York: Oxford University Press, 1978.

Lake, Anthony. *Somoza Falling.* Boston, MA: Houghton Mifflin, 1989.

Leiken, Robert S., and Barry Rubin. *The Central American Crisis Reader.* New York: Summit Books, 1987.

Levinson, Jerome, and Juan de Onis. *The Alliance That Lost Its Way.* Chicago, IL: Quadrangle Books, 1970.

Linowitz, Sol M. *The Making of a Public Man: A Memoir.* Boston, MA: Little, Brown, 1985.

Logan, John A., Jr. *No Transfer: An American Security Principle.* New Haven, CT: Yale University Press, 1961.

Lowenthal, Abraham F. *The Dominican Intervention.* Cambridge, MA: Harvard University Press, 1972.

———. *Partners in Conflict.* Baltimore, MD: The Johns Hopkins University Press, 1987.

McLellan, David S., and David C. Acheson. *Among Friends: Personal Letters of Dean Acheson.* New York: Dodd, Mead, 1980.

McNeil, Frank. *War and Peace in Central America.* New York: Scribners, 1988.

Marchetti, Victor, and John D. Marks. *The CIA and the Cult of Intelligence.* New York: Alfred A. Knopf, 1974.

Martin, John Bartlow. *Overtaken by Events: The Dominican Crisis from the Fall of Trujillo to the Civil War.* Garden City, NY: Doubleday, 1966.

Martz, John D., ed. *United States Policy in Latin America: A Quarter Century of Crisis and Challenge.* Lincoln: University of Nebraska Press, 1988.

Martz, John D., and Lars Schoultz, eds. *Latin America, the United States and the Inter-American System.* Boulder, CO: Westview Press, 1981.

May, Ernest R. *The Making of the Monroe Doctrine.* Cambridge, MA: Harvard University Press, 1975.

Menges, Constantine C. *Inside the National Security Council.* New York: Simon & Schuster, 1988.

Middlebrook, Kevin J., and Carlos Rico, eds. *The United States and Latin America in the 1980s.* Pittsburgh, PA: University of Pittsburgh Press, 1986.

Miscamble, Wilson D. *George F. Kennan and the Making of American Foreign Policy, 1947–1950.* Princeton, NJ: Princeton University Press, 1992.

Moffett, George D., III. *The Limits of Victory: The Ratification of the Panama Canal Treaties.* Ithaca, NY: Cornell University Press, 1985.

Morley, Morris H. *Imperial State and Revolution: The United States and Cuba, 1952–1986.* Cambridge, England: Cambridge University Press, 1987.

Murphy, Robert K. *Diplomat Among Warriors.* Garden City, NY: Doubleday, 1964.

Nathan, James A., ed. *The Cuban Missile Crisis Revisited.* New York: St. Martin's Press, 1992.

Newsom, David D. *The Soviet Brigade in Cuba.* Bloomington: Indiana University Press, 1987.

Nixon, Richard. *RN: The Memoirs of Richard Nixon.* New York: Grossett & Dunlap, 1978.

———. *Six Crises.* Garden City, NY: Doubleday, 1962.

North, Oliver. *Under Fire.* New York: HarperCollins, 1991.

Nunn, Frederick M. *Yesterday's Soldiers: European Military Professionalism in South America, 1890–1940.* Lincoln: University of Nebraska Press, 1983.

Palmer, General Bruce, Jr. *Intervention in the Caribbean: The Dominican Crisis of 1965.* Lexington: The University Press of Kentucky, 1989.

Pastor, Robert A. *Condemned to Repetition: The United States and Nicaragua.* Princeton, NJ: Princeton University Press, 1987.

————. *Whirlpool: U.S. Foreign Policy toward Latin America and the Caribbean.* Princeton, NJ: Princeton University Press, 1992.

Pastor, Robert A., and Jorge G. Castaneda. *Limits to Friendship: The United States and Mexico.* New York: Alfred A. Knopf, 1988.

Perez, Louis A., Jr. *Cuba Between Empires, 1878–1902.* Pittsburgh, PA: University of Pittsburgh Press, 1983.

————. *Cuba under the Platt Amendment.* Pittsburgh, PA: University of Pittsburgh Press, 1986.

Perkins, Dexter. *A History of the Monroe Doctrine.* Boston, MA: Little, Brown, 1955.

————. *The Monroe Doctrine, 1823–1826.* Cambridge, MA: Harvard University Press, 1927.

————. *The Monroe Doctrine, 1826–1867.* Baltimore, MD: The Johns Hopkins University Press, 1933.

————. *The Monroe Doctrine, 1867–1907.* Baltimore, MD: The Johns Hopkins University Press, 1937.

Powers, Thomas. *The Man Who Kept the Secrets: Richard Helms and the CIA.* New York: Alfred A. Knopf, 1979.

Prizel, Ilya. *Latin America Through Soviet Eyes.* Cambridge, England: Cambridge University Press, 1990.

Rabe, Stephen G. *Eisenhower and Latin America: The Foreign Policy of Anticommunism.* Chapel Hill: University of North Carolina Press, 1988.

Reagan, Ronald. *An American Life.* New York: Simon & Schuster, 1990.

Riding, Alan. *Distant Neighbors.* New York: Vintage Books, 1986.

Russell, Ruth B. *A History of the United Nations Charter: The Role of the United States, 1940–1945.* Washington, DC: The Brookings Institution, 1958.

Scheman, L. Ronald, ed. *The Alliance for Progress: A Retrospective.* New York: Praeger, 1988.

Schlesinger, Arthur M., Jr. *Robert Kennedy and His Times.* Boston, MA: Houghton Mifflin, 1978.

Schlesinger, Stephen, and Stephen Kinser. *Bitter Fruit.* Garden City, NY: Doubleday, 1982.

Schoultz, Lars. *Human Rights and United States Policy toward Latin America.* Princeton, NJ: Princeton University Press, 1981.

————. *National Security and United States Policy toward Latin America*. Princeton, NJ: Princeton University Press, 1987.

Scott, Peter Dale, and Jonathan Marshall. *Cocaine Politics: Drugs, Armies, and the CIA in Central America*. Berkeley: University of California Press, 1991.

Seymour, Charles, ed. *The Intimate Papers of Colonel House*. Vol. 1. Boston, MA: Houghton Mifflin, 1926.

Shultz, George P. *Turmoil and Triumph: My Years as Secretary of State*. New York: Scribners, 1993.

Skidmore, Thomas E. *Politics in Brazil, 1930–1964*. New York: Oxford University Press, 1967.

Smith, Gaddis. *Morality, Reason, and Power: American Diplomacy in the Carter Years*. New York: Hill and Wang, 1986.

Smith, Wayne S. *The Closest of Enemies: A Personal and Diplomatic History of the Castro Years*. New York: Norton, 1987.

————, ed. *The Russians Aren't Coming: New Soviet Policy in Latin America*. Boulder, CO: Lynne Reiner Publishers, 1992.

Thatcher, Margaret. *The Downing Street Years*. New York: Harper-Collins, 1993.

Thomas, Hugh. *Cuba: The Pursuit of Freedom*. New York: Harper & Row, 1971.

Tuchman, Barbara. *The Zimmermann Telegram*. New York: Viking, 1958.

Vance, Cyrus. *Hard Choices: Critical Years in America's Foreign Policy*. New York: Simon & Schuster, 1983.

Vandenberg, Arthur Hendrick. *The Trail of a Tradition*. New York: G. P. Putnam's Sons, 1926.

Vandenberg, Arthur H., Jr., ed. *The Private Papers of Senator Vandenberg*. Boston, MA: Houghton Mifflin, 1952.

Varas, Augusto, ed. *Soviet–Latin American Relations in the 1980s*. Boulder, CO: Westview Press, 1987.

Walters, Vernon A. *Silent Missions*. Garden City, NY: Doubleday, 1978.

Welch, Richard E., Jr. *Response to Revolution: The United States and the Cuban Revolution, 1959–1961*. Chapel Hill: University of North Carolina Press, 1985.

Wood, Bryce. *The Dismantling of the Good Neighbor Policy*. Austin: University of Texas Press, 1985.

——. *The Making of the Good Neighbor Policy*. New York: Columbia University Press, 1961.

Wyden, Peter. *Bay of Pigs*. New York: Simon & Schuster, 1979.

INDEX